Hyperledger Fabric In-Depth

Learn, Build and Deploy Blockchain Applications Using Hyperledger Fabric

Ashwani Kumar

FIRST EDITION 2020

Copyright © BPB Publications, India

ISBN: 978-93-89328-226

Distributors:

BPB PUBLICATIONS
20, Ansari Road, Darya Ganj
New Delhi-110002
Ph: 23254990/23254991

DECCAN AGENCIES
4-3-329, Bank Street,
Hyderabad-500195
Ph: 24756967/24756400

MICRO MEDIA
Shop No. 5, Mahendra Chambers,
150 DN Rd. Next to Capital Cinema,
V.T. (C.S.T.) Station, MUMBAI-400 001
Ph: 22078296/22078297

BPB BOOK CENTRE
376 Old Lajpat Rai Market,
Delhi-110006
Ph: 23861747

Published by Manish Jain for BPB Publications, 20 Ansari Road, Darya Ganj, New Delhi-110002 and Printed by him at Repro India Ltd, Mumbai

Dedicated to

My wife Harpreet and kids Viniti and especially younger one Naman,
both have always encouraged me to walk the extra mile.

About the Author

Ashwani Kumar is a technologist by profession having 19+ years of experience working in large enterprise-grade solutions. He was instrumental in architecting, designing, developing, and delivering multiple solutions for numerous industry verticals. His area of expertise involves J2EE and cloud computing technologies. Ashwani holds a Bachelor of Engineering Degree in Computer Technology from Nagpur University.

Though Ashwani has worked on several technologies throughout his tenure, however chancing upon Blockchain a couple of years ago brought up an interesting point in his zeal of learning new and emerging technologies. Blockchain and specifically Hyperledger Fabric was till then into nascent stages from understanding and application perspective. Ashwani has spent considerable time working and exploring Hyperledger Fabric, which is most sought after permissioned blockchain and has seen it evolve release after releases. Ashwani is a firm believer in sharing knowledge and believes sharing increases your own outlook and hence this book.

About the Reviewer

Manav Gupta is an IBM Distinguished Engineer, Master Inventor and published author. In his current role as CTO Cloud (Canada), Manav provides guidance to develop a digital strategy for clients across North America, by leveraging cloud, analytics and cognitive platforms. He has published several books on service management, cloud computing and big data and Blockchain. Most recently, he authored "Blockchain for the Enterprise".

Acknowledgement

I have always wondered while reading a book as to what it would have taken to write it. The very first thought of being able to write a book and that too on niche technology was not that enthusiastic. However, consistent push and show of belief in me by family and friends made me took over the journey of writing a book. As rightly said in one of the great quotes, **'In vain have you acquired knowledge if you have not imparted it to others.'**

First and foremost, I would like to thank everyone at BPB Publications for giving me this opportunity to publish my book and encouraging me to write a book on Hyperledger Fabric even when it was just at its nascent stages. A big thank you to the BPB editorial team attached to me who was always there with me all the time and pushing me every time I thought am clueless about writing.

Special thanks to my wife Harpreet, who has always mentioned to me that 'time is the key' and I should press all my energies in writing and completing the book. Great thanks to my kids Viniti and Naman, who have always shown trust in me and kept reminding me I should not take a pause in my journey until it's complete.

A special mention of thanks to Som Shekhar Singh, DoT Publicis Sapient, for bringing me into the world of blockchain and giving me a free hand to explore the Hyperledger Fabric. He kept asking me questions, which led me to explore more of this.

Last but not least, thanks to Manav Gupta, Director & Distinguished Engineer at IBM, who himself is an author for technical review of the book and providing valuable feedback.

– Ashwani Kumar

Preface

Blockchain has certainly moved from being a Buzzword and now has reached the stage where it has provided the avenues to rethink as to how trust works. From the time the blockchain came into existence as a by-product of the invention of Bitcoin, it has made inroads in the enterprise worlds, helping to define new ways of doing collaborative business processes and trusting each other. Blockchain, for sure, is not only limited to cryptocurrency rather has proved to be a solid foundation for real-world enterprise use cases. Hyperledger Fabric, an enterprise blockchain platform, has evolved a lot since inception and is now deployed in many production-grade applications with companies' world over making use of it.

This book covers the understanding and working of Hyperledger Fabric. This book is divided into two logical sections: the first part of the book covers topics around Blockchain with taking reference from Bitcoin and Ethereum at times. This is a foundational concept section before we go deep dive into Hyperledger Fabric. The second section gets into Fabric with an attempt to make concepts easy to understand. This book also covers a lot of examples to set up networks and then writing smart contracts. All examples are supported separately with code samples. This book is divided into 11 chapters, and it provides a detailed description of the core concepts of Blockchain and Hyperledger Fabric.

Chapter 1 introduces the basics of Blockchain. It describes the building blocks of blockchain and minutest of details as to how all moving parts work together. It talks of the reason for the existence of blockchain and what challenges of the real-world it solves. It also focuses on identifying types of blockchain and details about them. Taking a cue from Bitcoin, it explains key terms used such as Forking, Mining, Rewards, Difficulty level, and so on.

Chapter 2 covers decentralization that is one of the core building blocks of Blockchain. It talks about how it is leveraged in the blockchain solution. It also covers the various aspects of decentralization while comparing it with distributed and centralized systems.

Chapter 3 introduces you to cryptography in general. Cryptography plays an important role in blockchain from establishing identities, generating keys, or chaining blocks together. This covers cryptographic primitives and other important functions such as hashing and working of Merkle tree and so on.

Chapter 4 introduces you to the aspect and importance of consensus in decentralized systems. It takes you through various consensus algorithms that are vital in understanding of how the blockchain system works in the context of consensus. This chapter covers the various consensus algorithms.

Chapter 5 introduces you to a perfect oxymoron, a journey into enterprise blockchain. This chapter talks about the need for private blockchains and considerations that an enterprise needs to take before jumping into the blockchain bandwagon. This chapter also lists the successful products/platforms available for readily use and real-world use cases.

Chapter 6 sets the foundation stone for the understanding of Hyperledger Fabric. It covers the core concepts of Hyperledger Fabric. This chapter ensures that reader understands the basic concepts, key components, and all moving parts thoroughly before applying them to make a working application.

Chapter 7 introduces you to the architectural concepts and design philosophy of Hyperledger Fabric. Taking a cue from the last chapter, this shows how different components knit and work together to work as a blockchain platform. This chapter also provides internal details of transaction workflow, which is a multi-step process and includes multiple entities.

Chapter 8 helps you to get your hands dirty in setting up of Hyperledger Fabric blockchain network and what it takes on the ground to set that up. It provides a reference to a lot of code samples specifically written to support this chapter. It talks a lot about system requirements, configuration files, and chaincode that does the actual magic.

Chapter 9 covers the details of writing smart contracts (chaincode) for the Hyperledger network. It also addresses the aspects of installing, instantiating, and upgrading of chain codes. Provide enough samples to ensure readers understand development, unit testing, and dev mode deployment for quick turnaround.

Chapter 10 covers security and privacy in detail, in general, for Blockchain and specifically for Hyperledger. It goes on in detail, making readers understand various privacy and security considerations available in Hyperledger and how they can be leveraged.

Chapter 11 gives you the brief introduction to the recent changes and enhancements introduced in Hyperledger Fabric v 2.0.

Downloading the code bundle and coloured images:

Please follow the link to download the
Code Bundle and the *Coloured Images* of the book:

https://rebrand.ly/cbgth5m

Errata

We take immense pride in our work at BPB Publications and follow best practices to ensure the accuracy of our content to provide with an indulging reading experience to our subscribers. Our readers are our mirrors, and we use their inputs to reflect and improve upon human errors if any, occurred during the publishing processes involved. To let us maintain the quality and help us reach out to any readers who might be having difficulties due to any unforeseen errors, please write to us at :

errata@bpbonline.com

Your support, suggestions and feedbacks are highly appreciated by the BPB Publications' Family.

Table of Contents

CHAPTER 1
Understanding Blockchain

This book is intended to discuss and share knowledge specifically around Hyperledger Fabric, which is at the forefront among leading enterprise Blockchain platforms. However, before we go deep into exploring Hyperledger, we must try to learn and understand about Blockchain basics and relatively advanced concepts. This chapter talks about Blockchain in general, and how the exchange of value has evolved over a period owing to socio-economic changes that eventually lead to the innovation of Bitcoin, the first-ever Blockchain implementation. We would then cover details about Blockchain internals, which is brief know-how of the working of Blockchain, and then we shall also look into the types of Blockchain that have come into existence to full-fill different real-world use cases.

Let's get started.

Structure

- Blockchain
- History
- Working of Blockchain
- Blockchain types

Objective

The objective of the chapter is to cover most basics of the Blockchain. It would describe the building blocks of Blockchain and explains key terms used in Blockchain.

Blockchain

Blockchain has certainly moved away from just being a buzzword; it is no longer a hype. At the time of writing this book, Enterprise Blockchain has already been implemented at various industrial verticals to address real-time business problems other than public Blockchain (for now read cryptocurrency), which already holds a right amount of market share symbolizing its acceptance and usage.

It is imperative to understand Blockchain at the core level, to realize its benefits and how it addresses the various real-time problems.

According to Wikipedia, *"Blockchain is a growing list of records, called blocks, which are linked using cryptography. Each block contains a cryptographic hash of the previous block, a timestamp, and transaction data (generally represented as a Merkle tree root hash)."*

At a higher level, this definition sums up the basic definition of Blockchain and introduces a couple of terms such as block, Merkle tree root, cryptographic hash, and so on. All of these new words, we would decipher and understand in detail in due course of going through this book.

In simplest terms, "Blockchain is a data structure; it is an ordered, back-linked list of blocks of transactions." Yes, essentially, it is a data structure where blocks (think of container which holds transactions in body and metadata in the header) that are back linked to the previous block through a cryptographic hash key.

The following image shows how various blocks in a Blockchain are linked together and what constitutes an individual block. The body contains transactions, and they are hashed together to become what is called a Merkle root, which gets included in the header along with many other things. For now, see that the hash of the previous block is present in the current block header, which keeps the blocks together in the Blockchain:

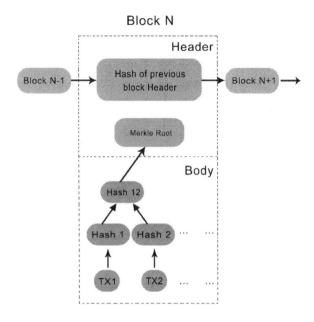

Figure 1.1: Block structure

In reality, Blockchain is much more than a simple data structure; however, it's okay to assume this as a data structure. Blocks are linked together through cryptographic hash keys, and there is a strong reason for it. Cryptographic hash functions can be used as an integrity check to detect changes in data. Hash functions have got several properties which make it best to use for Blockchain:

- **Pre-image (input) resistance**: Hash functions are one-way functions that are given any input; there shall be a single output, and looking at the output, there is no way of finding out what could be the input.

- **Collision-free:** It merely means it's hard to find out two different inputs that could result in the same output.

- **Second pre-image resistance:** Even with having an input and hash, it is difficult to have another pre-image that could produce the same hash.

So, in a block, we would have multiple transactions recorded and their cumulative hash stored as Merkle root tree along with other header attributes that creates a unique hash value for that block. This hash value is stored as the previous block hash in the next child block. Previous block hash is part of the block header, which binds it with the parent block. The uniqueness of the hash and its linking to parent block using previous block hash is the reason that gives one of the key characteristics of the Blockchain, that is, immutability.

If there is any change in any of the transactions in a block, then it would result in a change in the transaction hash, hence subsequently change in Merkle tree root hash. Since Merkle tree root hash is part of the block header, so Merkle root tree change (because of transaction hash change) leads to block header hash change. In children block (N block) hash where parent block (N-1 block) hash is stored as previous block hash, this change stimulates the change in the current block, and likewise, it triggers the change in the entire rest of the blocks in Blockchain. This is virtually impossible as it requires defying the consensus in Blockchain, which is virtually impossible in a peer to peer network.

The below figure represents on a high level, the Bitcoin block structure, the content is actual and has been taken out using publicly available bitcoin explorer. In the first block, having height 614,555, there are two sections, a header and a set of transactions. In this header, there is a value of previous block header hash, which is the actual hash of block 614,554. And subsequently, in block header of 614,554, we could see the previous block header hash of 614,553.

The header hash of any block is computed using different fields present in the header, such as previous block header, Nonce, Timestamp, Merkle Root, and so on. Merkle root is the computed hash of the transaction hashes. So, any change in any transactions leads to change in Merkle Root and then change in the hash of header and so it subsequently it affects its children or next block, and this creates a ripple effect in the Blockchain hence flagging an attempt to change the content of Blockchain and hence challenging its immutability:

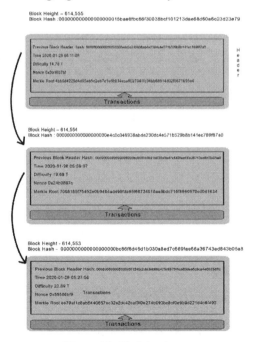

Figure 1.2: Block headers

Having understood about Blockchain as a data structure and how the use of cryptographic hash function provides immutability, it is also evident that a program running standalone playing around with this data structure doesn't make it fit as a Blockchain for peer to peer transactions.

While Blockchain is a data structure at the core level, Blockchain is also a scheme of things which were put together to have a system where peer to peer transaction can happen without the help of an intermediary. The idea of Blockchain coming into existence was purely to have a system where the exchange of value can happen between peer to peer even if they don't trust each other and that too without an intermediary.

Exchange of value is way different from the exchange of information; for instance, sending a document to somebody else, it is essentially a copy of the document and not the document itself that is being sent or shared. So, anyone can distribute multiple copies of a document, image, or email, and many more. But this cannot be the case with the 'value,' think of something of value, for instance, money. If you had 10 dollars in your account and you send this to someone else, then the receiving person would have that money, and you would leave with none. To ensure this atomicity and prevent double-spending, we need intermediaries. Because intermediaries such as banks, settlement houses provide trust between parties, ensuring that double-spend doesn't happen. Though all this comes with a cost and requires time, the biggest challenge yet is to achieve prevention of double-spending.

The consensus is the way by which the Blockchain system prevents double-spending. Various consensus algorithms are used in various Blockchain systems. **Proof of Work (PoW)** is the one that was used in the first-ever Blockchain system, that is, Bitcoin, the world's first and widely used cryptocurrency. We shall discuss consensus in detail in the coming chapters with a look at PoW and what is being used in Enterprise Blockchain for achieving consensus.

So, while we understood the concept of immutability in Blockchain as the data written cannot be altered, so writing meaningful data becomes important such that authentic transactions should get recorded into Blockchain, and that is where consensus model comes into play.

Let's take a step back and understand one more definition of Blockchain and would try to see what we have covered so far and what we need to go through yet:

- Blockchain is a decentralized, peer to peer, trustless, global network where each node stores a copy of distributed ledger of the append-only real-time approved consensus transactions bundled together in blocks which are hash linked using cryptography.

Looking at what we have covered so far, some of the terms have not been discussed until now. We will try to cover those terms, and by the end of it, we would have a clear understanding of it.

Blockchain is a decentralized network, which simply means a network of computer systems where no one is in control, no one owns the network, it is contrary to the centralized systems where big corporations offer services through centralized systems, and they are the sole owner of the system. Take an example of significant e-retailer such as Amazon or eBay, and a small-time retailer providing goods and services to its set of the customer through them. If, for any reason, e-retailer suspends the individual retailer account, then that would jeopardize the entire business of the retailer.

In the Blockchain network (see we have moved from a data structure to a network), every participant is the equal owner and can join or leave the network at its will and convenience. Bitcoin and Ethereum are perfect examples of Blockchain network where anyone can simply bring up a client (Bitcoin client or Geth for Ethereum) and join the network. You only need software and internet connectivity to be part of the Blockchain network. No one is a regulator or in authority to allow or deny you to join the network.

Blockchain is a decentralized network. There are various axes basis which decentralization works, in one of the blog Vitalik Buterin (Ethereum co-founder) has very elegantly described decentralization. I particularly like one of the statements which goes as "Blockchains are politically decentralized (no one controls them) and architecturally decentralized (no *central infrastructural* point of failure) but they are logically centralized (there is one commonly agreed state and the system behaves like a single computer)."

The next term that we did encounter was peer-to-peer; following on the lines of decentralization, a network is made up of peer nodes, and it's the peer that talks among themselves are essentially sending transactions among each other. So, as soon as a peer receives a transaction, it sends out that transaction to the peer in its vicinity, and it goes on and on, and every peer in the network gets the same transaction no matter how geographically they are distributed.

In a public network, since anyone can join in at will, no one knows about other peers, so there is no way or reason for trusting another peer, and that is why it is referred to as a trustless network. The critical question to answer here is how transactions are processed if Blockchain is a trustless network? The answer lies in the mix of consensus and cryptography.

A consensus algorithm is a process that is used to achieve agreement on a state of values among distributed systems. According to Vitalik, the purpose of consensus is to "allow for the secure updating of a state according to some specific state transition rules, where the right to perform the state transitions is distributed among some economic set." Blockchain node or peer is nothing but at the end is a software and consensus is a set of rule which every node follows to ensure the agreement is reached on the validity of transaction that can be appended on the ledger.

We shall cover consensus algorithms in detail later in a chapter where we would also discuss the Byzantine General's Problem, which is analogous to consensus issues in Blockchain and how this problem is solved using different consensus algorithm such as Proof of Work, Proof of Stake, and so on.

Cryptography has an essential and very vital role to play in Blockchain; it is an important pillar and part of the Blockchain system. Cryptography is a branch of computer science which talks about various techniques of disguising and revealing information either in transit or at rest. Blockchain uses cryptography mainly at securing the identity of the sender of transactions, which generally happens through the generation of the public and private keys. Also, it ensures that data is not tampered with, which generally happens through the use of hash functions. However, with the advancement of Blockchain networks, new cryptography techniques are also used, such as Zero-Knowledge proof, and so on.

The last part that is remaining to understand from the definition is distributed ledger. Every node, where can receive, distribute, and validate transactions, it does have storage as well that keeps the record of all transactions and is called a ledger. Bitcoin, for instance, maintains LevelDB as a database or ledger for maintaining the transactions. An interesting point to note here is that all nodes in the network maintain the same copy of the ledger, which contains the same set of transactions. So, at any point in time, any node would act as the same source of truth, think of Blockchain data structure and consensus that helps us achieve this.

Given that information is shared across all the nodes and every node maintains the same copy, so even if any node or even multiple nodes leave the network, there shall be no impact as the rest of the nodes can still keep the network running. Whenever any node joins back the network, it first synchronizes with other peer nodes and gets all the data, updates the ledger, and can start participating in the transaction receiving, distribution, and validation.

In the following image, we could see that various nodes are connected, whereas all maintain the same copy of the database among themselves:

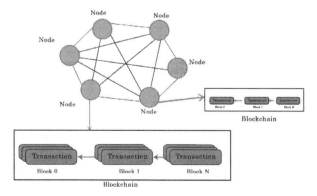

Figure 1.3: Node and Blockchain database

To sum up, in this section, we have tried to cover what Blockchain is and how the culmination of various technologies and new invention has brought to the world a new paradigm of transaction and recording of data with the sole intention of making transaction free from an intermediary, less costly and faster.

History

There always has been a reason for something to come into existence, and that is why invention happens. Inventions happen to solve problems or when a curious mind sees beyond what is already known. The invention also happens when concepts from different realms are brought together to solve a problem that would typically be not put together. Same way, Bitcoin was the culmination of over the year's research in cryptography and distributed computing. Blockchain is the by-product of Bitcoin.

Most of us, who mainly are reading this, living in the age when the internet was invented. It all started with a couple of computers wired together, and now we are witnessing exponential growth and usage of growth that probably it's difficult to think life without internet.

Human history has witnessed several gaps over some time, and there have been inventions along the time that has closed this gap, and humanity has changed forever after these inventions. Few notable ones are:

- **Knowledge gap**: There was a time around the 1400s when reading and knowledge was only available and accessible to High & Mighty. Then Press was invented, and it brought the knowledge and information to masses, and we see development revolutions.

- **Power gap:** In the 1800s, a time where slaves and the workforce were the only sources of manufacturing, the engine was invented, and it closed the power gap.

- **Distance gap**: Late 90's and early 2000s, when information, media, banking, and communication seemed far apart among users, then the internet came, and it closed the distance gap, and for once, everything looked accessible.

- **Trust gap**: Interestingly, we are living in the age of Trust gap now. We are heavily dependent on intermediaries to help execute and complete our transactions. Simply, to transfer money from one account to another account we need banks, we need agencies to get a document validated. Likewise, many other intermediaries verify our information for others and other's information for us, only to provide us with trust so that we can proceed with a transaction.

Bitcoin, the first implementation of Blockchain, was invented to fill the trust gap that exists mainly in monetary systems. However, with other Blockchain systems coming into action over the last ten years after the invention of Bitcoin, now has moved from purely monetary transactions to any transaction that involves the exchange of value.

The trust gap is the reason of how human behavior has evolved from ancient times to modern times. Whereas, there has been an evolution in the representation of value (think money), corresponding social behavior changes have been observed as to how they respond to the transaction due to various social, geographical changes.

The following image is trying to represent the evolution of the value exchange system over some time. There were numerous other inventions as well along the time, such as Banking, Gold Standard, and Online Banking, and so on, which have been instrumental and became milestone as to how people were exchanging value among themselves. In this picture, we have just kept a couple of notable ones just to give the flavor of change:

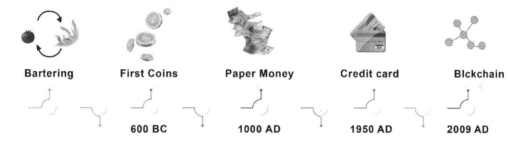

Figure 1.4: *Value exchange evolution*

Let us understand the figure more elaborately:

- **Bartering**: Before money, there existed a bartering system where assets or goods were exchanged for goods. For example, if you are a crop producer and your neighbor is a vegetable seller, both of you could get into a transaction and exchange assets. The trust level was high as the transaction was happening person to person, and goods were available instantly.

  With the issues arising from the difference in exact needs at a particular point of time, for instance, a person with crops might not want vegetables at the moment, and instead of looking for milk, bartering at times was not fulfilling. Then there was a time when commodity money existed for some time; commodity money was mostly carrying something which everybody would need, such as seeds, salt, livestock, and so on; however, it still had its share of issues.

- **Coins**: After some time, in search of ease of doing a transaction and to be able to trade in different geographies, coins came into existence. These coins used to have holes in the middle so that people can carry them easily by hanging around their necks. They were imprinted with the faces of emperors and gods to show the value.

Until the bartering system, the exchange was more around with something that has actual tangible as an intrinsic value, whatever was being exchanged was directly seen as something of consumption, say, exchanging a cattle for a bag of fruits. With coins, there was an invention of abstraction where the exchange of value now changed from actual consumption to something that referred to as value.

Now, coins carry value, a promise that can be used to buy things. This is how human behavior changed regard to the exchange of value with need mismatch and geographical disparity for carrying out the trade.

- **Paper money:** With the challenge of carrying coins or precious metals, there came another change. Trade needs were evolving; trust mismatch was rising, and so was human behavior. Then someone came up with the idea that if I deposit my precious metal\gold with someone trustworthy and get a paperback, which shows that I have this much gold with them and I can trade this piece of paper.

  It was much easier to carry; however, at the cost of trust that my gold is safe with the so-called trustworthy. With this in practice, it took almost centuries when paper money started being accepted widely, and banknote becomes acceptable at a broader level. Paper money or generally called as the banknote is a type of promissory note or only its future promise of value that having a banknote with someone holds a promise from the issuing authority that the value would be full filled.

- **Plastic money:** Then, after a long time, there was an invention called plastic money. Diners club in the United States was the first to present with the idea of plastic money. With great hesitation, as with other transformations, people started moving through with trust in financial institutions for the promised value that this plastic money would give.

- **Bitcoin**: This was more around how the human behavior changes and the challenges being faced by people from the middleman, primarily financial institutions. Considering, transactions between peers required trust and financial institutions were the sole owners of providing that trust; however, that trust causes a good amount of overhead in terms of time and money. Today, trillions of dollars are sent across the world as part of cross border payment. If you worked in one corner of the US and needed to send money back to your family in London, you might end up paying USD 20-30 flat fee for a wire transfer plus additional fees on top of suffering from fluctuating exchange rates between currencies. In the end, your bank in London might take up to 3-5 days for registering the transaction.

Facilitating payments is a significant revenue generator and a highly profitable business for financial institutions, providing them with the used amount of transactions and charges. According to one of the facts, during the year 2016, cross-border transactions, from payments to letters of credit, generated 40% of global payments transactional revenues. It's just not cross border payment, but clearance and settlement systems, securities, trade finance are other functions where financial institutions rake up a lot of money just because they provide trust services between transacting parties.

Bitcoin is the system that challenges the very notion of money and how trust works. Bitcoin was invented as a separate currency and a payment system that manages its currency. It is an independent payment system, meaning that there is no central entity that owns and controls its operation. Using Bitcoin, anyone can send payment to anyone who does have a valid bitcoin address. What you need is an internet connection, a digital wallet that contains keys, and the receiver's valid address. These eliminate the disadvantages that financial institutions facilitate, such as transaction cost and delay. Bitcoin transaction does cost you fees, but it is very nominal and charged by miners, and the time delay is usually limited to minutes or max to hours.

Bitcoin was invented in the year 2008 with the publication of a paper titled "Bitcoin: A Peer-to-Peer Electronic Cash System," someone with the pseudonym Satoshi Nakamoto. No one to date knows the identity of Satoshi Nakamoto; no one knows if it was a single person or a group of people.

Nakamoto combined several prior inventions, and most obvious ones were Wei Dai's B-money and Adam Back's HashCash for creating a decentralized electronic cash system that did not have a central authority for currency issuance and validation of transactions.

HashCash is a proof-of-work algorithm, which was invented to be used as a denial-of-service countermeasure technique for several systems. Around 1997, HashCash was initially proposed as a mechanism to regulate systematic exploitation of un-metered internet resources such as email. One of the core concepts that it came out was Cost-Functions; the HashCash CPU cost-function computes a token, which can be used as a proof-of-work, a cost-function should be efficiently correct, but quite expensive to compute.

The first use of HashCash was to limit email spamming, because as the popularity of emails grew, so did spams. With HashCash, the metadata of an email, mainly the *from* address, the *to* address, the time, and so on, were formalized as a protocol. On top of that, the sender of an email must add something called *nonce* to this metadata; a nonce is generally a random number which, when added with this metadata used to generate a hash. It was further tricked by asking to generate a hash that starts with a predefined number of '0's in binary format.

To generate a valid hash, the sender has to adopt the brute force method, that is, trial and error of generating a nonce added with metadata than generating a hash value such that it meets specific criteria of predefined leading number of 0's in front of the binary value of the generated hash. The sender needs to try different nonces until he could come up with a valid combination; otherwise, the email could be rejected by the recipient's email client.

This is where the idea of Cost-Function comes into effect, generating hash number would need a certain amount of CPU to be spent so if a spammer wants to send hundreds of thousands of emails as valid email then he needs to calculate the hash value for all the emails to look them like valid emails, which would undoubtedly require him to spend CPU cycles and hence monetary expense to buy power to run those CPU cycles. As we have already seen that, hash algorithms are a one-way hashing function. It is challenging to generate a hash requiring a specific pattern, whereas it is not expensive to validate a message against the hash to check its validity.

Proof of Work proved to be one of the cornerstones for the Bitcoin platform, which was realized using HashCash's invention. However, in Bitcoin, Proof-Of-Work, a version of HashCash is used in a very different way. Proof of Work uses HashCash techniques to enable a race among miners in Bitcoin. A miner who wins the race, that is, becomes the first one to produce a valid proof of work — a hash of a Bitcoin block after accepting and validating transactions gets to decide which transactions go through.

Once a new block has been mined, confirming a set of valid transactions, these transactions cannot be or is an expensive affair to be reversed. Any malicious node would have to prove at least as much work as required to find the block in the first place, with subsequently adding up for every additional block that has been added so far, which under normal circumstances becomes exponentially harder over time. The real-world resources, usually energy that has gone to compute hash, required to be spent on reversing the transaction in someone's favor turns out to be way higher than the potential profit that can one make by doing the fraudulent activity.

These are how, in Bitcoin, HashCash became the stepping stone for the Bitcoin invention. It solves the double-spending problem by ensuring someone wants to do fraud knows the mathematics of return on investment that he needs to put to cheat in a decentralized way. Previously, the double-spend problem was a weakness of digital currency and was addressed by clearing all transactions through a middleman or central clearinghouse, which again has the disadvantages of expensive cost and delay in settling the transactions.

The Proof-Of-Work in one or another form used widely in popular public Blockchain systems and is not applicable in enterprise Blockchain platforms. Still, the idea of covering this in a short note was to understand the importance of the consensus algorithm invalidating the transaction and appending the Blockchain ledger. Enterprise Blockchain platforms do use consensus algorithms but in some other fashion following the same philosophical principle of reaching an agreement among participating nodes before writing a transaction permanently on a ledger.

Bitcoin is not the first digital money that was invented and put in use; there were earlier attempts as well. B-Money being one of them, the proposal came from Wei Dai, a computer scientist from Washington University. Around November 1998, just after graduating from university, he came up with an idea of "Efficient cooperation requires a medium of exchange (money) and a way to enforce contracts," and this proposal was called B-Money. In this, Dai gave two alternatives to implement the digital cash system.

B-Money introduced a network model for distributing transaction data, plus the use of cryptographic signatures to send money. However, it was never implemented. Yet, Dai's proposal was not forgotten; B-money ended up as the first reference in the Bitcoin white paper.

Bitcoin is the successful implementation of a decentralized money system. There were a couple of other implementations that happened before Bitcoin, most notably one is Ecash by the company name DigiCash which was founded by David Chaum in 1989. For one or another reason, this didn't go through. Bitcoin all started with the publication of a white paper on October 31, 2008, and the source code was published on January 3, 2009. On the same day first genesis block was created, that is, the first block of any Blockchain and then after this and Bitcoin never looked back. There are an estimated 10 million unique users of Bitcoin with daily trading volume running into billions of dollars.

The reason that Bitcoin has been surviving for all these years and is popular because this is a complete decentralized financial system with no government, authority, or financial system controlling this. It is a censorship-resistant, borderless system. It is a purely peer to peer system where every peer/node is equal. This is purely anonymous, doesn't have any registration process, and doesn't require any permission to join the network and as well can leave at will. There is a system, which is purely driven by mathematics and so not on people's wish, so there is no provision of freezing an account as in the case of financial institutions where they can simply freeze your account on authority's notice and even on a falsified complaint.

"The Times 03/Jan/2009 Chancellor on brink of second bailout for banks" was the message in the genesis block (first block) of Bitcoin, which closely links to the global financial crisis that shook the world in 2008. It resulted in a financial bailout to the central banks by the governments in the form of printing the large sum of cash, which leads to hyperinflation in the system. This all happens because people's funds are being managed by the authorities that, at times, work under the influence of government and central institutions, which may try to manipulate the system.

Bitcoin at that time came as a financial system where people can manage their money by themselves. And that is the sole reason the popularity of Bitcoin is gaining over some time.

Interestingly to note here is that the invention of Bitcoin, which was purely due to the very reason of opaqueness in the financial system gave birth to technologies that are virtually being used to address various industry issues. That is the reason, on the back of Blockchain technologies, several enterprise platforms have come up that can solve challenges of Supply Chain Finance, Trade Finance, Healthcare records, and many more.

Working of Blockchain

Bitcoin, being the first implementation of Blockchain, makes the best case to understand how Blockchain works. So far, we have seen what Blockchain is, by going deep inside with so far a reasonable definition, understanding its core components. Also, the evolution of money and human behavior, along with it, gave us a strong foundation as to why Blockchain came into existence. In this section, we would go along how bitcoin works at the lower level what techniques and computer science have been amalgamated to make this work.

The fundamental of working of Bitcoin can be summed up like, each node does have the same version of the software which maintains the same state all the time, and all this happens in a decentralized fashion. In Bitcoin, you can anytime bring up your node (Bitcoin client software) and connect the main Bitcoin network. This is a decentralized network with no one having the sole authority of any sort. So, in a truly decentralized system, anyone can join or leave that on will. The connection and disconnection of nodes occur independently and doesn't impact any other node or network as a whole.

Remember, Blockchain is a decentralized medium to eliminate middleman whose role was to ensure trust in a transaction. The Bitcoin system is based on decentralized trust, and trust is achieved as an output of the interactions of different nodes in the Bitcoin system.

In Bitcoin, every node does have a local copy of the distributed shared ledger, think of this a database organized as Blockchain consisting of blocks with validated and ordered transactions. As soon as one node initiates a transaction, it reaches to all the nodes in the network, and it remains in the memory pool till the time they are confirmed. Once consensus is reached, transactions are confirmed, they are added into Blockchain, and once written in Blockchain, there is no way of going back. As more blocks keep getting added in Blockchain, the transactions are considered to be more permanent/confirmed with much nil or little chances of going back again.

Now, we would be talking about a bitcoin transaction, which would give us enough understanding of how Blockchain works in general; most of the Blockchain that has come after Bitcoin works on the same principle with certain changes as to address specific concerns not handled by Bitcoin. For instance, in Ethereum, smart contracts came into existence as it intended to move from the simple transaction of exchange of value to have an exchange of assets of value and that too with custom agreement conditions that can be programmed.

The below image is a high-level representation of steps that are involved in a Bitcoin transaction:

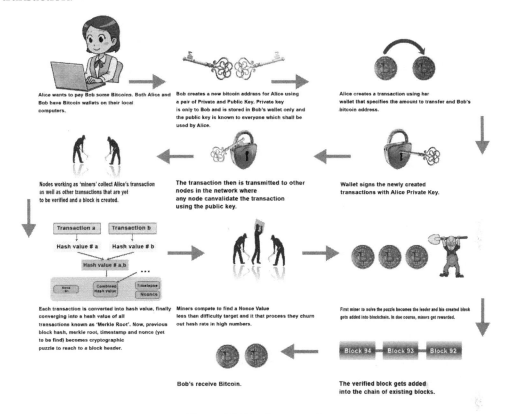

Figure 1.5: *Bitcoin transaction*

The transaction is at the core of Bitcoin, which, when validated and approved, gets added in a block, which then becomes part of long Blockchain. Assuming, Alice wants to send some bitcoins to Bob. Both have bitcoin wallets that can connect to the Bitcoin network. Think of a wallet as a specialized software (client program) that can connect to Blockchain, generate keys, and send a transaction to the Bitcoin network.

To send Bitcoin, one needs to have some identity, which is a bitcoin address. As mentioned earlier, at times, the invention is the culmination of even many existing things that have existed before but independently, so decentralization and cryptography have existed long before. Cryptography plays a vital role in Bitcoin or for that in any other public or private Blockchain. We will limit our discussion here to the use of cryptography for Bitcoin, but then we would elaborate it further for Hyperledger when we reach there.

Public key cryptography is used extensively in the Blockchain for creating keys that are used to generate identity for a node/peer/user who then initiate a transaction with the proof that he is the sole owner of the bitcoin (an asset in another network). A private key is usually a 256-bit random key that can be created by virtually any method, even by writing 0 and 1 256 times. There are various methods by which private keys can be generated, specific tools are also present, which can help you generate a private key. Public keys are generated based on private keys. There are specific methods that can be used to generate public keys; most notable ones are prime number exponentiation and elliptic curve multiplication. These functions are mathematically based and are practically irreversible, which simply means that they are easy to calculate in one direction and near impossible to calculate in the opposite direction. Given private keys, you can generate public keys using any of the methods; however, given public keys, you cannot derive public keys:

Figure 1.6: *Bitcoin address generation process*

The combination of private/public plays a vital role in Blockchain, be it Bitcoin or other prominent Blockchains. In Bitcoin, the public key is used to receive funds, and the private key is used to sign transactions.

So, coming back to the transaction, whereas both Alice and Bob have their key pairs, Alice can use private keys to sign the transaction, and Bob can use key public key and digital signature to claim the Bitcoin further. However, as a decentralized system before Bob can make use of the bitcoins, this transaction needs to be approved and written on ledger so that Bob can go back and make use of funds. So far, before bitcoin (Blockchain), this was being done by middleman or banks.

Now, there is a process of consensus, which is an agreement by all participant nodes in the decentralized network that Alice owns the funds and can spend these coins to transfer to Bob. The consensus or agreement or writing on the shared permanent ledger is done by miners. Miners are a new concept here and are generally used in the preview of public Blockchain.

The concept of miner doesn't hold well in the case of private enterprise Blockchains such as Hyperledger Fabric. In enterprise Blockchains, there are various other ways by which consensus is done and is mostly pluggable algorithms depending on how the consortium of entities that are creating enterprise Blockchain wants to have consensus.

Coming back to Bitcoin consensus, miners are again the same software nodes that perform the task of validating transactions and adding validated transactions in a block and then spreading out the block to the entire network and when every node is happy that mined block is correct and authenticated then that gets added into the Blockchain in the ledger and the score of Blockchain increases by the same source of truth is visible on the entire network:

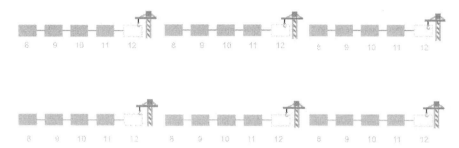

Figure 1.7: Nodes adding blocks

Creating a block is a crucial aspect of the consensus and to ensure that miner who is preparing the block is not a mala fide one, other than authenticating and approving transaction such that there is no double spend, miners need to solve a complex mathematical puzzle which requires humongous amount of energy. This algorithm is also called **Proof of Work** or **PoW** for short. This was also one of the greatest inventions in Blockchain as it is always difficult to reach consensus in a distributed architecture, and this problem has been generally coined as Byzantine General Problem. We shall discuss the Byzantine General Problem and how PoW has helped achieve the solution to the problem.

The solving of this complex puzzle provides inherent security to the Blockchain as one would not want to spend energy in the hope of doing any dubious transaction as if the block gets rejected by the peers in the network, the amount of energy spent would be wasted, and hence there could be monetary losses to the miners.

Once transactions are approved, validated, and added into the block and block has been accepted and added into Blockchain of all the nodes, then this becomes a permanent record:

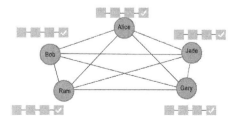

Figure 1.8: Final block acceptance

In this case of Alice sending Bitcoin to Bob, once this transaction is approved and added in Blockchain, then the transfer of ownership is now with Bob, who can spend this Bitcoins, and Alice has relinquished the ownership of Bitcoin. So, this way, transfer of value happens over a peer to peer network without any need of a middleman.

The transaction in the real world is not as simple as it just sounded, but still, it gives a fair idea of how the transfer of value can be achieved in a decentralized network. In reality, there is a lot of cryptography, sophisticated mathematics, and script execution that happens, which ensures the smooth function of bitcoin Blockchain.

This section has allowed us to understand key terms that were invented and being used in the Blockchain network, as this basis a common ground for all the Blockchain networks that came after Bitcoin.

Enterprise Blockchain, while following the same fundamentals, follows a different implementation and strategies at times to achieve the Blockchain functionality. Whereas we would be referring back to the techniques that we have learned here in the following sections, we would also be learning the difference as to why Enterprise Blockchain decided to go differently.

Blockchain types

Blockchain is not just only about technology. Instead, it is an ecosystem, a combination of human behavior, business principles, economics practices, game theory, cryptography, and computer science:

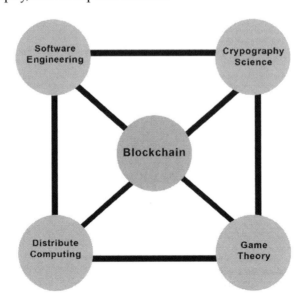

Figure 1.9: *Blockchain – an ecosystem*

A Blockchain overall exhibits specific characteristics such as:

- **Decentralization**: One of the primary characteristics of Blockchain is decentralization, which involves decentralization of infrastructure, which means no one controls the infrastructure; there is no single point of failure. All nodes are individual and equal, have the full flexibility to join and leave at will. Decentralization also involves decentralization of power, which means no single entity or a group of entities is in charge of the system; there is no need to take permission to join the network. There is no one in control of any data.

- **Transparency**: The transparency of the Blockchain comes from the fact that every node maintains the same copy of the ledger as everyone else. All transactions are visible to everyone, which includes where the transaction is coming from.

- **Immutability**: This is probably one of the unique property where no participant can tamper with a transaction after it has been recorded on the ledger. If a transaction is in error, a new transaction with correct values can be added to reverse the error, and both transactions are then visible.

- **Consensus**: For a transaction to be valid, all participants must agree on its validity.

- **Provenance**: Participants know where the asset came from and how its ownership has changed over time. This is more visible in enterprise Blockchain.

- **Finality**: A single, shared ledger provides one place to go to determine the ownership of an asset or the completion of a transaction. This is also more applicable to Enterprise Blockchain.

The idea of discussing characteristics of Blockchain is to be able to distinguish different types of Blockchains where one special favor more over another.

On a high level, there are three categories of Blockchain:

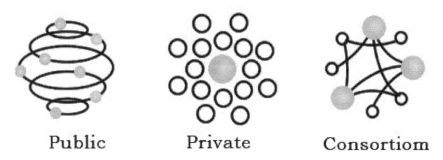

Public   Private   Consortiom

Figure 1.10: Blockchain types

- **Public Blockchain**: A Public Blockchain, first-ever Blockchain the came into existence, is a genuinely public Blockchain; anyone in the world can join, read, send transactions that anyone can see, and validate. And anyone in the world can participate in the consensus process - the process for determining what blocks get added to the Blockchain and what the current state is. They are borderless, neutral, and censorship-resistant. They are considered to be permissionless as you don't need permission for any operation. The simplest way to be part of the network is to download the compatible version of the node software, run that, and execute that to join the network. Once up and running, your node would be contacting with other peers in the network and shall download the latest and updated Blockchain ledger.

  Examples are – Bitcoin, Ethereum, Litecoin, Monero, and so on.

- **Federated Blockchain:** They are also known as consortium network. They are generally initiative or collaboration of several entities who have been in business with one another; however, they still maintain their ledgers resulting in the redundancy of data, a lot of reconciliation effort, and so on. The most successful example of this kind of Blockchain is the financial sector. In this, not anyone having internet access can come and join the network. Instead, a group of entities decides about the network, roles, and permission of joining participants; for example, any governing party might only need to view and validate the data. They might not have a say in the transactions. Most importantly, a consensus algorithm is mostly configurable, as nodes can decide who would be entitled to sign the transaction before it can be written on the permanent ledger.

  Example – R3 Corda.

  These Blockchains are more concerned about transaction privacy and are partially decentralized.

- **Private Blockchain:** These are more restrictive Blockchain, where decentralization is not at its best, and features such as immutability, transaction privacy might outweigh decentralization. In this case, write permissions are centralized at one entity, whereas viewing permission can be arbitrarily extended to the node or group of nodes. The best way to understand this is to think about private Blockchain is a traditional centralized system with a degree of cryptographic auditability attached.

Conclusion

This chapter is the first in the book was more around theoretical concepts covering Blockchain. We started with Blockchain being a data structure and then saw getting that transformed into a network. We did briefly touched upon the role of cryptographic hash function and how it helps secure the Blockchain. We took references from Bitcoin, being the first practical implementation of Blockchain. A brief about the role of Private and Public Keys were also discussed in the chapter to help understand how the transaction works in the Bitcoin. We also looked into a complete cycle of Bitcoin transfer to understand the role of wallet, keys, miners, and then successful changes in the Blockchain.

A brief journey of history and how the exchange of value have seen transitions over some time due to innovations at different point of time along with the socio-economical changes in the community that drives the trust in the partners.

In the last, we did discuss various characteristics of Blockchain and different types of Blockchain networks in existence that are meant to solve different domain problems with established platform examples in different types.

Hoping that this chapter would have given you a good start in understanding the basics of Blockchain and as we move ahead with the next chapter, surely you would get a good understanding of the related concepts.

CHAPTER 2
World of Decentralization

Decentralization is one of the core building blocks of the blockchain. This chapter shall cover the basics of decentralization and how that is being leveraged in the Blockchain solution. It also covers the various aspects of decentralization.

Structure

- Centralization first
- Understanding decentralization
- Distributed versus Decentralized
- Types of decentralization
- Decentralization in Blockchain
- Advantages and limitations of decentralization

Objective

The sole objective of this chapter is to make you familiar with one of the core characteristics of blockchain, that is, decentralization. While we would go through the decentralization concept, at the same time, in this chapter, we shall also see a comparison of a decentralized system with a centralized system. We would extend this comparison to a distributed system. A comparison drawn between these systems would help us understand the concept at its core.

Centralization first

Decentralization is the key to Blockchain and probably one of the essential characteristics. To understand decentralization, it is vital to understand the concept of centralization, which we have been living for years.

We, human beings, live and operate in societies that work on structures, most notably hierarchical structures. In this structure, we have layers and layers on top of one another, with the shrinking top as we move upwards, much like a pyramid structure. These are something we have been accustomed to for all our lives. These are the structure we do see everywhere. We see this in our schools, higher institutions, corporate organizations, and then at a broader scale, that is, at government level. The biggest challenge this structure poses is, we end up having decision making bodies centered at the very top. Ironically, the information on the basis, which decisions are made comes from the bottom side layers. As a result, power usually gets concentrated at the top.

The following figure simply demonstrates a typical hierarchical structure of an organization, where we have employees at the bottom, middle layer management, and on top of they being run by a usually short layer of Vice Presidents. And then these Vice presidents reporting into CEO of the company who usually would take almost all the decisions that are followed by the entire company:

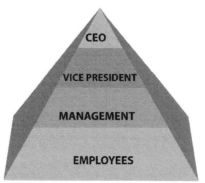

Figure 2.1: Hierarchical structure

As an apparent phenomenon, there is a drop in quality of information; there is the filtration of data as it moves upward, and usually, we end up in a situation, having decisions being made with diluted impact at the ground level gets formalized. This structure inherently gives more reliable power to people sitting at the top to make decisions for someone who is at the lower level.

At times, this leads to corruption at the higher up level and instances of influences in the decision-making process, which eventually leads to a failed institution. The core of this kind of prevailing hierarchy is centralization, power centralization.

Our software architectures have so far been following the more or less same structure. Melvin Conway, a computer programmer, introduced an idea that has become popular as Conway Law.

"Organizations which design systems ... are constrained to produce designs which are copies of the communication structures of these organizations."

— M. Conway

This was more oriented towards the software system basis, the organization where it is being conceptualized and developed. However, the structure of organizations, institutions derive their characteristics and behavior from society, which follows a layered setup.

As an example setup, if we consider one of the biggest e-retailer such as Amazon, the software system is centralized, there is usually centralized setup, that is, a cluster of servers that controls the processing, information flow, data storage, and so on, within a group of servers which are mainly owned, operate and maintained by a single entity or a corporate organization. At any point in time, if Amazon decides to bar an individual retailer from its site, they can do on their own, even for a little reason such as we have a complaint against you. Another biggest example of a centralized system is the banking system.

The following image shows a very typical setup of a centralized system:

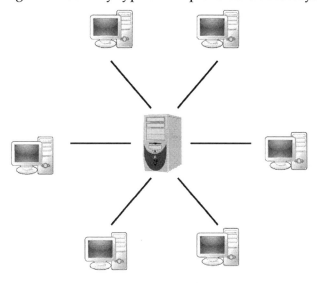

Figure 2.2: Centralized system

However, people may argue that such a bigger setup doesn't run on a centralized system; instead, they have a distributed set of systems to support complete functionality. So, whereas there might be somewhat architecture decentralization (will talk about this soon) but not political decentralization. Also, the core purpose of architectural decentralization is to provide resiliency, a property in the architecture where if there is an issue with any of the components/systems of the network, there is no business impact, and that is generally achieved through redundancy.

Redundancy is achieved by making the systems reliable, master-slave setup could be a good example; clustering is another one though it solves other purposes as well. So, redundancy is an implicit feature of distributed whereas, in a centralized system, redundancy may or may not be there. Also, the owning organization does have control of both primary and redundant systems in a centralized system. In contrast, in the decentralized system, every participant controls the same instance, so redundancy is, by default, present there.

Before we delve into talking about what decentralized systems are, how they came into existence, and a bit of discussion about new decentralized systems, let's have a look at the challenges and issues that we have with a centralized system.

Manipulation is seen as one of the most significant weaknesses of the centralized system, having a single authority as an owner of the complete setup would have the complete control over the data at flow as well at rest. Under the influence of government authorities, these centralized systems are forced to make decisions that are against the transparency, privacy, and fair practices of doing business. For example, at one point in time, Wikileaks was not able to get a donation from the public through the most significant payment systems at the behest of government authorities. So, the centralized system has the issue of manipulating certain things at their wish or under some inappropriate governance.

Control or ownership is the next biggest challenge; users of the system have near to no control over the data even if they were the sole owner of that. Assuming you are uploading your photos or other media content on social media websites, and one day your account is barred from accessing the website under the pretext of any condition.

Hacking is also one of the reasons for centralized system vulnerability. Given that centralized systems are limited to several systems, they are more prone to hacking. Once a hacker gets control of the system, he might have the reason to manipulate data or steal sensitive information of users, and so on.

Centralized systems are not censorship-resistant, the content can get censored at the operating party will, only means if they don't want to show any content even though that might be too personal to the user who has created and uploaded that, centralized systems can choose to bar that citing their policies. The simplest example could be a real opinion.

A decentralized system is free from all these issues. They cannot be manipulated as there is no one owner of the system, and it's a vast network of equal weightage participants or peers of the network. The consensus is the way by which any change in the data can be achieved; the consensus is the process of reaching an agreement as to what should be written on the ledger or database of transactions. Also, since there is no one system and preferably a group of systems with everyone having the same copy of the information, it is rather difficult or next to impossible to hack such a system.

There is no single authority that controls the system, so there is no means by which the entire network can be sabotaged by influencing.

Understanding Decentralization

Decentralization is pretty much the opposite of centralization. Everything is distributed in a decentralized system such as storage, computation, or for that matter, even the decision-making process. Decentralization removes the need to have a central server, and all participants in the network are equally capable and carry the same weightage.

Decentralization also eliminates the issues that we have seen from the regular hierarchical structure and how that impacts other users in the system. In a decentralized system, participants coordinate among themselves, and the entire network is governed by the agreed rules written down in software. Blockchain is a decentralized system that also follows the same pattern and probably goes beyond by making use of mathematics and cryptography to cement it further.

Decentralization has got its fair share of history and has been thought of, exercised, and practiced to address various aspects of software architecture, storage, and sharing, and so on. The first case that comes close to have a decentralized system was Usenet, which was developed somewhere around the late '70s by university going students.

Usenet came into existence as an improvement/replacement for **Bulletin Board System (BBS)**. BBS was a centrally run software program where users can connect to servers using the terminal program and then can upload and download data, mostly messages. Usenet was mainly intended to deliver messages reliably, and have a couple of computer systems connected; there was no central system in place. As soon as one of the users post anything on Usenet, then the local server would connect to another server, send the post, download the new messages, and this goes on for all the computers connecting in the network until the message has reached to every computer connected on the network.

Usenet was later integrated into ARPANet, and then this laid down the foundation of the modern-day internet. The internet is a truly decentralized network, where data packet delivery is done through routers, and they work independently of each other. The applications developed on top of the internet are, at the time, centralized but not the internet itself.

Decentralization has also seen an evolution in other systems such as file sharing, data transmission systems, storage, and computing systems. Napster, BitTorrent are such examples where decentralization was used and peer to peer transfer of data; files were possible to some extent; however, there was still a reliance on the centralized system at times to keep the latest version of files.

Money is becoming more and more digital over some time, and eventually, it turned out to be a number in the database, was required to go through such an invention where it can change hands on a decentralized network. Money, a form of social trust so far needed intermediaries such as financial institutions to carry out the exchange between parties for most of the time, especially when there is a geographical outreach between the parties. Establishment of trust is one thing; secondly, money is not merely data like any other file or image; if someone has spent it once, he should not be able to do so again, substantially preventing double-spending.

So, decentralization of money has its share of issues, and it has gone through various inventions over time. With the invention of Bitcoin in 2009, where the culmination of a lot of earlier invention happened, and that resulted in the real decentralization of money, which can now change hands without the use of any intermediaries and solving the issue of the double-spend through cryptographic techniques and decentralized consensus.

Distributed versus Decentralized

While we have had a look at the centralized versus decentralized architecture, it is worthwhile to talk about distributed versus decentralized as most of the time; both are used interchangeably.

Let's have a look at the figure given below; this is something which has been used widely all over the places, looking at the decentralized network diagram it appears that there is a cluster of independent nodes working together, so whereas there processing may be shared or distributed across the nodes. Still, there may be decisions that may be centralized at cluster levels and maybe using some information at the intermediate level. At some point of time, peer to peer transactions may be routed through some centralized leader:

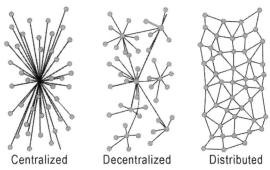

Centralized   Decentralized   Distributed

Figure 2.3: *Decentralization*

A near so perfect example of this could be gas companies such as British Petroleum or Shell; they have outlets spread across the geographic location which work independently of each other. Yet, they are controlled by a centralized unit.

The latest swarming technologies are usually decentralized to increase the robustness of the system, with a lot of nodes distributed around to carry out the specific dedicated task; however, even in that scenario, some of them would act as a centralized unit or leader, and all others must follow them. Similarly, in some control algorithms, we would notice multiple quad-copter control that is working in a distributed fashion, and a central node issues optimizations challenges to each of the participant copter to solve and then return the output. The central node will then issue instructions based on the collected and aggregated results.

So, far we must have started realizing the difference between distributed and decentralized systems. In the distributed system, as depicted in the above figure, we are not genuinely decentralized instead of a cluster of nodes that work on distributed principles yet connected through a central leader in some instances.

Now, let's have a look at the figure that is given below, and you would realize that distributed and decentralized are interchanged. It has started to make some sense now. In this image, decentralized looks truly decentralized where there is no central system, not even at a distributed level. So from architectural decentralization, that is, participating nodes are individually physical machines. Now, further, in this section, we would discuss other attributes of decentralization:

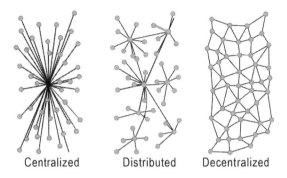

Centralized Distributed Decentralized

Figure 2.4

With the initial understanding of distributed versus decentralized architecture, we would now look into the types of decentralized architecture.

Types of Decentralization

Vitalik Buterin, the co-founder of Ethereum, has, in one of his blogs, explained the types of decentralization and has supplemented them with adequate examples. In this section, we would delve on to those points, and that would help us firm our understanding of decentralization and the type it enforces in a specific case.

Primarily, decentralization is broadly categorized into three types. However, they are independent of each other, but in real life, having one type of decentralization would mean that others also get followed to a more significant extent:

- **Architectural decentralization:** First and foremost is architectural decentralization; this infers that how the entire architecture is made up of in terms of physical nodes/computers. How distinct computers are running, maintaining communication with them, and how the entire system behaves if the number of physical systems goes down.

- **Political decentralization**: The second one is political decentralization; this comes to the fact how many people of the organization control the network made up of computer systems. In a truly decentralized system, there shall be no one person or organization that controls the system. Bitcoin is the perfect example of this as no CEO/organization in Bitcoin who runs and controls the systems in the network. Though we have been discussing the network systems, this generally applies to the real-life as well, in a top-down organization structure we had referred earlier as well, it is politically centralized as it has one CEO that controls all the operation.

- **Logical decentralization**: The last one is logical decentralization, a bit tricky to understand. An excellent example to understand this is, Ethereum, which is generally termed as 'World's Computer.' It presents one view of the interface and data that is stored across multiple systems that are part of the network. No matter which system has been queried for specific data, it comes out the same. So, there is a logically agreed state that all machines share, so in a real sense, blockchains are not logically decentralized.

There have been instances and blockchains in making that shall be genuinely logically decentralized. It is more visible across file-sharing decentralized systems such as **InterPlanetary File System (IPFS),** where other than being architecturally and politically decentralized, they are moving towards being logically decentralized where a copy of the same data set may not be available on every node. However, it would have still had the potential to get the data that is requested.

Decentralization in Blockchain

Decentralization is the key attribute of blockchains. However, it is interesting to note that since no one is in control of managing the Blockchain, that is, no one can take any individual decision rather its member or community-driven, and everyone weighs equal and have equal right to say, blockchains are politically decentralized.

Similarly, no one institution or person that is putting up the entire infrastructure or set of machines\nodes that form a right Blockchain (read Permissionless), instead it's the node that is becoming part of a network on their will by putting up their machines or infrastructure, Blockchain networks are truly architecturally decentralized, which simply means there is no single point of failure and member can leave whenever they want and even then network would keep running. The best example is Bitcoin, which has been running for the last ten years with no company or person responsible for creating or managing the Bitcoin network.

Content Delivery Network (CDN) is an example of logical decentralization. A CDN maintains and stores the cached version of its content at multiple locations spread across geography. Every time a user request for content on the World Wide Web, it's generally gets served from CDN, and if data is not found that it would connect to the origin server and get the data. So, there is no single machine or node that maintains the complete set of data that is required to be served; instead, it can get the data to be served.

The following image represents how a CDN works and how content is presented to the end-user; in the figure, we could see that content is being presented to the end-user through the Cache Server to help to reduce the load time of content. And only in the case, if the content is not present in the CDN, then it would go back to the origin server to get the data, and even once it gets placed in Cache Server, then further requests shall be served from there. It shows how logical decentralization is achieved by making sure that content is distributed across the servers and how that helps achieve low latency for end-users:

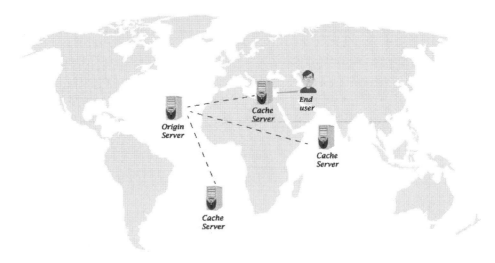

Figure 2.5: CDN

In Blockchain, every node maintains the full copy of the dataset. Hence, they are not in real sense are logically decentralized, that is, they do maintain a commonly agreed state that is replicated across all computers and hence behave as a world computer.

Advantages of Decentralization

Like any other system or architecture, decentralization has got its share of benefits and limitations. In this section, we would briefly touch upon the advantages of decentralization and would realize how these benefits are realized in the making of Blockchain systems:

- **No owner**: One of the most critical benefits that can be derived from the decentralized system is, there is no owner of the system, and everyone is the owner of the system. There is no concept of a central authority; there is no single party that controls the entire system and has the power and fancy of bringing down or manipulating the system. Every participant would play in the role of deciding what should be stored in the system and has equal rights in the decision-making process. Everyone is in equal control as to how the system should evolve.

- **Censorship resistant**: Decentralized systems are censorship-resistant; no one does have the power to censor any user or content of any of the nodes. It is the opposite of the centralized system where the operating party can censor individual user's data citing their policy or even without giving a reason.

- **No single point of failure**: Fault Tolerance is another most significant advantage that is observed in decentralized systems. There is no single point of failure; if a node or for that matter a group of nodes go down there shall not be any impact on the system, it would still keep running and working as desired. In a centralized system, if database or group of servers holding instances of databases go down then entire system go down and become unusable, however, in case of a decentralized system, since every node maintains a copy of the same set of data, there is no loss of information if one of the systems goes down. As soon as this system comes back up, it can restore the copy of data by synchronizing with its peers.

- **Permissionless**: This holds good, especially in the case of decentralized blockchain systems that are public. Anyone can join the system without needing permission from anyone. Generally, in the decentralized blockchain system, anyone brings up the node by merely installing and running the software node and then can join the network. Also, any node can leave the network at its will and join back again. There is no need to take permission from anyone as there is no central authority, and no one is in control.

- **Trustless**: Decentralized systems, especially Blockchain, are often termed as a trustless system. There is no need to trust anyone as to how data would be stored and processed. The use of cryptography and mathematics ensures the correctness and validation of data. Also, the more the number of participants in the decentralized system more is the security of the system without needing any centralized or third-party intermediator for enforcing the trust in the system.

Limitations of Decentralization

While we have talked about the advantages of a decentralized system, it is worthwhile to have an understanding of some of the limitations of the decentralized system as well:

- **High maintenance**: With the notion of distributed shared ledger, all nodes are expected to maintain a copy of the same data with them (we have some exceptions now), but considering a generic behavior, all nodes should have the full copy of the data with them. At the time of writing this book, the size of the bitcoin has grown beyond 200 GB. So, this means that node needs to have more and more resources to maintain this size of data and as well need to have more dedicated resources to operate on the data such as search, and so on.

- **Low scalability**: To write data permanently on all nodes need to reach a consensus that is an agreement, and given this is a distributed system and as well spread geographically wide, it becomes more and more challenging or a performance degradation with the increase of the number of nodes in the system.

There have been mechanisms in place to control the size of block and time to add a block in the Blockchain, but as a software bitcoin does control adjustment of timing in block addition to make sure that average is maintained. The increasing number of nodes in Blockchain is not fully solved yet, and there have been other layers of protocols being established to contain this challenge. **Segregated Witness (SegWit)** is an example of such an option in place.

- **Lack of support**: Blockchain networks so far are software-driven, and no support mechanism can help in case anything goes wrong. Extensive cryptography is used in maintaining and transfer of funds, and assets and **Public Key Infrastructure (PKI)** is at the core of the Blockchain. Nodes would maintain a pair of public and private keys to carry out transactions, but in case of the lost private key, your access and ownership of funds are also lost, and there is no way you can get hold of your funds back.

- **Irreversibility**: Blockchain data, once written on the ledger, is immutable/permanent and cannot be changed. So, any mistake on the side of a node carrying out a transaction such as transfer of funds cannot be reversed back in any circumstances.

- **Slow protocol changes**: Blockchain network works on the protocol/software code that runs individual nodes. All rules that are expected to be around transaction flow, validation, authorization, and so on are written in code only. Any up-gradation of the node software code requires agreement with most of the users (nodes) of the system, which often is a slow and tedious process compare to the centralized solution.

Conclusion

The entire idea of going through this chapter was to understand decentralization and how it plays a vital role in Blockchain networks. Decentralization is one of the fundamental pillars of the Blockchain. We did discuss centralization first and how centralization has been the core of how we live and operate. The centralized structure has been omnipresent for years to the date from our education institutions to governing bodies, and even then to a broader level where many countries/governments at times come together to serve a purpose, European Union is a classic example of that.

Whereas centralization has been in practice for over many decades, this kind of system poses its challenges and has its limitations. One of the foremost challenges that we observed was dilution and filtration of information as it moves from lower level to higher up level. The top layer in centralized systems often produces results that are based on half information and result in impacts a broader group of people. Additionally, there have been instances of influence or biased decisions under the behest of a group having self-interest.

Software systems and architecture have also been following the same structure with more of a centralized architecture where a group of servers owned and controlled by an entity or organization at times dictates the data and flow and at rest. We talked about an example of e-retailer in the context and how their decisions can impact others. We also discussed the issues with centralized software systems such as a single point of failure, hacking issue, data manipulation, and so on.

Moving on, we discussed decentralization, talked about the brief history of decentralization as to why it came into existence, given the challenges with the centralized systems. There had been various progress made on different aspects of a software system with regards to decentralization like storage, computing, or decision-making systems. However, the decentralization of money remained an issue for a long time, and we saw with the invention of Bitcoin. With the culmination of many inventions, Bitcoin was able to bring the decentralization of money; preferably, the internet moved from the internet of information to the internet of value. Decentralization has a significant role to play in the invention.

We did briefly touch about the advantages and limitations of decentralization, which were equally important to understand as we foray into the world of Blockchain. Like decentralization is an essential characteristic in Blockchain, there is another computer science field that has been in existence for decades but has a substantial impact on Blockchain and is used at the core of Blockchain. These new characteristics are Cryptography; we shall be going deep into cryptography in the next chapter.

CHAPTER 3

Cryptography – A Pillar

Cryptography plays a vital role in blockchain, be it for establishing identities, generating keys, or addressing or chaining block together. Cryptography, by itself, is a vast field with a lot of algorithms and applications. In this chapter, we would try to understand cryptographic primitives and other vital functions such as hashing and working of the Merkle tree.

Structure

- Cryptography
- Cryptography Primitives
    - o Symmetric Cryptography
    - o Asymmetric Cryptography
    - o Hashing Function
- Blockchain and Cryptography
- Cryptography Techniques in Hyperledger Fabric

Objective

The objective of this chapter is to help you navigate through various cryptographic primitives and how they are relevant to Blockchain. Blockchain, at its core, is a peer to peer system with distributed ledger having no central authority, so it becomes more imperative in such a system to have a provision that how information is transmitted, processed, and stored. With the invention of Bitcoin and hence Blockchain coming into existence, it was more desirable to have a security system to avoid problems such as double-spending. Cryptography has answers to all these questions and is considered one of the strongest pillars in the system.

In this chapter, whereas we would understand how cryptography plays a role in the blockchain-based system at the same time, we would look into basic cryptographic primitives such that we understand it fully.

Cryptography

Cryptography is the science of developing techniques for protecting data in rest and in-transit through the use of mathematical models such that the person responsible for accessing the information can only view and process that information. In the literal sense, cryptography means *secret writing* in Greek; however, the science of cryptography has moved way forward than just secret writing, which is also referred to as encryption.

It started with the objective where cryptography helped solved the issue of confidentiality when transferring and storing data. To address this issue, techniques such as character shuffling, mixing of symbols, use of alternative alphabets, and so on, were used.

For instance, Caesar Cipher is a famous cipher used by Julius Caesar, which was meant to communicate with his generals securely. The cipher *shifts* each letter in a message by a certain amount – with a shift of 3, B would become E, D would become G, and so on. It seems pretty simple and straightforward; however, nowadays, in Cryptography, the techniques which are used to protect information are obtained from mathematical models and a set of rule-based calculations known as algorithms. These models and algorithms are used to encrypt (convert) messages in ways that make it hard to decode it.

Whereas one or other means of cryptography has been in existence for quite some time, but within the last two decades, with the revolution of internet coming into existence and expansion of computer networks, the use of information has reached a new level. People now use computer systems and networks more often than before, and that includes online shopping, exchanging sensitive information over the network, and also carrying out financial transactions. That simply means network these days carry both personal and financial data and so it becomes essential that network and data are secure so that unauthorized users cannot get hold of sensitive data and use that for their malicious purpose.

Cryptography follows the CIA triad at the fundamental level:

- **Confidentiality**: Confidentiality means maintaining the secrecy of the information that is being transmitted over a network. The objective is that only the sender and the intended recipient should be able to read and understand the message. Malicious users (eavesdroppers) should not be able to read or modify the content of the message. To achieve confidentiality in a network, the message is transmitted over the network in an encrypted form.

- **Integrity**: Integrity simply means no distortion in the content; the idea is that any message sent over the network must reach the intended receiver in its original form, that is, without any modification made to it. If any eavesdropper maliciously makes any changes in the content, the receiver must be able to figure out that there are changes in the original message. Integrity can be achieved by attaching a digest (checksum) to the message. This checksum ensures that an attacker cannot alter the message.

- **Availability**: Another essential aspect is availability, which means that information created and stored should remain available all the time to intended users. Availability is also a critical factor for organizations' business continuity because the unavailability of information can severely impact an organization's day-to-day operations. For instance, a financial institution such as bank reputation would be at stake if its customers are unable to make transactions using their accounts.

While the CIA remains the foundational principles of the cryptography (and network security), there are other essential aspects which are worth mentioning:

- **Non-repudiation**: Non-repudiation relates not to be able to deny the ownership of a message sent or received. Once a message has been sent or received, the sender or receiver should not be able to deny the fact about the sending and receiving of the message. The receiver should be able to prove that the message has come from the intended sender and not from anyone else. Also, the receiver should be able to prove that the received message's contents are the same as sent by the sender.

- **Access Control**: The term access means any action corresponding to reading, writing, executing, and modifying. So, access control determines and controls who can access what. Access control regulates which user has access to a specific resource, and under what circumstances the access is permissible and which operations the user is allowed to perform on a specific resource. For example, we can specify that an entity or user X is allowed only to view the records in an information system but not to modify them. However, user Y is allowed to update the records along with read access rights.

- **Authentication**: Authentication is the process of establishing the fact that whether someone or something is, is the real one, who or what it pronounces itself to be. Authentication is necessary to ensure that the receiver has received the message from the actual sender, and not from any malicious user or middleman attacker. That is, the receiver should be able to authenticate the sender, which can be achieved by sharing a common secret code word by sending digital signatures or by the use of digital certificates.

According to X.800 (The International Telecommunication Union-Telecommunication Standardization Sector), also known as ITU-T, security services are divided into five categories. The following picture on a high level talks about the major categories in the Security services and then various other services under specific areas. We shall be talking about categories in general and wouldn't go into detail of each service as that is out of scope for this book:

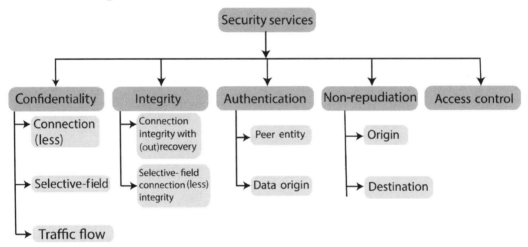

Figure 3.1: Security services

Whereas cryptography now includes a lot of things, including Symmetric Key Cryptography, Asymmetric Key cryptography, Hash Functions, Zero-Knowledge proofs, post-quantum cryptography, but we would keep our focus on the primary type of cryptography. We would elaborate on how they are being leveraged in blockchain these days.

Cryptographic primitives

Cryptographic primitives are generally known as proven, widely used, and low-level cryptographic algorithms to build cryptographic protocols for computer security systems. In this section, we would talk about the cryptographic suite of techniques that are used in general and in the blockchain system that makes it one of the pillars of the blockchain.

Symmetric Key Cryptography

Symmetric key cryptography is also known as a private key algorithm is an encryption system where the sender and receiver of message both use a single shared key to encrypt and decrypt messages. The key itself is required to be shared between the sender and the receiver, and this process is also called the **key exchange**. Symmetric Key Systems are faster and more straightforward; however, the problem is that both the parties have to exchange somehow keys is a secure manner.

With the use of symmetric encryption algorithms, data destined to be sent is first converted in such a fashion that cannot be understood by anyone who does not have the same secret key to decrypt it. Once the intended recipient who possesses the key receives the message, the symmetric algorithm would reverse its action so that the message can be made to come back to its original and understandable form. The secret key that the sender and receiver both trying to use could be a specific code, or it could be a random string of characters or numbers that have been generated by a secure random number generator.

Symmetric key cryptography supports two types of encryption algorithm:

- **Block algorithm**: A block cipher takes a fixed length of bits as input, then known as a block, in the plaintext message and encrypts that block. Generally, blocks are composed of 64 bits. Still, it can be of variable length depending on the particular algorithm being used and the various modes in which the algorithm might be capable of operating. As the data is being encrypted, the system holds the data in its memory as it waits for complete blocks.

  Block ciphers are slower in operations than stream ciphers; however, they turned out to be more efficient. Since block ciphers operate on larger blocks of the message at a given time, they are more resource-intensive and are regarded to be more complicated than stream ciphers to be implemented. Most of the encryption algorithms present in symmetric key algorithms are block ciphers. Usually, block ciphers are considered better for use in a fixed size of the message that is well known in advance; a good example could be encrypting a file or have message sizes that are already known in protocol headers.

- **Stream algorithm**: A stream cipher encrypts each bit in the plaintext message, 1 bit at a time. In this case, since data is encrypted in streams, no data is retained in the system's memory. Stream ciphers are considered to be better for use in situations where data is of unknown size, or the data is in a continuous stream.

  The following figure describes the symmetric key cryptography at a very high level. In this, we have a plaintext or unencrypted message which we wish to send to someone else. With the use of a key and encryption algorithm, the plaintext is converted into ciphertext. This ciphertext is unreadable for anyone who trespasses in between. Once the ciphertext reaches the intended recipient than with the use of the Shared Key and decryption algorithm, the recipient can decrypt the message from ciphertext to plain text:

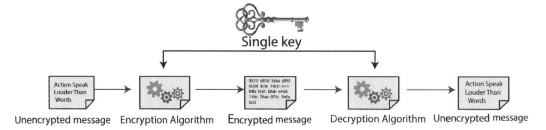

Figure 3.2: Symmetric Key Encryption

Some of the well-known symmetric algorithms are:

- AES (Advanced Encryption Standard)
- DES (Data Encryption Standard)
- Blowfish
- RC4 (Rivest Cipher 4), RC5 (Rivest Cipher 5), RC6 (Rivest Cipher 6)

Asymmetric Key Cryptography

Asymmetric cryptography is a cryptographic system that uses a pair of keys, a public key, and a private key. It is called asymmetric because private and public keys are different, unlike in Symmetric key where there is a single that gets used by both sender and receiver. It is also known as public-key cryptography, and it came into existence later than symmetric key cryptography. The public key is supposed to be widely distributed, whereas the private key is meant to be known and remain securely with its owner. Keys are always created in a pair – every public key must have a corresponding private key. Recipient's public key is used to encrypt the plain text by the sender, and the recipient uses its private key to decrypt the resultant ciphertext that has been communicated.

In this system, the recipient is responsible for the generation of both the Public Key and the Private Key. To understand this, Public Key could be referred to as **pk** and the Private Key as **sk**. To represent both of these keys together, they shall be mathematically represented together as (pk, sk). The sender uses the Public Key (pk) of the recipient to encrypt the plain text message that needs to be sent across to the receiving party. The recipient then makes use of the corresponding Private Key (sk), whom the recipient is the sole owner and has kept securely to decrypt the encrypted ciphertext from the sender.

One of the advantages of asymmetric cryptography over symmetric cryptography is to avoid the need for both the sender and the receiver from having to meet face to face to decide on how to protect (or encrypt) their lines communications with each other. However, this still poses the question, how does the sender know about the public key? It can be done in the following ways:

- The receiver can willing let the sender know of its Public Key (pk) on a public channel so that the communications can be initiated and then further established for the transfer of data in a secure way

- The sender and the receiver may not know about each other in advance. In that scenario, the receiver makes it Public Key is known on a global basis so that whoever wishes to communicate with the receiver party can communicate

In the below given rudimentary example, let's say Alice and Bob want to communicate in secure manner, and Alice wants to send a text message to Bob. So, Bob would have his Public/Private Key generated and shall share the Public key with Alice. When Alice wants to send a message to Bob, then she can encrypt the message with Bob's public key, and Bob, in turn, on receiving the ciphertext can decrypt the message using his private key:

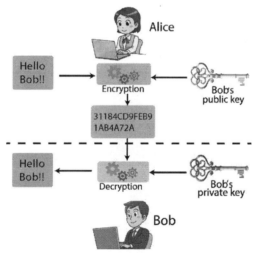

Figure 3.3: Asymmetric Key Encryption

Some of the well-known asymmetric algorithms are:

- Diffie-Hellman
- RSA (Rivest–Shamir–Adleman)
- DSA (Digital Signature Algorithm)
- Elliptic Key Cryptography

Public key cryptography has some limitations as well, most notable ones are, asymmetric key cryptography are slow compared to symmetric cryptography, and it doesn't fit well where a large amount of data needs to be encrypted.

At the same time, asymmetric cryptography because of the multiple key nature lets the receiver keep only one private key to communicate with the multiple senders.

A couple of examples where Public key cryptography is used:

- **HTTPS protocol:** Used in SSL/TLS, for example, for key agreement
- **SSH:** Protocol that allows creating a terminal connection securely
- **Bitcoin:** Virtual currency
- **DNSSEC**: Provides integrity for DNS

Hash functions

It is better known as cryptographic hashing function or keyless cryptography. There is no use of a key in hash functions; instead, they are used to create a theoretically unique fingerprint of the message, which helps us determine if the message has been altered from its original form.

Widespread use of an extension of the hash function is digital signatures that allow us to not only create a hash to ensure that the message has not been altered but also encrypt the hash with the public key of an asymmetric algorithm to ensure that the message was sent by the expected party and to provide for non-repudiation.

Hash functions are a set of a mathematical algorithm that can take input data of any arbitrary length and produces an output of a bit string of fixed length size. The input to the Hash function is called message and output is known as hash, message digest, or simply digest.

The following image gives us an illustration of how an input change leads to the change in the output:

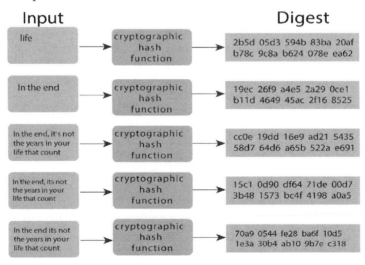

Figure 3.4: Hash function

In the first instance, we are just passing one world; however, we are getting fixed length of output as we would be getting when we would pass input of different lengths, in this example, we are still passing a limited string set as an input however if we do pass the content of a complete book we shall still be getting the fixed-length output.

Another observation is changing one character in the entire input leads to the variable output. We can very well make out that changing one character in word (see word 'end' in input) is resulting in fixed-length yet unpredictable output.

The first two inputs, even being smaller in length than the rest of the input content resulting in the same length output. Difference between 3rd and 4th input is quite small; notice that in 4th input, we have just changed it's to its, and the output completely changed, and there is no way to figure out from both the output's that their inputs were relatively similar. In the same fashion, in 5th input, the only change is we have just removed a comma afterword end, and then again, there is the total change in output and that too with no predictability. The output has been generated using the SHA1 algorithm on a windows machine.

Hashing function possesses a couple of fundamental properties which makes it worthwhile to use in cryptographic functions:

- **One-way function**: Hashing functions are one-way functions, which simply mean that there is no way that given an output, we can figure out the input (challenging to find). It is also known as **Pre Image Resistance.**
- **Collision resistance**: Hashing function ensures that if two inputs are different, then their output would always be different. Also known as **Collision Free.**
- **Deterministic output**: Regardless of how many times we provide the specific and same input to the hashing function, it shall always give the same output. It is termed as **Second Pre Image Resistance.**

Other than this, there are other properties in the hash functions, which are also useful in blockchain applications.

- **Puzzle friendly**: Whereas it is difficult to figure out the input based on the output, it is quite efficient in calculating the output for comparison if the input is given. It is something that is used in Bitcoin for validation when a nonce is produced after meeting the difficulty level.
- **Hiding**: a minor change in input message could change the hash value so extensively that the new digest appears uncorrelated with the old hash value; this is also known as the avalanche effect.

Some of the cryptographic hash algorithms are:
- MD5 (Message-Digest Algorithm 5)
- SHA-1 (Secure Hash Algorithm 1)

- SHA-2 (Secure Hash Algorithm 2)
- SHA-3 (Secure Hash Algorithm 3)
- RIPEMD-160 (RIPE Message Digest)

Essential applications of cryptographic hashing algorithm are:

- **Message integrity**: This is often used for file verification. The process of comparing the message digest before and after transmission helps verify if the content of the message or file is intact and has not been tampered with.

- **Digital signature**: Digital signature is performed on the message digest of the message to be transmitted. The received message is deemed authentic if the signature verification succeeds, provided the signature, and recalculated hash digest over the message. That way, the message integrity property of the cryptographic hash is used to create secure and efficient digital signature schemes.

- **Password verification**: It is a great threat of massive security breaches if file/ storage containing user credentials as plain text is compromised. To tackle this, there is a practice to only store the hash digest of each credential. To authenticate the user, the password presented by the user is converted into a hash using a cryptographic hashing function and then is compared with the stored hash.

- **Proof of Work**: Other than being used in a different system in different forms and shapes, the hashing function is being leveraged in well-known public blockchain systems such as Bitcoin and Ethereum. Every node is required to perform some work to prove that it has found a valid block. One of the key features of this scheme is their asymmetry: the work would be moderately hard on the requester side but comparatively easy to validate at the receiver end. That is why miners do end up spending a significant amount of resources while other nodes validating the block can quickly compute the validity.

With a level of basic understanding built around cryptography and its primitives, we shall now spend some time around to see how cryptography is being used in the blockchain and its related systems.

Blockchain and Cryptography

Whereas we have briefly touched upon the cryptography in the above section and did talk about primitives as well, in this section, we would try to cover cryptography and its application in various forms in current blockchain platforms.

The use of cryptography in private transactions goes back to the early 1990s when the eCash system was conceived by David Chaum, where eCash was being used for shopping at the establishments which were accepting it. This system was not successful because of various reasons such as it was still a centralized system being controlled by a trusted third party, and so on. At the same time, there were other inventions of cryptographic ideas going around, most notably one cryptographic concept, and their implementations are from Adam Back's 'hashcash' proposal, Wei Dai's 'b-money' and Nick Szabo's 'Bitgold' proposal. These concepts became the foundation of the Bitcoin for Nakamoto. Then there were a lot other blockchain platform came into existing learning and improving on Bitcoin cryptographic usage and implementation.

Generally, cryptographic primitives in blockchain are categorized into two parts, primary and optional. The first part includes cryptographic hashes and standard digital signatures that are essential for ensuring the blockchain as an immutable global ledger with the feature of public verifiability and can achieve consensus. On the other side, an optional category is mainly used for enhancing the privacy and anonymity of blockchain-based transactions. It uses the concept of unique signatures like ring signatures, zero-knowledge proofs, and so on. Furthermore, other cryptographic primitives, such as secret sharing and oblivious transfer, are also indirectly used.

Cryptographic Hash Function

The hash function is one of the most used primary cryptographic primitives in blockchain, though we have discussed this in the earlier section, now we would delve more into this from the perspective of blockchain.

A hash function H is a function that takes an input of an arbitrary length and produces a fixed-length output. It possesses the following properties:

- Collision resistance
- Preimage resistance
- Second pre-image resistance

Cryptographic hash functions in blockchain are used for various purposes, including the following:

- In cryptographic computing puzzles, for example, Proof of Work (POW) in Bitcoin
- Address generation (for public and private keys)
- Shortening the size of the public addresses
- Message digests in signatures
- Merkle Root Hash

Merkle Root hash is an essential ingredient in the block header that provides the cumulative hash of all the transactions:

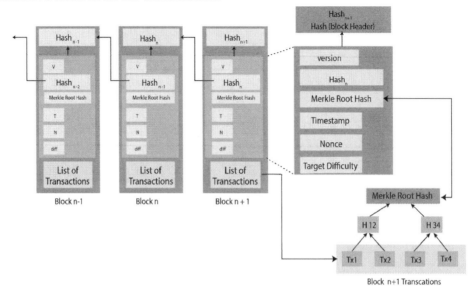

Figure 3.5: Merkle Root Hash

Digital Signatures

One of another cryptographic primitive that is equally important and used widely in the blockchain is Digital Signature. The idea of Digital Signature came into existence somewhere around 1976, with the introduction of public-key cryptography by Diffie and Hellman. Digital Signature ensures authentication of source, message integrity, and also non-repudiation of the sender. Digital Signature helps create shortcodes, also known as signatures of digital messages using the private key. And then, these signatures can only be verified by the corresponding public key. The digital signature ensures message integrity by helping safeguard against malafide modification of digital messages. In the blockchain, digital signature plays an important role, as it is used to sign transactions. That way, it helps in providing transaction integrity, non-repudiation of the sender.

The following figure represents a general workflow of how a user signs a transaction using his private key. It is used in the same way in the blockchain as well for signing transactions:

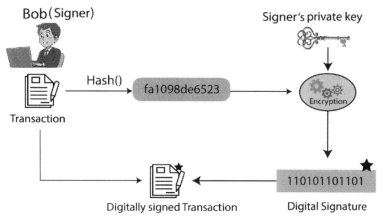

Figure 3.6: Digital signature

Similarly, the next diagram shows how other nodes, mostly verifiers verify the signature of the transaction is valid by using the transaction signer's public key. Digital Signature is decrypted using the signer's public key, which results in the message digest or hash of the transaction, which was encrypted. It gives surety of the transaction being signed by the expected user. And then hashing the transaction and comparing it with the decrypted message digest ensures that data has not been tampered with:

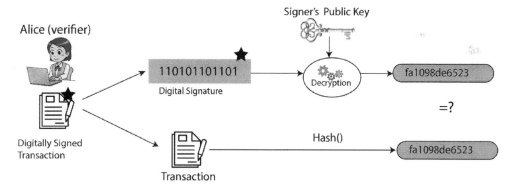

Figure 3.7: Verification

ECDSA (Elliptic Curve Digital Signature Algorithm) and **EdDSA (Edwards-curve Digital Signature Algorithm)** are the two digital signature schemes frequently used in blockchain. In principle, both of them are based on the hardness of the elliptic curve version of the discrete logarithm problem. ECDSA works over a general elliptic curve and is now used in Bitcoin and Ethereum. In contrast, EdDSA works over a (twisted) Edward curve and is now used in cryptocurrency such as Monero. Elliptic curve cryptography is a type of asymmetric or public-key cryptography based on the discrete logarithm problem as expressed by addition and multiplication on the points of an elliptic curve.

So, whereas we have seen how hash functions and digital signatures from public key cryptography as part of primitive cryptography play an essential part in blockchain, there are other essential aspects of cryptography that are being leveraged to enhance the privacy and anonymity of transactions, some advanced signature primitives are also being used.

A couple of examples are:

- Multi-Signature
- Blind Signature
- Ring Signature
- Threshold Signature

Zero-knowledge Proofs

Blockchain precisely cryptocurrencies follow the principle of anonymity of participants, and for that, the idea is to protect the privacy and anonymity of the transaction is to make transactions unlinkable. However, such systems need to verify whether the spender has the secret corresponding to the address the money comes from. To address this, the zero-knowledge proof came into existence and is being used quite extensively in a lot of cryptocurrencies in some shape or form.

In the algorithm of the Zero-knowledge proof, two participants, a prover and a verifier, participate. For the ease of understanding, an image has been shown down. Assuming Bob acting as a verifier wants to verify if Alice (prover) can prove a statement. Alice asserts some statements and proves its validity to the verifier without revealing any other information except the statement. It goes through a set of phases, that is, Witness, Challenge, and Response phase.

Zero-knowledge protocols are beneficial cryptographic protocols for achieving secrecy in the applications. They can be used to provide the confidentiality of an asset (transaction data) in the blockchain while keeping the details of the asset secret in the blockchain:

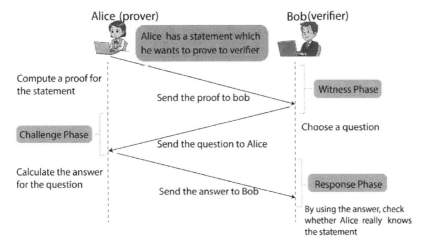

Figure 3.8: *Zero-Knowledge Proof*

There are public blockchains available that use zero-knowledge proofs; for example, Zerocoin uses this for providing un-traceability and unlinkability in transactions.

Access Control

It is by design that in the public and permissionless blockchain that all information is shared across the distributed public ledger, and everyone can see that. However, in the case of a private and permissioned blockchain platform, a selective restriction is anticipated based on some agreed criteria between the participants. There are different access control mechanisms available such as role-based, attribute-based, and organizational-based, that can be used in blockchain. Nowadays, access control techniques are profoundly used in blockchain-based platforms. Prominent use cases are medical applications or insurance industry applications where data is relatively sensitive and must only be accessible to trusted and authorized parties.

There are different types of access control mechanisms that are utilized in blockchain applications; some of these mechanisms are explained to be used in the blockchain:

- **Role-based Access Control (RBAC):** RBAC scheme provides a mechanism of restricting participants to control the access of resources or information based on their defined roles in the system. The same can be extended in the blockchain framework where access control is required based on user roles.

  The following figure depicts the role-based access control in a private healthcare blockchain. Depending on the role, each participant has got its access rights. A patient could request for his medical data, however only the doctor associated with the patient should only be able to modify the patient's health record in the blockchain. A Research Company, on the other hand, can request patients' data for any disease for research purposes:

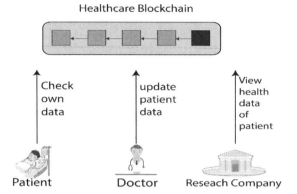

Figure 3.9: Access Control

- **Attribute-based Access Control (ABAC):** ABAC is based on the attribute structure, that is, access is granted if specific attributes are present in the request. These attributes could be user-specific, environment-specific, and so on. For instance, in a blockchain network setup between various departments of an organization, 'department' could be an attribute through which the access of the blockchain data could be restricted. In an insurance providing organization, the claims processing department could have a different view of the blockchain compared to the other department. ABAC can be used in a fair access blockchain model by keeping attributes in the policy.

Other than the access mentioned above control systems, other mechanisms can be used in other blockchain platforms, such as **Organization-based Access Control (OrBAC),** which are being used in blockchain for IoT based projects.

Obfuscation

Obfuscation simply means making something unclear. It is one of the secure cryptographic technology. The technique used in obfuscation is converting a program in such a fashion that the program still holds the same internal logic and gives out the same desired output; however, there is no way of finding the details of the program. Obfuscation makes the reverse engineering process difficult such that no one can decode the internal structure and logic of the program. It is being applied in the blockchain to make smart contracts turn into a kind of black box that is hard to decipher. Alongside, these obfuscated smart contracts can also make use of the secret key to decrypt an encrypted output. It could be a great enhancer to the privacy in the blockchain where smart contracts are generally publicly visible to everyone.

In the following figure, there is an obfuscated smart contract which stores the private key corresponding to a public key. The public key is used to encrypt the transaction data. It is hard to get the corresponding private key because of the obfuscated smart contract:

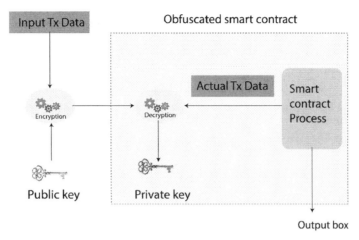

Figure 3.10: *Smart Contract Obfuscation*

A good example of partial implementation of obfuscation is Pay to Script has transactions (P2SH) in bitcoin.

Verifiable Random Function (VRF)

Many Proofs of Stake blockchains use VRF to perform secret cryptographic sortition in the process of electing leader and committee as part of the underlying consensus protocol. VRF provides a pseudorandom function that helps generate a verifiable public proof of its output based on public input and private key. It helps map inputs to verifiable pseudorandom outputs.

Algorand and Witnet network protocol are examples of blockchain platforms that employ VRF to conduct secret cryptographic sortition.

In this section, we have tried to cover various primary and optional cryptographic primitives in the context of blockchain, which is being used in various blockchain platforms. Still, this list is not complete, and there are a lot of other cryptographic schemes that are currently in use. Couple of them are listed here:

- Lightweight Cryptography
- Secure Multi-party Computation (SMPC)
- Secret Sharing
- Commitment Scheme
- Accumulator (used in Zerocoin)
- Oblivious Transfer (used in Searchain)

- Oblivious RAM
- Proof of Retrievability (POR) – Storj uses this approach

Cryptographic Techniques in Hyperledger Fabric

Given cryptography has been an integral part of the blockchain platform, various functions and so for Hyperledger Fabric. There are various primitives and optional cryptographic schemes that get applied in Hyperledger Fabric.

The main focus areas for Hyperledger Fabric which we would see are as follows:

- Participants Identity
- Access Control
- Identity Mixer
- Ledger Integrity (Hashing)
- Authenticity of transactions

Participants Identity

Hyperledger Fabric is a permissioned blockchain which inherently means that all parties in the fabric network are known in advance and at times known to each other. The different participants in the network primarily are peers, orderers, client applications, administrators and users, and so on. Each participant in the network has a digital identity encapsulated in an X.509 digital certificate.

X.509 digital certificate is a document that holds a set of attributes relating to the holder of the certificate. For a participant identity to be valid, it must be issued from a trusted authority, and trusted authorities are also known as Certificate Authority:

Figure 3.11: Identity Issuance

Issuance of certificates is part of **Public Key Infrastructure (PKI),** think of public-key cryptography primitive who issues digital certificates to participant nodes, who then use them to authenticate themselves in the messages they exchange with their environment. Although a blockchain network is more than just a communications network, it strongly banks on the PKI standard to ensure secure communication between various network participant entities, and to ensure that messages posted on the blockchain are duly authenticated.

Whereas in Hyperledger Fabric, the identities can be issued from well know PKI. At the same time, the fabric itself provides an in-house CA by the name of Hyperledger Fabric CA that can be used to generate and issuance of certificates.

Access Control

We did talk about this cryptographic primitive in one of our earlier sections and how this can help controlled access to the resources in the blockchain network. Hyperledger Fabric extends the idea of participant identity to determine the exact permissions over resources and access to information that actors have in a blockchain network.

Hyperledger Fabric has come up with something that is called **Attribute-Based Access Control** or **ABAC.** In an attribute-based access control scheme, any type of attributes, such as user attributes or resource attributes, is configured to define and determine access. Specific Key-value attributes can be assigned while registering and enrolling the user, and the same can be checked during the invocation of resources.

Identity Mixer

We did talk about anonymity and unlinkability in Zero-knowledge proof; on the same lines, Hyperledger Fabric uses *Idemix*. Idemix is a cryptographic protocol suite that provides the facility of anonymity and unlinkability. With privacy-preserving features such as anonymity, it facilitates the ability to do the transaction without revealing the identity of the transactor. At the same time, it provides unlinkability that is the ability of a single identity to send multiple transactions without revealing that the transactions were sent by the same identity:

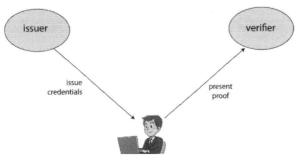

Figure 3.12: Identity Mixer

Same as we saw in Zero-Knowledge Proof:

- An issuer or trusted authority certifies a set of user's attributes that are issued in the form of a digital certificate, also known as the **credential**.

- The user then generates a **zero-knowledge proof** of possession of the credential and also selectively discloses only the attributes the user wants to disclose. The proof, because it is zero-knowledge, does not disclose any additional information to anyone, be it verifier or issuer.

As of now, only Fabric Java SDK provides support for Idemix, which is planned to be extended further in the next releases.

Hashing

Hashing is one of the most used cryptographic primitives in blockchain platforms and so in Hyperledger Fabric. We know that a blockchain is structured as a sequential log of interlinked blocks, where each block contains a sequence of transactions. One of the principal constituents of the block is the header, and each block's header includes a hash of the block's transactions, as well as a copy of the hash of the previous block's header. In this way, all transactions on the ledger are sequenced and cryptographically linked together. The hashing technique used in Fabric is SHA256:

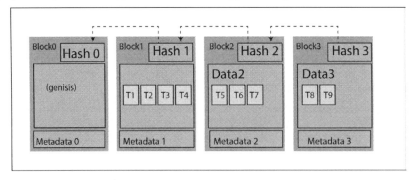

Figure 3.13: Block Hashing

Digital signature

Hyperledger Fabric follows steps of the sequence, also known as Transaction Flow, right from the starting when a client initiates it to the point when this transaction finally makes it to the ledger. In this process, there is a step of Endorsement, which is part of the consensus algorithm that Hyperledger Fabric follows, whereby endorsing the client endorses the incoming transaction and verifies the signature. Though transaction flow has been explained in different chapters in detail, the objective of this section is that the Digital Signature cryptographic scheme is an essential part of the transaction.

Just to give you a glimpse, the following figure shows the first step of the transaction flow. Don't worry if you do not understand it thoroughly; we shall cover this in detail in the coming chapters.

A Client is sending a request to targets **peer A** and **peer B**. The transaction proposal is constructed where the proposal is a request to invoke a chaincode function with specific input parameters, having the intent of reading and/or updating the fabric ledger. Along with input, the proposal takes the user's cryptographic credentials to produce a unique signature for this transaction proposal:

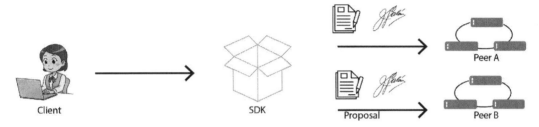

Figure 3.14: *Transaction proposal submission*

Now, the below-given diagram is the second step of the transaction where endorsing peer verifies the transaction, among other things. In this step, the endorsing peer also verifies if the signatures are valid:

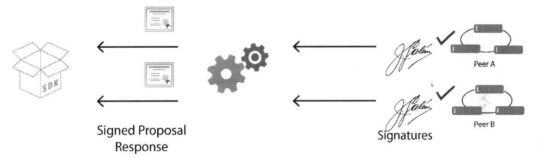

Figure 3.15*: Transaction proposal response*

There is more to this, which we shall cover in the chapter, which talks about privacy and security in Hyperledger Fabric.

Conclusion

With this, we come to an end for this chapter, where we talked about Cryptography. Cryptography by itself is a vast field, and covering it in its entirety would need a separate book. The idea was to make sure that essential features and techniques are covered in this chapter, with no intention of going through detailed internals of every technique. The knowledge imparted in this chapter is sufficient to forget going with blockchain and Hyperledger Fabric because, as application developers, we shall be using these techniques that too wrapped in mostly SDKs.

So, cryptography is an essential pillar of Blockchain platforms, and without the use of cryptography and related primitive and optional techniques, no blockchain platform can be thought of. In this chapter, we tried to cover the basics of Cryptography and basic primitives involved in it. With that, we moved on to understand the use of cryptography in blockchain and saw how various techniques are being used at the basic and advanced levels.

Hyperledger Fabric is a permissioned blockchain, so where cryptography is necessarily required for the ledger, transaction, and so on, it has to take care of the participant identity and access control, which we have covered in this chapter briefly. Though this chapter was explicitly about cryptography, so we have explicitly mentioned these. We shall try to cover such concepts in the entire book as and when we would see the need to discuss them.

Another vital characteristic of the Blockchain platform is consensus; in the next chapter, we shall cover consensus is detail.

CHAPTER 4
Consensus Algorithms

In a decentralized system, consensus plays a crucial role in determining what should be written permanently in a tamper-proof way. An understanding of the consensus algorithm is vital to understand how the blockchain system works. This chapter covers various consensus algorithms.

Structure

- Consensus Algorithms
- Decentralized Consensus Challenges
- History of Consensus Algorithm
- PAXOS
- RAFT
- Byzantine General's Problem
- Nakamoto Consensus

Objective

The objective of this chapter is to help you go through and understand an essential aspect of the decentralized system, that is, consensus or simply put, way to reach an agreement between different sets of participants.

Consensus Algorithms

A consensus in simplest of terms is about reaching an agreement by a group of participants regardless of the mechanism that they might have used. The result of reaching a consensus is that participants agree on the result, state of something which could be agreed upon by all, and this agreed state becomes the basis of the next set of transactions. The consensus then becomes accepted decision among a group of participants. Importantly, there is a process adopted by participants as to what rules or methodologies they shall follow to reach consensus, for computer science thinks of this as algorithm and output state of the agreement is consensus. So, combining the two, a defined process or set of rules for reaching an agreement is broadly or roughly known as a consensus algorithm.

A terrible example of this could be a group of college students planning to go to a coffee shop, and they have a couple of options as to which café would they want to have their coffee. They all could have a leader whom they trust, and the leader can decide where they all should be going. Alternatively, they could raise their hands for a specific option, and by counting the numbers where most people want to go, they can close the option. The result or consensus is that they finally reached an agreement of the selection of a café.

So, when a lot of members are taking part in a system, and they need to agree on something, they need to follow specific rules to achieve that. In a system, though, it might be a distributed one. Still, it is controlled by a single entity that everyone can trust, so there is no need or slight requirement of dealing with consensus. In a decentralized network, where there is no single entity that controls the data, peers might not trust each other than every peer that is part of the network need to agree on the way to verify the transaction, and agree on the order as to how these records should be persisted, necessarily agreeing on the final state of the output.

In a distributed system, achieving consensus has always been a challenge where a lot of people kept on proposing ways to solve the issue and achieve consensus. In a distributed network, there could be a challenge of nodes going down, network getting partitioned or the biggest one was where nodes might behave maliciously, reaching to consensus was difficult to achieve until the invention of Bitcoin where Satoshi Nakamoto gave an acceptable way of solving the problem of **Byzantine Fault Tolerance (BFT)** by way of **Proof of Work (PoW)** consensus algorithm. Following the suit, there has been a lot of algorithms that have come out to overcome some of the limitations of the PoW algorithm.

Decentralized Consensus Challenges

On the contrary to a centralized system, where one is in control to perform any action, a decentralized system is a set of nodes working and coordinating together to achieve a common objective. Whereas we have discussed the benefits of the decentralized system earlier in detail, there are a couple of consequences that come as part of having a decentralized system in place. The following are the consequences.

Concurrency

In a decentralized system, participant nodes work as separate processes, and they operate concurrently, which simply implies that there shall be multiple events that would be co-occurring. To be able to sync with others, they need to work in coordination with each other.

No Global Clock

To maintain consistency across the participating nodes in the network, it is essential to determine the sequence of events that have happened over a period, which is difficult to achieve in the absence of a single global clock across the network. Having a global clock and then timestamping the event would have helped figure out the sequence of events, however due to the phenomena of *clock drift* where the situation may arise that a clock does not run correctly at the same rate as a reference clock. So, we might end up getting ordering of events wrong as they do not follow a global clock.

In the same way, it is difficult to identify the event sequence based on when the events were received and when they were sent.

Independent Failures

Another consequence of having a decentralized system is that system can fail at any point in time for various reasons beyond control. The failures could be:

- **Crash-fail**: The node can stop working because of software/hardware failure.

- **Network partitioning**: A subset of a network could be partitioned, and a group of nodes can get disconnected, and as a result, the message could start getting dropped. The following figure shows a network partitioning between **Server A, Server B, and Server C:**

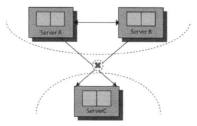

***Figure 4.1**: Network partitioning*

Byzantine

Any node in the network may choose to behave maliciously and could start acting arbitrarily. That simply means it may decide to send wrong messages, block, or alter messages in the network.

Messaging

Lastly, one of the vital aspects of the decentralized system of how peers or nodes communicate with each other. So, they communicate with each other through passing messages between themselves. Messages can be exchanged through any one of the available protocols, be it HTTP, RPC, GRPC, or any other custom protocol. They could be of two types of message exchange patterns:

- **Synchronous Message Exchange:** In a synchronous system, it is known that messages would be sent across or delivered within a time-bound fashion. In this scenario, systems are generally less complex as peers would be sure that once they have sent a message, it would be received by another peer. However, this might not be a realistic scenario in real-world deployments where systems can crash, go offline, or messages could be lost or delayed.

- **Asynchronous**: In an asynchronous system, it is reasonably assumed that message could be lost in the network, there might be a long delay or messages could be received by recipients in totally out of order.

With all these consequences that a distributed network could have it is essential to have design considerations in the decentralized system so that they are still able to achieve a common goal and more importantly consensus in the system so that all the nodes in the system have a consistent view of the state of transactions.

To achieve consensus in a distributed network, the consensus is defined as an assurance of the following properties in a distributed system:

- **Validity**: Any value decided upon must be proposed by one of the processes
- **Agreement:** All non-faulty nodes must decide\agree on the same output value
- **Termination**: All non-faulty nodes eventually decide on some output value

History of Consensus Algorithms

With the ever-growing use of computing infrastructure, architectures are becoming more and more distributed. A single machine has its limitation, and it has a limit as to what it can handle. With the increase of usage of systems and higher volumes of data and traffic, there is a need for systems to be able to handle things in parallelism fashion to scale better and to address the need for high traffic, which a single system may not be able to achieve. We need **Scalability** there. Other than

Scalability, systems are expected to be highly available all the time, even if there are varied traffic and load and also if there are failures. Business Continuity is an essential aspect that most systems, correctly enterprise deployed applications, look to achieve. To address the need for **High Availability**, systems need to be resilient, and often, this can be achieved by having multiple redundant machines that work on the principle of replication. Latency is a third important aspect where services having global coverage would want to have consistent client experience and to keep **Latency** in check; the request would tend to be served from the replicated instances that are geographically closer to the requester.

With the apparent need to have distributed architecture and the challenges that we have just seen above of message delay, network partition, and so on, how can we be sure that all systems would have the same state of the system? In a nutshell, consensus becomes a fundamental general-purpose need of the distributed systems, it ensures the useful guarantee of getting all the systems of a network to reach to an agreement on a state, provided a certain number of failures is not exceeded. In the end, the ultimate goal of consensus is not that of the negotiation of an optimal value of a state, but the collective agreement on some value that was previously proposed by one of the participating servers in that round of the consensus algorithm.

To achieve this, work has been done for many decades.

One of the earliest works that were done and got published in 1985 by Fischer, Lynch, and Patterson. Their short paper' Impossibility of Distributed Consensus with One Faulty Process' described what is possible to achieve with distributed processes in the asynchronous environment.

In summary:

- No consensus can be guaranteed in an asynchronous communication system in the presence of any failures
- A failed process could just be slow and can be active again at precisely the wrong time

Mostly, there was a trade-off between liveness and safety. Liveness assumes that nodes are free to accept different values in subsequent rounds. However, safety requires that once some round has succeeded, no subsequent round can change it.

Most notably, it was from Leslie Lamport who came up with PAXOS after several attempts and then RAFT. We shall be discussing these two in detail in the following section. Then we would also talk about a couple of other consensus algorithms that are not only Crash Fault Tolerant or can work with network partitions but with Byzantine nodes as well in the system.

PAXOS

PAXOS has a rather colorful history that span decades:

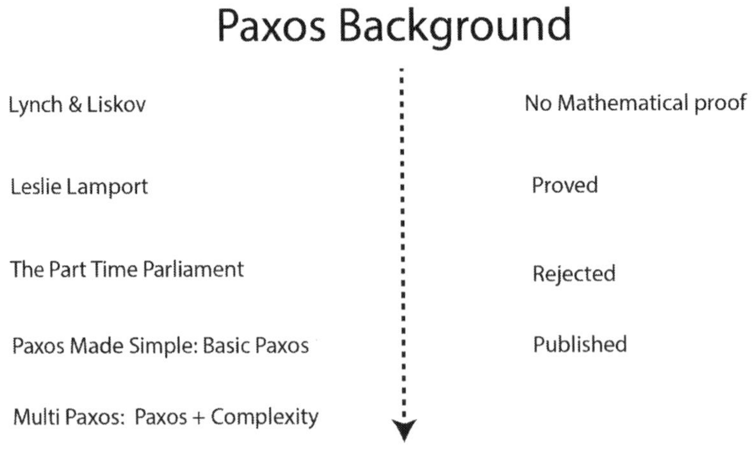

Paxos Background

Lynch & Liskov	No Mathematical proof
Leslie Lamport	Proved
The Part Time Parliament	Rejected
Paxos Made Simple: Basic Paxos	Published
Multi Paxos: Paxos + Complexity	

Figure 4.2: PAXOS evolution

The principles of Paxos have derived from earlier works of Nancy Lynch and Barbara Liskov and others somewhere around in the 1980s about consensus and distributed transactions in partially synchronous systems. Yet there was no formal mathematical proof existed until a classical version of PAXOS written by Leslie Lamport that was mathematically proved to be correct.

The idea of PAXOS initially came into existence with a paper by the name of *The Part-Time Parliament* sometimes in 1998 by Leslie Lamport. This paper was submitted to ACM Transactions on Computer Systems. This paper was rejected at this stage.

Whereas this paper tried to solve the distributed consensus problem; however, it cast the algorithm in terms of a parliament on an ancient Greek Land. Whereas it was fun to read, but it still could not help people understand the algorithm effectively. People were so engrossed in Pseudo-Greek names used in the algorithm that they found it very hard to understand.

It was not until in 2001 wherein a conference, Lamport, a conversation had with a bunch of people and had a chance to explain what PAXOS is? On returning, he wrote down the entire explanation as a short note, and then came a simplistic and shorter version of PAXOS by the name of *PAXOS made Simple*.

As of date, there are multiple variants of PAXOS, namely:
- Basic Paxos
- Multi-Paxos
- Cheap Paxos

- Fast Paxos
- Generalized Paxos
- Byzantine Paxos

Out of the complete paper, below is the excerpt from the original paper that displays the gist of the entire PAXOS algorithm. Please note that this is only from getting an understanding of the algorithm than to claim that it's all:

Phase 1. (a) A proposer selects a proposal number n and sends a *prepare* request with number n to a majority of acceptors.

(b) If an acceptor receives a *prepare* request with number n greater than that of any *prepare* request to which it has already responded, then it responds to the request with a promise not to accept any more proposals numbered less than n and with the highest-numbered proposal (if any) that it has accepted.

Phase 2. (a) If the proposer receives a response to its *prepare* requests (numbered n) from a majority of acceptors, then it sends an *accept* request to each of those acceptors for a proposal numbered n with a value v, where v is the value of the highest-numbered proposal among the responses, or is any value if the responses reported no proposals.

(b) If an acceptor receives an *accept* request for a proposal numbered n, it accepts the proposal unless it has already responded to a *prepare* request having a number greater than n.

Phase 3.

To learn that a value has been chosen, a learner must find out that a proposal has been accepted by a majority of acceptors. The obvious algorithm is to have each acceptor, whenever it accepts a proposal, respond to all learners, sending them the proposal.

Figure 4.3

PAXOS Consensus Algorithm

Paxos is a simple consensus algorithm that assumes a collection of processes that can propose values. PAXOS consensus algorithm ensures that a single one among the proposed value is chosen:

- If no value has been proposed, then no value should be chosen
- If a value has been chosen than processes should learn the chosen value

Going back to FLP outcome, asynchronous consensus protocols cannot guarantee both safety and liveness, so they all come with their inherent trade-offs and Paxos was one of the first distributed fault-tolerant consensus protocols to guarantee the safety and also attempts to produce liveness by ensuring that a proposed value is eventually selected by the group of participants in a consensus around.

There are couple of properties/essential aspects that are linked with PAXOS:

- PAXOS is an asynchronous consensus algorithm, and it takes into consideration the distributed system characteristics that we discussed in the above section, that is, there is no global clock or a shared notion of time.
    - o Also, nodes may restart/may fail by stopping
    - o Operate at arbitrary speed
- There is no way to know how long a message would take to get from Point A to Point B.
    - o Messages can take arbitrarily long to be delivered
    - o Message can be lost/duplicated
- Safety: PAXOS ensures once consensus is reached, it is never violated, that is, the agreed value is not changed.
- Liveness: PAXOS doesn't guarantee liveness, and the consensus is reached if a large subnetwork is no faulty for enough time.

In PAXOS, nodes assume three roles and known as **agents**:

- **Proposers**:
    - o It sends a proposed value to a set of acceptors
- **Acceptors**:
    - o May accept the proposed value
    - o Value is chosen when a large enough number of acceptors accept the value
- **Learners**:
    - o Its role is to find a proposal that has been accepted by the acceptors
    - o It learns the value

The conditions laid out in the PAXOS algorithm are:

1. An acceptor must accept the first proposal that it receives:

    However, there could be a situation where several proposers are sending proposed values at the same time that are accepted by acceptors, and it could turn out that all of them accept no majority value since they are accepting the first proposed value. Paxos suggest solving this by uniquely indexing each proposed value that an acceptor receives, which allows them to accept more than one proposal. Also, there could be an issue where every acceptor has accepted value, but no single value is accepted by a majority of them. Then another issue could be, if there are two proposed values and if each has been accepted by about half of the acceptors.

    To address this, a proposal is defined with a unique number, and the network selects a value once a specific proposed value is accepted by the majority of the acceptors, known as the chosen value. Multiple values can be chosen; however, it orders to comply with safety requirements; all these proposals should have the same value.

The second requirement of PAXOS that ensures safety is:

2. If a proposal with value v is chosen, then every higher-numbered proposal that is chosen has value v.

   On a rudimentary level, to just understand the working of PAXOS given now, we have the understanding of roles and basic requirements. Please note that this is not the extended elaboration of the PAXOS algorithm; the idea is just to make you understand how PAXOS works at a high level.

   PAXOS is a two-phase protocol that simply means that proposers interact with the acceptors twice:

   - **Phase 1:** A proposer asks all the acceptor nodes in the system if they have already received a proposal. If the answer is NO, then, it proposes a value. It is also known as PREPARE-PROMISE phase:

     - **Phase 1a:** PREPARE – A proposer initiates a PREPARE message, picking a unique, incrementing value.

     - **Phase 1b:** PROMISE – An acceptor receives a PREPARE (uniqueID) message.

   - **Phase 2**: Once the proposer receives a PROMISE message from the majority of acceptors, it then tells acceptors to accept that proposal. If not, then the process of the PAXOS run starts over again.

     - **Phase 2a**: PROPOSE – The proposer would now check for if it can use its proposal or if it has to use the highest-numbered one it received from among all responses

     - **Phase 2b**: Each acceptor would now receive a PROPOSE(ID, VALUE) message from the proposer. If the ID is the highest number that it has processed, then it accepts the proposal and propagates the value to the proposer and all the learners. Once the majority of acceptors accept ID, value, then consensus is reached. The consensus is on the value.

Again, this explanation is more of a very high-level overview and working of PAXOS; you can get abundant of resources on the public domain, which gives an excellent understanding of the PAXOS. Apache Zookeeper and Google Chubby are examples of Paxos.

RAFT

The RAFT is a distributed consensus protocol that was developed by Diego Ongaro and John Ousterhout. The RAFT was designed as an alternative to the PAXOS algorithm, which was considered to be challenging to understand and implement. The primary goal of developing RAFT was understandability and implement ability. It tends to solve the issue of having multiple servers agree on a shared state, even in the case of crash fault or network partitioning.

RAFT takes into all the distributed consensus challenge that we discussed in the section above. The authors of RAFT mentioned that consensus is usually used in the context of replicated state machines, which is again the most commonly used pattern in a distributed system.

Before we delve into the RAFT consensus algorithm working, shall get an understanding of the concepts that RAFT uses, which are:

- Emphasis on Leadership
- Roles
- Importance of Term Number
- RAFT RPC
- Server Timeouts

Emphasis on Leadership: RAFT makes a lot of focus on strong leadership, Raft integrates leader election as an essential part of the consensus protocol. Once a leader is elected in the system, then all decision-making abilities within the protocol must then be driven only by the leader. There could be only one leader at any point in time, and log entries can only flow from the leader to the followers.

It adds the following constraints in leader driven system:

- All message exchanges can only be initialized and initiated by the leader or a system trying to become a leader. It is enforced in the protocols specification through the modeling of all communications as RPCs.
- All clients of the application shall communicate with the leader directly, and the leader shall take care of all those communications.
- The system is only available when a leader has been elected and is alive. Otherwise, a new leader will be elected, and the system will remain unavailable for the duration of the vote.

Roles: RAFT model works on the concept of roles, which are Leader, Candidate, and Follower:

- **Leader**: The leader sends heartbeats, which are empty AppendEntries RPCs to all followers in the network; this is done to prevent timeouts during idle periods. For every command that comes from the client, it appends into the local log. It then starts the process of replicating that log entry, in case of replication at least a majority of the servers, commit, and then it applies committed entry to its leader state machine, and then return the result to the client.

- **Candidate**: Candidates are the one who starts a new election, incrementing the term, requesting a vote, and voting for themselves. Depending on the outcome of the election, become leader, follower (be outvoted or receive RPC from valid leader), or restart these steps (within a new term). Only a candidate with a log that contains all committed commands can become a leader.

- **Follower**: Followers are there only to respond to RPCs, but do not initiate any communication.

All of these roles have a randomized time-out, which is around 150 ms – 300 ms, on the, elapse of which all roles would assume that the leader has crashed and would then convert to be candidates, triggering a new election and incrementing the current term.

Importance of term number: As we saw one of the challenges in a distributed system is of a global clock, to avoid issues with clock synchronization in asynchronous systems or to avoid clock skew, RAFT uses a logical clock in the form of terms. Logical time uses the insight that no exact notion of time is needed to keep track of causality in a system. Each server has its local view of time that is represented by its current term. This current term number increases monotonically over time, meaning that it can only go up.

Each new term starts with an election process to find out a new leader of the system. The candidate nodes, after voting themselves, request for votes from other follower nodes to gather the majority. If the majority is achieved, then the candidate becomes the leader for the current term.

Following high-level tasks gets executed by observing the term number of each node:

- If servers (nodes) in the system find out that their term number is lesser than the term number of other servers in the cluster, then they would update their term number. It implies that whenever a new term begins, then the term numbers are matched with the leader or the candidate and are updated to reflect the latest.

- Candidate\Leader node demotes to the Follower state if their term number is out of date (less than others).

- The term number of the servers is also communicated; if a request is achieved with a stale term number, the said request is rejected. It means that a server node will not accept requests from a server with a lower term number.

RAFT RPC: RAFT algorithm uses two types of **Remote Procedure Calls (RPCs)** to carry out the functions:

- RequestVotes RPC as the name denotes is used by the candidate node to send the request to other nodes in the system to gather votes during an election.

- AppendEntries is used by the leader node as a heartbeat mechanism to check if a server is still up and as well for replicating the log entries. If the follower node responds to the heartbeat, then the node is considered up else, it is down.

Server timeouts: RAFT uses a concept of election timeouts to ensure that there is a rare occurrence of split votes (multiple candidates getting the same number of votes to become a leader), and even if that happens, it could be resolved quickly. To prevent this from happening, election time out is usually chosen randomly from an interval of 150 ms – 300 ms. It works out in such a fashion that in most cases, only a single server would time out, that is, it increases its possibilities of winning an election and hence less chance of split voting. Then leader starts sending out a heartbeat to all the systems before any system could time out and may become a candidate.

RAFT Consensus Algorithm

With the understanding of core concepts of the terminology of RAFT and its key concepts, on a high level, following is the depiction of the complete process that how shall it look like. In the later section, we shall use images to cover the vital aspect of the RAFT protocol:

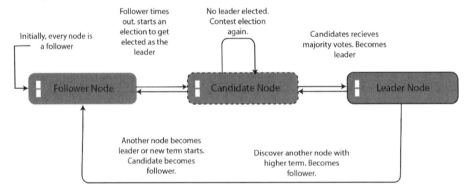

Figure 4.4: RAFT

The essential steps of the consensus algorithm are:

- Leader Election
- Log Replication
- Safety

Leader election

Electing a leader is an essential milestone of the RAFT algorithm. A leader assumes the role of the central authority in the network, and it keeps sending heartbeat to other follower nodes in the network to maintain supremacy. The leader election process triggers off if a follower node times out (usually called election timeout) while waiting for a heartbeat message from the leader node. If a node doesn't receive a heartbeat within the election time out period, then that follower node changes it state to a candidate state. After that candidate node votes for itself and issues RequestVotes RPC to other nodes in the network to garner majority and attempt to become the Leader.

Following things happens during the election process:

- A follower node becomes a candidate node if the election timeout expires. The candidate node request for votes from other nodes in the network and becomes the leader by receiving the majority of votes. Now, this leader node starts sending heartbeats to notify other nodes in the system of the new leader.

- The candidate node may not receive a majority of votes during the election, and hence the term may end without any Leader in the system. And the candidate node returns to the follower state.

- If the term number of the candidate node that is trying to request the votes from other nodes in the system received fewer votes than any other candidate node in the cluster, the vote request is rejected, whereas other nodes retain their candidate status. If the term number is higher, the candidate node gets elected as the leader:

Follower		No border
Candidate		Dashed border
Leader		Solid border
Nodes with different election timeout		Less than a quarter of timeout is remaining
		More than 3/4th of timeout is remaining

Table 4.1

- Let's assume there is a network of three nodes, **Node A**, Node B, and **Node C.**

- All nodes are waiting for a heartbeat from the leader for the period as per the timeout setting. It is called election timeout, which means if any node doesn't hear from any other node in the network, then it can start taking part in the election process. Different sizes of the red line on top of the node suggest the leftover the time remaining with the node until it hears the heartbeat. As soon as a node hears a heartbeat from the leader of the group, it resets it timeout setting process starts again. In the figure, **Node B** seems to have less time remaining before it could get into the process of leader election:

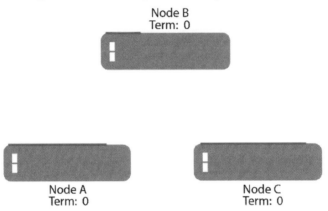

Figure 4.5: RAFT - Election timeout

- If the election timeout is over for a node without getting any heartbeat during that timeout and there is no leader by that time, then a follower can become a candidate. As shown in the below figure where **Node B** who had a minimum timeout left compared to **Node A** and **Node C**, and since it didn't hear any heartbeat, then it can become a candidate (Node with a dashed border) now, and then it votes to itself taking the vote count to 1:

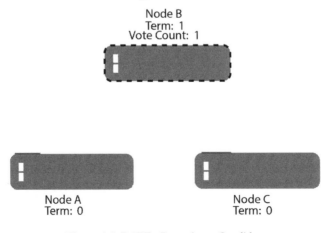

Figure 4.6: RAFT - Becoming a Candidate

- And then, the candidate node (**Node B**) sends out Request Vote messages to other nodes in the network. Other nodes are **Node A** and **Node C**, as shown in the picture. Note that **Node B** term has increased to 1, whereas **Node A** and **Node C** are still at Term 0. We could see a message going out from **Node B** to **Node A** and **Node C** requesting the vote:

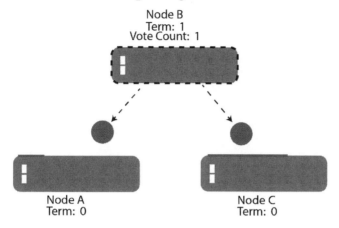

Figure 4.7: *RAFT - Request for a vote*

- If the receiving node hasn't voted yet in this term, then it votes for the candidate and as well increases the term. In the following picture, hollow red balls are being sent back as votes to **Node B**, who is the candidate node for this round:

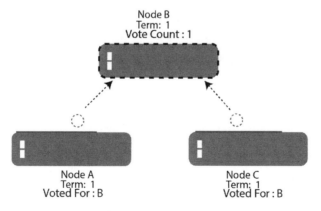

Figure 4.8: *RAFT - Vote from other nodes*

• Once a candidate has a majority of votes, then it becomes a leader. In this round, **Node B** has been able to collect three votes, including one from itself and one from **Node A** and **Node C** to become a leader. At the same time, the timeout session kicks off at other nodes while waiting for a heartbeat from the leader. A solid line around **Node B** shows that it has been elected as the leader of the group:

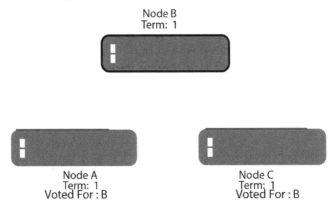

Figure 4.9: RAFT - Becoming a leader

• The leader then begins to send out AppendEntries messages to its followers, and the messages are sent in intervals specified by the heartbeat timeout:

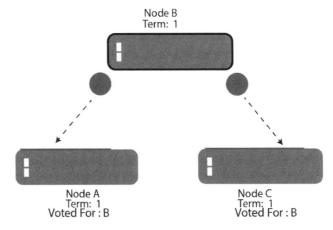

Figure 4.10: RAFT - Heartbeat messages

- Followers then respond to each AppendEntries message as they know that this is coming from the leader, and then they also reset timeout.

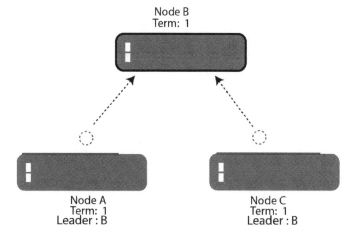

Figure 4.11: *RAFT - Heartbeat reply*

- This election term will continue until a follower stops receiving heartbeats and becomes a candidate.
- It is how the leader election process works, and nodes in the network follow the leader until the time they stop receiving heartbeat.
- The process has been depicted in the order of keeping the flow simple, yet an exhaustive process can be followed through extensive resources available online and elsewhere.

Log replication

Log replication is the second most crucial aspect of the RAFT algorithm consensus. A client makes requests only to the leader, and the leader stores all the requests made by the client in the logs. The log is then replicated to other follower nodes in the system. Usually, a log entry contains the following three pieces of information:

- Term number to determine the time of the entry of command. Remember, clock skew issue in a distributed system.
- The index is to identify the position of the entry in the log of the node. It starts at 1.
- Command: The request that the client has sent for execution.

There is a notion of entry commit in the algorithm. When the majority of nodes in the system have successfully copied the new entries in their respective log, it is assumed to be committed. At the same time, a leader also commits the entry in its log to confirm that it has been successfully replicated across the majority of nodes in the system. With this, all the previous entries in the log are considered committed. After the entry is committed, the leader then executes the entry and responds to the client with the result.

All the follower nodes execute the entries in the order they are received. It is guaranteed by the algorithm that if different logs specifically of leader and follower have identical index and term, they shall have the same command up to that index of the log.

RAFT is considered to be a crash fault and network partition tolerant consensus algorithm, so in the case of a leader crash, the log may become inconsistent. The leader then handles this inconsistency by forcing the follower's log to replicate its own. The leader node will look for the last matched index number between its log and follower's log, and then it shall try to overwrite any extra entries further from that index number with the new entries with the leader. It helps in Log matching the follower nodes with the leader.

The following set of the figure depicts how the log replication happens in a network, again the process has been kept simple to order to make it easy follow-through. In this network setup, we have three nodes **Node A**, **Node B**, and **Node C**, with a client by the name of Bob, who is trying to commit a value in the network:

- As described, all changes to the system now go through the leader. In the following figure, **Bob** (client) is sending the value of 8 to **Node A**, who is the leader of the system at this point:

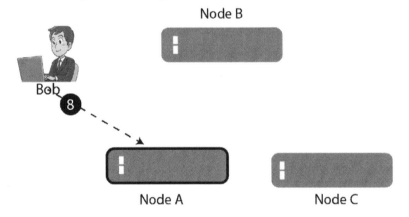

Figure 4.12: RAFT - Client request to the leader

- Each change is added as an entry in the leader node's log; at first, a log entry is currently uncommitted so that it won't update the node's value. In the following picture, you can see the **SET 8** is currently with **Node A** (leader) but with an uncommitted state. SET 8 has been displayed as a box with a dashed line:

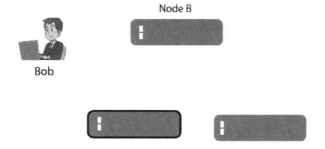

Figure 4.13: RAFT - Uncommitted entry

- To commit the entry, the node first replicates it to the follower nodes, red balls with values shown in the picture are the RPC commands that are being sent to the follower nodes to update the log as the process of log replication. **Node A** is the leader sending the value to the followers in the network, that is, **Node B** and **Node C**:

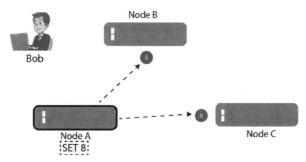

Figure 4.14: RAFT - Log replication across followers

- As a result, once the followers receive the new value, it gets reflected at the follower node, SET 8 command is now available with all the followers, that is, **Node B** and **Node C**, please note that SET 8 at **Node B** and **Node C** is uncommitted and being shown in dashed line:

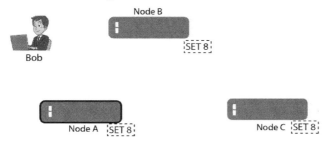

Figure 4.15: RAFT - Uncommitted state at every node

- Then the leader waits for the response from the majority of nodes until they have written the entry. In the following picture, follower nodes, that is, **Node B** and **Node C**, confirming back to the leader node (**Node A**) that they have written the value in the log:

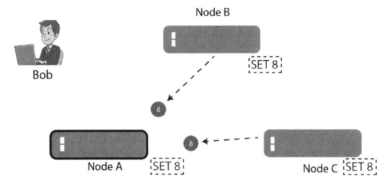

Figure 4.16: RAFT - Confirmation back to the leader node

- Once the leader gets back the reply, entry is now committed on the leader node, and the node state is **SET 8**. The committed entry is being shown as a solid line box with a tick around it:

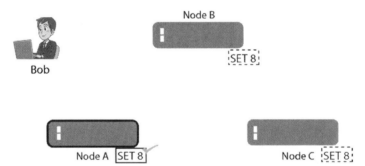

Figure 4.17: RAFT - Committed entry at Leader Node

- To commit the entry, the node first replicates it to the follower nodes:

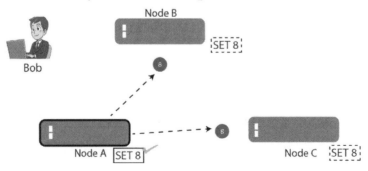

Figure 4.18: RAFT - Committing the values at follower nodes

- The leader then notifies the followers that entry is committed and follower node then commit the entry in their logs and as shown in the picture, SET 8 is now in solid line box with a green tick over it for all follower nodes.

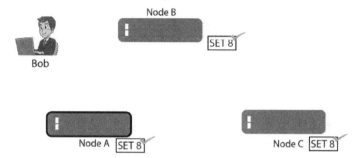

Figure 4.19: RAFT - Consensus completion

- With this, the cluster now has come to a consensus about the system state. This process is called log replication.

Safety

To ensure consistency in the cluster nodes, RAFT makes sure that the leader should have all the entries from the previous term and are committed to the log. It makes the aspect of Safety an essential consideration in the RAFT protocol. During the leader election process, the RequestVote RPC contains the term number. If the candidate node who is requesting for the vote has a lower term number than the follower from which it is requesting vote, in that case, the follower won't vote for the said candidate.

RAFT protocol safety rules: RAFT assumes design considerations in the protocol to ensure the safety of the network:

- **Leader Election**: There could be only one leader in the cluster for a specific term.

- **Log Matching**: As described earlier, if the leader and followers log has an entry with the same index and term, then these logs are guaranteed to be identical in all entries up to that given index.

- **Leader Completeness:** The log entries that are committed in a given term by a leader will always appear in the logs of the leaders following the said term.

- **State Machine**: A particular log entry applied by a node to its state machine shall have the guarantee that no other server in the system can apply a different command for the same log.

- **Follower Node Crash**: If a follower node crashes, then all the requests sent to the crashed node shall be ignored. The crashed node cannot take part in the election for obvious reasons, and when they come back up, they shall sync up its log with the server node.

That's how the consensus work in the RAFT algorithm, though the explanation here in the book, might not be a detailed one and may not have considered the minutest of the details. Still, then that was not the objective of this book, the idea was to make sure even if the reader is interested in Hyperledger fabric, but still, the reader should get a reasonable idea of the popular consensus algorithm such as RAFT.

Now, the following are some common and essential scenarios in the RAFT protocol.

1. **Split vote:** The split vote is the scenario in the RAFT protocol system when during the election, two nodes end up having the same number of votes, and hence the selection of a clear leader is not possible:

   - Let's see how a case of a split vote in the below figure; election timeout is going for all nodes where the system is in **Term: 3.** It is visible in the figure that **Node A** and **Node B** have a smaller election timeout left as compared to **Node C** and **Node D**:

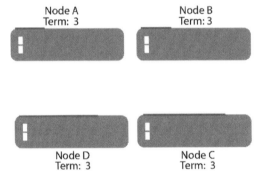

Figure 4.20: RAFT - Election timeout

   - Two nodes, **Node A** and **Node B**, become a candidate (see the dashed line along the node boundary) and start the election for the same term, **Node A** and **Node B** both vote for themselves and start requesting for votes. However, each reaches only a single follower before the other. Assume **Node A** request reaches to **Node D** first and **Node B** request reaches to **Node C** first:

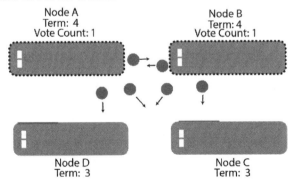

Figure 4.21: RAFT - Candidate Node requesting votes

- **Node D** responds to **Node A**, and **Node C** responds to **Node B**, so now each candidate has two votes and can receive no more for this term. **Node C** wouldn't respond to **Node A** as it has already voted for **Node B**, and similarly, **Node D** has voted for A so it won't reply to **Node A**. This is called split vote as no leader could be elected in this round:

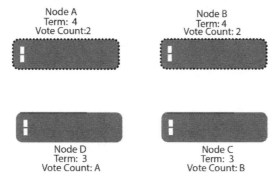

Figure 4.22: RAFT - Split vote

- Now, the election process would start over again, and as seen in the leader election section, any Node that receives a majority of votes would become a leader again.

2. **Network partition:** Machines can break at any point in time due to software/hardware failures. Similarly, networks can partition for various reasons, which simply means a subset of nodes gets disconnected from the leading network. For the time being, there is no communication happening between two sets of nodes. In this section, we would see how RAFT handles this system to make sure that consistency remains:

- The RAFT can even stay consistent in the face of network partitions; let's assume that there is a network of five nodes with **Node B** as the leader of the network. **Node B** is sending out heartbeat requests to all follower nodes in the network at regular intervals:

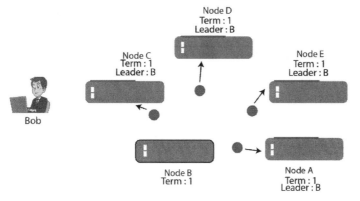

Figure 4.23: RAFT - A living system

- Communication is alive and kicking between a leader and follower node, and so other nodes in the network are responding:

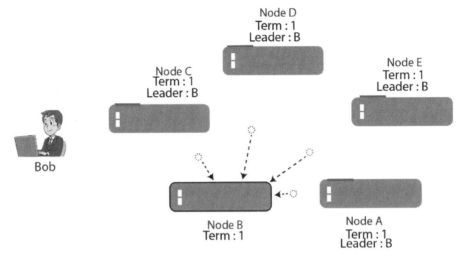

Figure 4.24: RAFT - Leader receiving heartbeat response

- Let's assume a scenario when there is an issue in the network, and a partition happens between two subsets of the entire network. In the following figure, a partition is added to separate A and B from C, D and E. Since **Node B** was already a leader, it continued to do so with the same Term but in another part of the network, in the absence of heartbeat as **Node B** now falls in another subset, **Node C** becomes a candidate. Eventually, a Leader and both are now sending heartbeats to their followers in the respective part of the network:

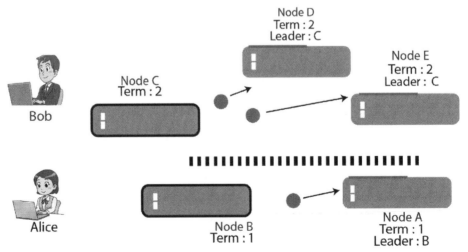

Figure 4.25: RAFT - consecutive heartbeat in a partitioned system

- In due time, before the partition could heal, and all nodes can come back into the leading network, there comes another client, **Alice. Node B** and **Node C** continue to be the leader of their group:

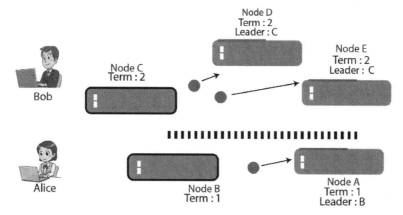

Figure 4.26: *RAFT - A new client in a partitioned system*

3. Alice would now try to set the value of node B to "3", as it is the leader of the network closest to Alice:

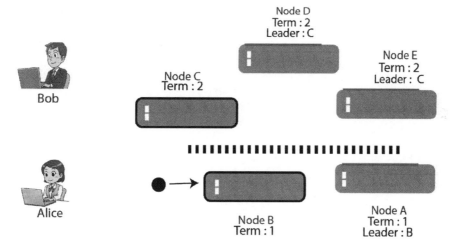

Figure 4.27: *RAFT - Alice sending a request*

- It would result in the uncommitted entry of **SET 3** on **Node B** and **Node A**; the entry couldn't be committed as there is no majority in the network:

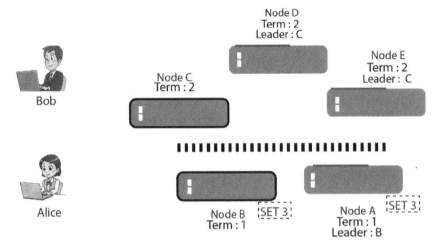

Figure 4.28: RAFT - Uncommitted entry in a partitioned network

- At the same time, another client, **Bob**, would try to set the value of **Node C** to "8", as he is closest to that network:

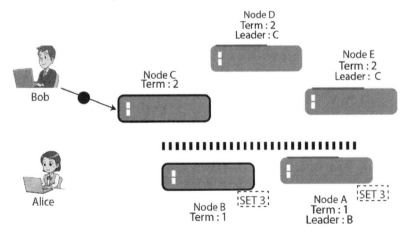

Figure 4.29: RAFT - Bob sending a request

- **SET 8** would be committed in the network as there were majority votes, and meanwhile, **Node B** network is unaware of any changes happening at another network:

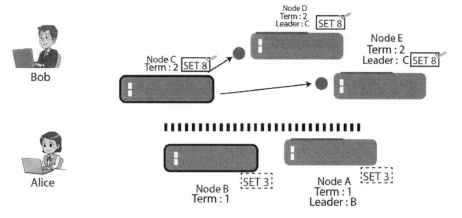

Figure 4.30: RAFT - Bob entry committed in a partitioned network

- With due course of the time, when the network partition heals, and now all nodes are again back in the same network. In the following figure, the network has healed, and nodes were interacting as they were before:

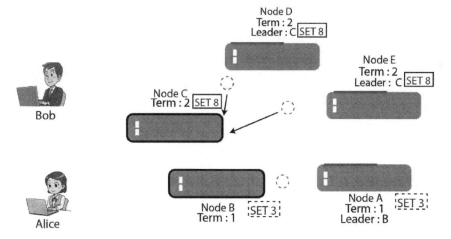

Figure 4.31: RAFT - Network partition healing

- **Node B** will see the higher election terms and step down, and at the same time, both nodes, **Node A** and **Node B**, will roll back their uncommitted entries and match the new leader's log. The log is now consistent across all peers in the cluster:

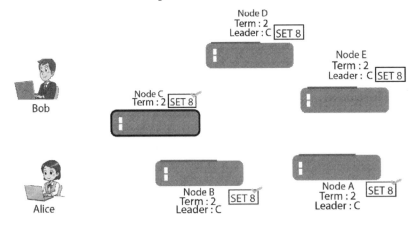

Figure 4.32: *RAFT - Healed network*

Still, we are not there

Whereas we have seen that consensus algorithms so far, that is, PAXOS and RAFT, can achieve the desired result in asynchronous environments using mainly timeouts; however, this only helps in crash fault-tolerant systems as we saw in this case of how RAFT handles consensus in network partitioning. In this case, the assumption is that nodes would not behave maliciously or act adversely. In a crash fault-tolerant system, a distributed system can be built with the assumption that a simple majority is enough to reach a consensus.

We still have not looked into the algorithms where nodes can go Byzantine. In a Byzantine system where nodes could have different incentives and act arbitrarily, we simply cannot assume a simple majority is enough to reach consensus. Half or more of the supposedly honest nodes can coordinate with each other to lie. In a distributed architecture, especially in a blockchain system where every node is an independent entity, it's hard to reach consensus if nodes turn malicious.

Byzantine General's Problem

On the same lines, The Byzantine Generals Problem is a term coined in computer science describing a situation where participant nodes must agree on a single strategy to avoid complete failure; however, there could be some of the participant nodes are corrupt and disseminating false information or are otherwise unreliable.

Before we delve into Byzantine General's Problem, let's have a look at *The Two general's problem.*

This problem describes a situation where two generals are planning to attack a common enemy. **General 1** is considered the leader, and the other is considered the follower. Each general's army on its own is not strong enough to defeat the enemy army successfully. Thus they both need to cooperate, agree, and attack at the same time to come out as a winner. It seems like a simple scenario, but there is one caveat:

Both Generals with their army on a different side of the mountain and the enemy city is in the valley. For them to communicate with each other and decide on a time, **General 1** has to send a messenger through the enemy city who is responsible for delivering the time of the attack to **General 2**. However, there is a possibility that the messenger might get captured or killed by the enemies, and thus, the message won't be delivered. That will result in **General 1** attacking while **General 2** and his army hold their grounds.

Even if the messenger can deliver the non-tampered first message safely, **General 2** has to acknowledge that he received the message, so he sends a messenger back, thus repeating the previous scenario where the messenger can get caught. It extends to infinite ACK's, and thus, the generals are unable to reach an agreement.

There is no way to guarantee the second requirement that each general is sure the other has agreed to the attack plan. Both generals will always be left wondering whether their last messenger got through:

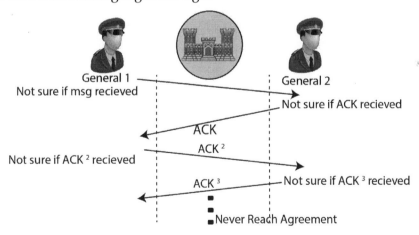

Figure 4.33: Two General's Problem

The two general problems have been proven to be unsolvable.

Byzantine General's Problem is a more generalized version of Two General's problem with a tweak; it was described in 1982 by Lamport, Shostak, and Pease. It takes into consideration more than two generals who need to agree on a time to attack their enemy. With this, they assume the scenario of one or more generals who could be traitors. The leader-follower paradigm that we have seen so far in other algorithms have been replaced here by commander-lieutenant setup. The objective here is to reach an agreement or consensus; they both need to agree on the same decision, which would be either attack or retreat.

Following the same story setup of army deciding to attack common enemy, however this time, this army has many divisions being led by generals. The army generals communicate with other lieutenants camped at other divisions only through messengers.

It is required that all the generals have to agree upon either one of the two plans of action, that is, attack or retreat. They need to agree on the exact time to attack all at once or retreat at the same time. If the attack is without full strength, then it means only one thing, they would have to accept brutal defeat. If all generals are trustworthy, then reaching an agreement is simple, and they are confident of winning. However, some of the generals could be traitors; there could be spies or enemy soldiers or in between who could pass the wrong message across.

Consider a case where there are a commander and two lieutenants, and the messages are only attack or retreat, which all need to agree on to reach the consensus:

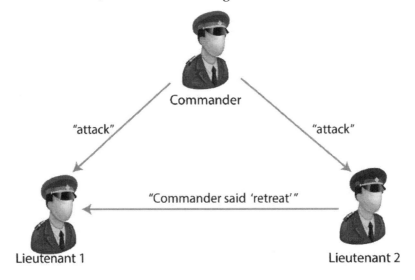

Figure 4.34: Byzantine Lieutenant

In the above figure, **Lieutenant 2** is a traitor who purposely changes the message that gets passed to **Lieutenant 1**. Now, in this case, Lieutenant 1 has received two messages and does not know which one to follow. Basis the assumption that **Lieutenant 1** follows only the **Commander** because of strict hierarchy in the army. Still, 1/3rd of the army is weaker by force as **Lieutenant 2** is a traitor, and this would lead to failure:

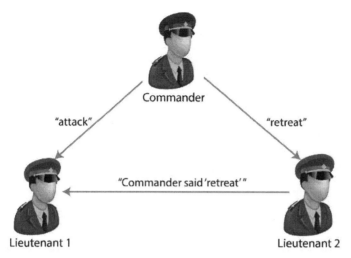

Figure 4.35: Byzantine Commander

Now, in this figure, the commander himself is traitor and is passing different messages to lieutenants. In this case, 2/3rd of the army has followed the incorrect order and might not reach consensus. Both cases are similar to **Lieutenant 1;** there is no way of figuring out if the message coming from another Lieutenant is wrong, or message from commander Lieutenant is wrong. So, there is no way that this problem can be solved with three nodes with one going Byzantine.

So, the objective now is to figure out how many generals do we need so that we can tolerate a traitor (Byzantine node)?

In the paper, this has been discussed how many generals do we need to tolerate'm' traitor?

One of the snippets from the original paper says (The details of the paper can be found here at **https://people.eecs.berkeley.edu/~luca/cs174/byzantine.pdf):**

> *Byzantine Generals Problem.* A commanding general must send an order to his $n - 1$ lieutenant generals such that
>
> IC1. All loyal lieutenants obey the same order.
> IC2. If the commanding general is loyal, then every loyal lieutenant obeys the order he sends.

Figure 4.36

IC2 says even if the commander is a traitor, consensus must still be achieved. As a result, all lieutenants take the majority of the vote. The algorithm to reach consensus is based on the value of the majority of Lieutenant observing the value of the majority of decisions.

Theorem: For any m, Algorithm *OM(m)* reaches consensus if there are more than 3m generals and at most m traitors.

It means that the algorithm can reach consensus as long as 2/3 of the nodes are honest. If the traitors are more than 1/3, the consensus is not reached, the armies would not be able to coordinate their attack, and the enemy shall win.

Another snapshot of the algorithm states:

Algorithm OM (0).

(1) The commander sends his value to every lieutenant.
(2) Each lieutenant uses the value he receives from the commander, or uses the value RETREAT if he receives no value.

Algorithm OM (m), m > 0.

(1) The commander sends his value to every lieutenant.
(2) For each i, let v_i be the value Lieutenant i receives from the commander, or else be RETREAT if he receives no value. Lieutenant i acts as the commander in Algorithm OM($m - 1$) to send the value v_i to each of the $n - 2$ other lieutenants.
(3) For each i, and each $j \neq i$, let v_j be the value Lieutenant i received from Lieutenant j in step (2) (using Algorithm OM($m - 1$)), or else RETREAT if he received no such value. Lieutenant i uses the value $majority(v_1, \ldots, v_{n-1})$.

Figure 4.37

A simplified view of this is, m denotes the traitor nodes; in the first case, *m = 0*, which means no traitors and each lieutenant obeys. In case *m > 0*, each lieutenant's final choice comes from the majority of all lieutenants' choice.

This theorem can be understood easily with the help of a visual diagram and its explanation, as given below.

Let's assume there is a network of a commander and three lieutenants, let C be the commander and L{i} be the Lieutenant i:

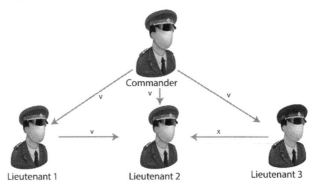

Figure 4.38: Byzantine Lieutenant in BGP

In this case, **Lieutenant 3** is the traitor, so OM (1):

- Commander sends v to all Lieutenants
- L1 sends v to L2, and L3 sends x to L2
- For L2 majority (v,v,x) comes out to v

The final decision is the majority of the vote from L1, L2, and L3, and as a result, a consensus has achieved. One of the important consideration here is that majority of the lieutenants need to choose the same decision and not a specific one.

Another case could be when the commander is behaving like a traitor:

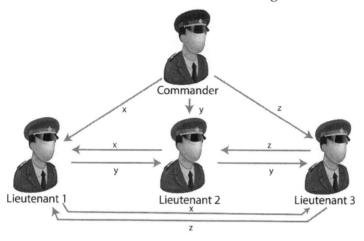

Figure 4.39: Byzantine Commander in BGP

In this case, the algorithm applies as OM(1):

- Since commander is a traitor, so it sends different values to all the lieutenants, that is, x to Lieutenant 1, y to Lieutenant 2, and z to Lieutenant 3.
- Then, L1 sends x to L2 and L3.
- L2 sends y to L1 and L3.
- And L3 sends z to L1 and L2.
- For L1, the majority is (x,y,z)
- Similarly, for L2, the majority is (x,y,z) and for L3 is the majority is (x,y,z)

They all have the same value; thus, the consensus seems to be achieved. But since x, y and z are different commands, assuming no value has been received and then as per the algorithm nodes choose to RETREAT.

In this paper only, Leslie Lamport, Robert Shostak, and Marshall Pease came up with the first-ever proof to solve the Byzantine General's problem, which demonstrated that a system with x Byzantine nodes must have at least $3x + 1$ total nodes to reach consensus.

If *x* nodes are faulty, then the system still should operate correctly after coordinating with *n* minus *x* nodes (since *x* nodes might be faulty/Byzantine and not responding). However, we must prepare for the possibility that the *x* that doesn't respond may not be faulty; instead, it could be another way around, and it could be the *x* that does respond. If we want the number of non-faulty nodes to outnumber the number of faulty nodes.

Then we should have at least *n minus x minus x > x. [n − x −x > x, that is, n > x +2x, so n > 3x].*

Hence, $n > 3x + 1$ is optimal.

One of the assumptions for this to work was to have a synchronous environment. So, we could see where we have the capability to handle either Byzantine OR Asynchronous system, not a system which is Byzantine AND Asynchronous.

Nakamoto Consensus

We have observed that most Byzantine fault-tolerant consensus protocols end up using some form of synchrony assumption to overcome FLP impossibility. Also, in traditional consensus, it is defined that a proposer and a group of acceptors must all coordinate and communicate to decide on the next agreement of value. It happens to be a complicated process because it needs every node to know all another node in the network to communicate (that is, quadratic communication overhead). However, the challenge is, it doesn't scale well and doesn't work in open, permissionless systems where anyone can join and leave the network at any time. So, we have got a set of challenges to solve that include the asynchronous environment, byzantine nodes, and ever-changing size of the network.

That is where Satoshi Nakamoto invented the consensus that applies to the distributed network of bitcoin nodes. The deterministic behavior paves the way for probabilistic. Instead of every node agreeing on a value, it works such that all of the nodes agree on the probability of the value is correct. It is also called **Proof of Work (PoW).**

Proof of Work (PoW)

In this consensus mechanism, instead of electing a leader and then doing the coordination with all nodes, the consensus is dependent on complex game theory. It is decided based on which node can solve the challenge or a computation puzzle thrown by the network in the fastest fashion.

Just to understand how PoW works, let's understand some basic primitive. The first thing would be the hash function.

A hash function is any function that accepts data of any arbitrary size and produces data of fixed size. The hash function is collision-free, which simply means that for any given input, there shall be only one output. There could no two inputs exist that can produce the same output. The output of a hash function is such that it is indistinguishable from random.

To illustrate, I have a file by the name of `hello.txt` on a local drive with text written as hello, and the output looks like:

```
Algorithm       Hash                                                              Path
---------       ----                                                              ----
SHA256          2CF24DBA5FB0A30E26E83B2AC5B9E29E1B161E5C1FA7425E73043362938B9824   C:\d\hello.txt
```

Figure 4.40: Hash of 'hello'

Changing `hello` to `hello1` makes the output looks like, with no way of figuring out by looking at the earlier message that even changing one character could lead to unpredictable outcome of the hash value:

```
Algorithm       Hash                                                              Path
---------       ----                                                              ----
SHA256          91E9240F415223982EDC345532630710E94A7F52CD5F48F5EE1AFC555078F0AB   C:\d\hello.txt
```

Figure 4.41: Hash of 'hello1'

Somehow, on the rudimentary level, think of this concept that is used to elect a leader in the PoW consensus algorithm. However, in actual, this is much more of a complex than it looks, and this includes a lot of steps such as independent verification of the transaction, aggregation of transactions, verification of new block, and so on. So, the challenge that is thrown on the network to come up with a number as a probabilistic measure to be able to become a leader and send through a block of transactions to all peers looks something like Puzzle - Given data B, find a number x such as that the hash of x appended to A results in a number less than A, assume A to be 10, and B to be *'hello'*:

$hash(B) = hash('hello') = 0x0f = 15 > 10$

$hash(B+1) = hash('hello1') = 0xff = 255 > 10$

$hash(B+2) = hash('hello2') = 0x09 = 9 < 10$, seems that appending 2 with B has solved the problem since hash is less than A.

[Please note that the above calculation of hash is not real and is being just to help us understand how this works.]

Since the hash functions are cryptographically secure, the only way to find a solution to that problem is by brute-force that is trying all possible combinations. Once a node finds the required value, then it would send the block of transactions across the network who can validate the puzzle and as well validate the transaction. And subsequently, the new block is added in the blockchain at every node level. The network keeps on building on this timestamped chain, and the chain with the most cumulative computation effort expended.

In a nutshell, the consensus is a new artifact of the asynchronous interaction of thousands of independent nodes, all following simple rules. (that is, cumulative difficulty).

Nakamoto consensus seems to be Byzantine fault-tolerant in the practical sense. However, the way it achieved consensus was way different from how researchers have talked about and demonstrated so far. It has proven to be simpler than already existing consensus algorithms in terms of going through leader election, quadratic communication overhead, and so on.

Conclusion

Distributed systems have become the need of the hour as usage and complexity of the system grew over some time. Due to limitations of a single machine and limitation of CPU power, only a limited functionality could be achieved, which may not be relevant in the current world of increasing traffic load and low latency expectations. Scalability, High Availability, and Latency have been the key attributes that were required to make the distributed system work properly. However, with the growth of the distributed system, we also saw the challenges kept coming up because of concurrency, no global clock, independent failures, and faulty messaging.

With all these challenges around, there was a need to have a mechanism to be in place for achieving consensus in a distributed system such that there shall be a uniform view to the users across these systems. To resolve the distributed consensus system, a lot of research has been done for an extended period. Whereas FLP theory mentioned that it is impossible to achieve consensus in the asynchronous system, Laslie Lamport came up with the PAXOS algorithm with a particular assumption to solve the distributed consensus problem. With difficulty in understanding the PAXOS, a new algorithm by the name of RAFT came into existence. However, whereas both PAXOS and RAFT were considered to be sustainable in the asynchronous environment, they still were not able to handle Byzantine nodes. We also discussed the Byzantine General Problem and as well Byzantine Fault Tolerance algorithm.

It was only Nakamoto consensus that took the approach of probabilistic outcome and solved Byzantine General Problem in a very novel way and that pave the way for the Blockchain coming into existence and solving the distributed consensus problem given that there is no central authority and nodes can join and leave the network at will. Proof Of Work, as it is commonly known, has been the leading algorithm for distributed consensus, especially in Blockchain platforms where the network is both asynchronous and Byzantine nodes could exist. Though there are certain shortcomings in the PoW, one could be throughput and were a lot of organizations and academics have been continuing with the research and advancements in the space.

The entire objective of going through this chapter was to understand the distributed consensus at its core and what all challenges we do see in the space. I hope after reading through this chapter, you must have got a good understanding of the consensus algorithm. From next chapter, we would start focusing on building a foundation for Hyperledger Fabric, in next chapter we shall have a look at the enterprise version of blockchain and what is required for an enterprise blockchain to be a success that would set a ground for Hyperledger Fabric as an enterprise blockchain platform in upcoming chapters.

CHAPTER 5
Blockchain in Enterprises

It is the first chapter in the new section where we step in to use of Blockchain in Enterprises, a perfect OXYMORON. This chapter talks about the need for private blockchains and considerations that the Enterprise needs to take before jumping into the blockchain bandwagon. This chapter also lists down the successful products/platforms available for readily use and real-world use cases.

Structure

- A new era - Permissioned blockchains
- Blockchain in Enterprise
- Business drivers
- Leading platforms
- Use cases/examples

Objective

After reading through blockchain in general, understanding core concepts and the role of decentralization, consensus, cryptography, we shall now move into understanding Hyperledger Fabric, which this book is intended for.

Introduction

So far, we have learned through core concepts of blockchain with regards to public and permissionless blockchain, specifically around Bitcoin or, at times, Ethereum. However, as discussed in the last chapter, whereas Enterprises intend to use blockchain for addressing their core issues around interaction and transactions with other organizations to carry out their usual business, they would want to have business-critical data secure and private. No organization would want to disclose its transactional detail in public. Other than data, trade rules and agreements are also of importance to them, which they can put together in the form of Smart Contracts, and they would want to execute these smart contracts or do transactions between intended parties and not in the view of the public. For instance, in Ethereum, being an open and public blockchain, all smart contracts can be viewed by anyone.

So, there needs to be a balance between exploring blockchain capabilities yet keeping data, transactions, and execution rules in closed-loop, which is where enterprise blockchain comes into the picture. A better way of think about enterprise blockchain as it gives a streamlined way of sharing the process and data across the members of an ecosystem in such a fashion that no single entity is in charge and control of the data. All the participants do have a say in how that data is supposed to be governed, and those involved in consensus would have a complete copy of the ledger.

Another essential aspect that the enterprise blockchain platform brings is the capability to transform business agreements and transaction rules to be coded in smart contracts that can be run on top of the blockchain platform. The shared processes are codified to establish a business flow that determines who can do what to move the status of an asset. When a transaction related to any business operation is proposed to update the ledger, a consensus mechanism comes into the picture, so that all the members of the network can come into agreement as to what should be the state of an asset as it moves through agreed and required shared process.

A new era – Permissioned blockchains

Public blockchain rise could be very well attributed to the emergence of cryptocurrencies as its first practical implementation. The core focus remained decentralization, security, peer to peer communication, among other aspects. With all nodes being equal with no central authority or intermediatory helped achieved decentralization. The phenomenon of network incentivization by way of mining helped security grow.

In the public or open blockchain, since there is no central authority that controls the network so anyone can join the network, there is no need for explicit permission to join. Participants in the public blockchain network are not known to each other in any way other than means of pseudonymous identity in the form of public addresses. The reliance is on economics and game theory incentives to make sure that participants in the network behave honestly and play according to the rules. Consensus plays an important role here through which honest participants are rewarded economically through incentives. In contrast, malicious participants could end up incur work or cost, with no possibility of recovering that cost.

For instance, consider a network of a couple of entities who work together. Still, they all maintain their copy of records, which often turns out to be inefficient, expensive, and vulnerable to mistakes and failures:

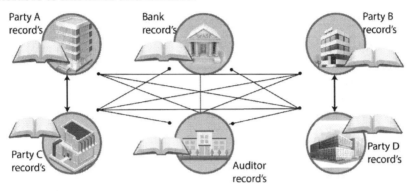

Figure 5.1: *Traditional systems*

The same set of participants while collaborating on a blockchain platform shall have instant access to information with the features such as agreed consensus, provenance ability, immutability, and finality:

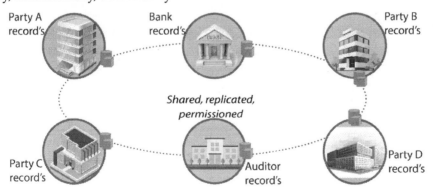

Figure 5.2: *Shared Ledger based system*

However, in the scenario of enterprises, business happens between known identities, participants know each other, and what organization they're associated with and what their role is. The assumption is participants behave fairly upholding business ethics; if not, then there are ways and means to figure that out, more so business continuation critically depends on the fairness of business process execution. So, whereas known identity is one of the prominent requirements for a blockchain like a setup but within a closed environment, so are others; let's have a look at some other requirements.

Throughput

Public blockchains such as Bitcoin or Ethereum do have low transaction throughput and that mainly because of time and computational requirement of confirming the transactions. Given the size of the network that is several nodes in the network, the entire process of adding transactions into a block, solving a puzzle, and disseminating the correct block to other nodes and then validation takes its own time before a transaction could be completed.

Moreover, the size of every block is limited to 1MB as of now for Bitcoin that also limits the number of transactions that could be added in one block; this all cumulatively leads to low throughput. For enterprises, this might not be acceptable and workable at the same time, so a solution leveraging the benefits of blockchain characteristics; however, with enterprise-level throughput was needed. A lot of enterprise blockchain platforms such as Hyperledger Fabric and Corda etc. achieve reasonable throughput as of now.

Efficient consensus

The consensus is the core of distributed ledger networks, and that is what ensures them to work without needing trusted central authority. Consensus algorithms are there to prevent fraudulent transactions that could be initiated by any malicious participant. Achieving consensus in distributed systems with the possibility of byzantine nodes in the network, Satoshi Nakamoto solved this with a novel way of Proof-of-Work mechanism, which is performing a large amount of computational work which in turn required a vast amount of computing resources to be spent that relied on power consumption. Whereas, POW on one side, provided the basis of the agreement through consensus algorithm as a by-product provided network security to the blockchain platform. However, the genesis of coming to share resource-intensive computation had unknown participants within the network.

However, in the case of private blockchains with a limited number of participants, POW may not be the consensus solution that is looked for, to carry out the shared business processes there was a need to come up with consensus algorithms that is not resource-intensive and preferably something that can be agreed upon by required participants in the network in an effective manner. Having limited and known membership dramatically reduces the need for extensive algorithms to prevent fraudulent activities on permissioned blockchains. Instead, private blockchain platforms were required to ensure that complex workflows and transactions are implemented correctly with a useful framework for having members agree to the very structure of the transaction itself.

For enterprise blockchain to gain momentum consensus algorithm used in public blockchain had to be rethought in terms of the effectiveness of resourcing capabilities. That is the reason most of the private blockchains have come up with their mechanism of consensus than using POW. Hyperledger Fabric uses Execute-Order-Validate consensus mechanism using Kafka based ordering system or RAFT based ordering system. R3 Corda uses notary nodes to achieve consensus.

Regulatory compliance support

Public blockchains inherently by design are censorship-resistant; that is, all nodes are equal, and there is no way any authority or any organization or any government controls the network; it is governed by the law of code. Whereas, in a business or enterprise network where all entities are equal, and they intend to establish a fair business network, abstracted from any manipulation and not governed by the interest of any specific organization.

Even then, businesses are required to abide by a regulatory framework that is enforced by various nominated bodies across the world. Enterprise networks, one one hand, were looking to achieve a manipulation free network, and at the same time, are required to be able to make regulatory bodies a part of the network even though in view-only mode. It probably was not possible and meant to be in public network, and that is the reason we saw the emergence of the private blockchain network, which could somewhat leverage the features of blockchain still being available for compliance support.

Controlled membership

A business network or group of participants who have come together to achieve a common business objective always would have logically common grounds. You would not expect the logistics partner to take part in a healthcare dominated business network. So, there needed a mechanism where membership is controlled in terms of who can join the network based on the fact that the value new partner shall bring to the network. Also, a new member who would join a network might have a subset of requirement in the entire network, think of trade flow where the carrier may have interest only in a limited set of information such as loading port, intended parties and may not be interested in business terms and conditions. Private blockchain help achieve this as there are set procedures for participants joining the network and the roles and access that can be granted to the joining members.

Practical applications

Public blockchains have come out mostly to solve a particular problem with most of them mainly trying addressing the peer to peer transfer of value mostly in the form of cryptocurrencies, Ethereum is a platform that offers transaction execution by way of smart contracts however then privacy remained a constraint there for enterprises. No enterprise would want to make their business agreement public to everyone.

For enterprises, there is a discrete set of business processes that they would want to optimize among themselves. With the private blockchain coming into existence, they offer to solve a varied range of real-world business problems that are not only limited to the cryptocurrency exchange. Choosing and using a platform primarily depends on how efficiently it can address their business needs, and private blockchain was created, taking a lot of organizations on board with developing the understanding as to what is required for business applications.

So, due to the above-given considerations, it came out very obvious that there is a need for private blockchain in the business organizations, and that led to the birth of private blockchain come into existence.

Blockchain in Enterprise - Considerations

Whereas permissioned blockchains did have a focus on optimizing shared business processes between intended participants and overcome friction, it fosters an ecosystem of collaboration where participants have full control over the access and governance of the shared data. Business agreements coded in smart contracts that run on top of the blockchain governs as to who is supposed to do what to be able to change the status of an asset as it takes part in the business process. Blockchain has been instrumental in allowing the transaction such that underlying asset can become shared & trusted data within participant organizations.

On top of that, privacy controls are put into place so that access is granted and limited. Participating in permissioned blockchain paved the way for a paradigm shift that enables players within an ecosystem to generate an interest to collaborate among themselves, including competitors in building trust, then to compete.

With enterprising increasingly collaborating to get the advantage of this new paradigm, there are other capabilities that blockchain in enterprises need to consider to make sure that the enterprise flavor of the application is not lost while overarching the newest technology adoption of blockchain.

A few other considerations are:
- **Enterprise Integration:** A permissioned blockchain system while being working as a connected ecosystem of enterprises need to make use of its internal enterprise applications. It is quite prudent that blockchain systems are capable of supporting existing enterprise applications such as CRM, reporting systems, and so on.
- **Monitoring**: Any enterprise system that comes into place has an inherent requirement of the monitoring system. It is required to make sure that the network remains highly available and accessible all the time Auditing:

Auditing and logging play an essential role in enterprise applications where the losing track of any single transaction could have monetary or otherwise impact. Other than that, having these properties in the blockchain system ensures technology failure root cause analysis, non-repudiation, and other needs that an enterprise may have.

- **Reporting**: There is always a requirement in enterprise systems to address regulatory and reporting needs, so enterprise blockchain platforms should support mechanisms either implicit or by way of supporting connectors such that regulatory and reporting can be taken care of.

The list and a brief description are given above is not the exhaustive list of making permissioned blockchain enterprise-ready instead there are a couple of pointers that needed to be kept in mind while trying to leverage blockchain in a closed environment to make sure that we do enable platform by some means such that these periphery features are available as well for consumption.

Business drivers

While we have discussed the coming up of private blockchain into existence basis what were the business needs that probably were not directly addressed by the public blockchains and at the same time, we also delved into a couple of points as to what a private blockchain should be able to provide to become to a real enterprise-grade platform. However, more importantly, for any business to start using the blockchain platform doesn't necessarily lie in the fact what technology can you in standalone fashion instead of in the business benefits that it brings to the table.

Blockchain might have exhibited the disruptive potential to be the basis of new operating models, but its initial impact will be to drive operational efficiencies. One of the best cost-benefit can be taken out of existing processes by getting away from intermediaries or the overhead cost and effort of record keeping and transaction reconciliation.

Further, in the section, we shall touch upon a couple of points that make a valid use case for blockchain platforms to be used in enterprises.

Increased efficiency – Reduction in time

In the real world, enterprises do business with other entities, where they exchange information in traditional, paper-heavy processes and in a time-intensive way, which is prone to human error. It usually gets overwhelmed and cumbersome if a single process spans across multiple organizations. Record keeping happens at multiple places, which are usually siloed systems of record of different participating organizations, and this is redundant data-keeping. In the event of any dispute, the reconciliation process happens, and at times, there is a need for intermediates helping to validate the transaction and record. All this leads to increased time for completing the business process as every single entity takes its own sweet time.

By streamlining and automating these processes with every participant on board on the blockchain platform, transactions can be completed faster and more efficiently. And given record-keeping is being done using a single digital ledger which is shared among participants, there does not arise a need to reconcile multiple ledgers. So, a resultant increased efficiency could be a more significant motive for interested parties to come over and establish a blockchain network.

Cost reduction

Cost reduction generally remains a prime factor for businesses, and it should be as it leads to more business gains, and that is the reason businesses are existing. Blockchain eliminates the need as many third parties or intermediaries which work as a source of trust partner in distrusting entities. Instead, blockchain data in a shared ledger becomes a source of truth by itself. Blockchain helps to get away from a lot of manual documentation to complete a business process as everyone will have access to a single, immutable version in real-time.

There have been real-world examples of significant cost reduction that has been noticed in various business segments across the industry. For instance, in the case of global supply chains, the use of blockchain has proven to help improve inventory management that has helped reduce costly data errors and delays. Now sellers have the real-time ability to accurately track capacity and costs, figure out the estimated delivery times for multiple routes, eventually helping them to make optimized decisions. Along with these cost-cutting benefits, the blockchain is helping transport providers to share details about routes and available capacity, which has helped in reducing costs and transport time.

Likewise, in financial services, blockchain helps reduce the need for manual intervention in aggregating, amending, and sharing data. Regulatory reporting and audit documents could become more comfortable, requiring less manual processing and reduction in cost. Post-trade reconciliation and settlement are other examples of time-consuming and expensive processes that financial institutions are getting rid of by leveraging blockchain technology.

Reduces risk

Blockchain does follow a consensus algorithm such that transactions must be agreed upon before they are recorded on the ledger, and once recorded, these records are immutable. Once a transaction is approved, it is cryptographically linked to the previous transaction or, more precisely, blocks. It enables blockchain to be more secure than other record-keeping systems.

Along with this, the fact that transactional data is stored across a network of computers then a single server, makes it very difficult for anyone to tamper with the transaction data. It makes a perfect use case for an industry where protecting sensitive data is crucial for business; such examples are financial services, healthcare, and so on, and their blockchain has an opportunity to make an impact as to how critical information is shared by helping to prevent fraud and unauthorized activity.

Increased visibility/transparency

One of the main benefits that blockchain technology provides is that transaction histories are more transparent now. All participants have the same copy of the ledger and hence the same set of records. The only option for updating the transaction record is through consensus, which means everyone has agreed to the new version of data being updated in ledger. Data stored on blockchain ledger; that's why because of this inherent design is correct, consistent, and thus provides transparency. Moreover, the same set of data is available to all, and members with permissioned access can view that. Maliciously changing the data in the blockchain is next to impossible, so it gives a kind of confidence that the data present is genuine and brings transparency across all participants.

With all the benefits deriving out of blockchain platform for enterprises where shared business processes span along with multiple organizations, it is becoming prudent for enterprises to adopt blockchain technology and many organizations have moved beyond prototyping and Proof Of Concept phase and have a solution implemented on production which are addressing their real-world business problems.

However, adoption of blockchain is not limited to being a technological decision; business decision significantly impacts this. While the intent of the application of technology in a particular use case is to help improve business processes is nothing new, earlier advancements of technology were mostly about the faster and more secure exchange of information. Blockchain, on the other hand, has made the possibility of exchange of value digitally with one another without depending on a third party to manage the transactions. Blockchain provides a paradigm shift in how we exchange value, and that is what is at the core of business processes among organizations, which is being seen as the main reason that is driving the adoption of blockchain in enterprises.

Leading platforms

With the need for increased adoption of blockchain technology across the industry, there are a lot of technology solutions that have been conceptualized and created to meet the demand. Most of the private blockchain platform was initially created with specific industry segments in mind. However, we have seen cases where they have gone beyond their initial purpose and now catering to a broader audience than initially thought for.

Here is the list of the popular platforms that are being widely used in the industry; a small note is also included to appraise readers on a high level what this platform does and is all about.

Please note that this is not an exhaustive list of available platforms.

Hyperledger Fabric

Hyperledger Fabric is an open-sourced project under the Hyperledger Umbrella promoted and maintained by the Linux Foundation. Linux foundation announced the creation of the Hyperledger Project around December 2015, and in early 2016 Fabric came into existence by combining the work of Digital Asset and IBM's OpenBlockchain. It was conceived as an enterprise-grade permissioned distributed ledger framework for developing blockchain solutions and applications. The design philosophy right from the start emphasized on modular and versatile design to be able to satisfy a broad range of industry use cases. It provides a distinct approach to a consensus that tends to enable performance at scale while preserving privacy.

The modularity design philosophy of the architecture enables network designers to plug in their preferred components like membership services, consensus, and ordering service to be able to address real-world issues about the broader range of use cases, and that is what distinguishes it from other blockchain solutions.

The participants within this network join the network through a well-defined policy and should be authorized and should have the credibility to take part in the blockchain. On a high level, Fabric has two more significant aspects; one is conceptualizing and creating a blockchain network representing the business network, where network designers play a more significant role. Secondly, smart contracts, which are also termed as chaincode, developers write and maintain chaincode, which often represents business agreements between participant organizations. Hyperledger Fabric supports Go Lang, NodeJS, and Java for writing smart contracts to enable readily available skills to be able to pick that up quickly. Hyperledger Fabric is primarily looking to work as an integration project where Distributed Leger Technology is required, and it offers various client-side SDK's to connect and interact with the blockchain network. As of today, Java and Node SDK are readily available with the support of Python, GO, and REST to be available soon.

While this book and section are concerned about Hyperledger Fabric, there is a lot of projects that are being worked upon under Hyperledger Umbrella to address different aspect.

They are as follows:
- Hyperledger Burrow

- Hyperledger Grid
- Hyperledger Indy
- Hyperledger Iroha
- Hyperledger Sawtooth

R3 Corda

Corda is a distributed ledger platform initially designed and developed for the financial services industry. It is an enterprise-grade permissioned private network DLT designed to record, manage and synchronize contracts and other shared data between participating members. It is an open-source platform that can be used to build apps or Cordapps as popularly known for the various industrial sector now, though, as mentioned, it started with financial services in mind.

Corda platform is created now being built and maintained by R3. R3 is an enterprise blockchain technology company headquartered in New York City and was founded in 2014 by David E Rutter. Corda is governed by the R3 consortium, which is a collaboration of numerous financial institutions. It fosters an ecosystem of different firms working together to build distributed applications on top of Corda for addressing and solving real-world use cases across different industries such as financial services, insurance, healthcare, trade finance, and digital assets. An important point to note here is that Corda is a distributed ledger technology and isn't a blockchain.

Corda platform has got many similarities and as well as differences with many existing blockchain/distributed ledger technology solutions. Corda does allow the creation of immutable records of transactional events. However, as in other blockchains, the transactions are carried out privately in Corda; that is, information is not sent across all the nodes and kept in distributed shared ledger; somewhat, it remains between the intended parties. Corda smart contracts can be written in Java and Kotlin.

Like in Hyperledger Fabric, Corda also follows its consensus algorithm, which is notary based. Corda uses the "Notary" infrastructure (Notary is a particular node in the network itself) for sequencing and validating of transactions. Since Corda doesn't maintain the same state across all nodes somewhat only between intended participants, it does not broadcast a transaction globally for validation purposes. A Corda network may choose to have multiple notaries, which can validate the transactions using different algorithms. Also, like Hyperledger, Corda doesn't have its cryptocurrency.

Corda's objective is to remove costly friction in business transactions by avoiding business intermediaries and enable businesses to transact with each other directly and that too in strict privacy using smart contracts, reducing transaction and record-keeping costs, and streamlining business operations. This unique approach helps gain performance and provides security advantage for Corda over other enterprise-level blockchain frameworks.

R3 provides two interoperable and fully compatible distributions of the platform – Corda open-source platform with source code available in GitHub under Apache 2 license and Corda Enterprise, which is a commercial version that comes with feature offerings and services fine-tuned for customized business needs.

Ripple

Ripple is a technology that includes a real-time gross settlement system, currency exchange, and remittance network created by Ripple Labs. So, it works both as a cryptocurrency and a digital payment network for financial transactions. Ripple operates on an open-source and peer-to-peer decentralized platform that allows for a seamless transfer of money in any form, whether USD, INR, or any other cryptocurrency such as bitcoin, and so on. Ripple's payment settlement asset exchange and remittance system are very much similar to the SWIFT system that is the main transfer backbone for international money and security transfers, which is primarily used by banks and financial institutions. Just for the sake of clarity, Ripple is an overloaded term:

- **Ripple**: It is the name of the firm that created and operate the Ripple platform
- **XRP**: The pre-mined native virtual currency that is developed to facilitate payments on Ripple
- **RippleNet**: The leading network that acts as a global settlement system which connects financial institutions, banks, and exchanges through the distributed ledger

Ripple does not have a concept of the mining as in other blockchain platforms for consensus. Instead, Ripple validates transactions and recommends its clients to use a list of identified, trusted participants to validate their transactions. Each server maintains a **unique node list (UNL)**, which is a set of trusted nodes. Only the votes of the other members of the UNL are considered when determining consensus as opposed to all participating nodes as in Bitcoin or Ethereum.

The UNL represents a subset of the network, which, when taken collectively, is trusted not to collude in an attempt to defraud the network.

Ripple was first released in 2012 and was co-founded by Chris Larsen and Jed McCaleb.

Quorum

Quorum is an open-source permissioned blockchain platform developed by J.P. Morgan that leverages the innovation of the public Ethereum with added enhancements to support enterprise needs. It provides a layer on top of Ethereum, which enables it to perform private transactions and makes it more robust by using different consensus algorithms.

Quorum was a spin-off of Go Ethereum, the base code for the Ethereum blockchain. It operates very similarly to Ethereum, however with clear distinctions in the following areas:

- Permissioned network
- Emphasis on transaction and contract privacy
- Different consensus mechanisms than PoW
- Improved performance

Stellar

Stellar is an open-source, decentralized protocol for digital currency to fiat money transfers, which allows cross-border transactions between any pair of currencies. With Stellar, one can move money across borders quite quickly, with reliability, and just for fractions of money. Stellar is a decentralized, peer-to-peer network and follows an open ledger system. Details of every transaction in Stellar is stored on the blockchain that acts as an open, transparent ledger. The ledger can be viewed by anyone in the network.

Stellar is a system that eventually helps track ownership. It makes use of an accounting ledger that is shared across a network of independent computer nodes to store two essential pieces of information for every account holder. These include the account balances and operations on balance, such as buy or sell offers.

Stellar uses the concept of Anchors, which act as a bridge between different currencies and stellar network. Stellar rely heaving on the anchors for its smooth functioning. 'Lumen' is the native token of stellar is represented as 'XLM.'

MultiChain

MultiChain is an off-the-shelf platform for helping and creating private blockchain between organizations or within departments of an organization. The objective of Multichain is to overcome a key obstacle to the deployment of blockchain technology in enterprise applications by providing the privacy and control required in a very easy to use way. Multichain is a node-based software that can be deployed on varied platforms such as Windows, Linux, and Mac-based systems. It provides a simple API and command-line interface for accessing the node and invoking different APIs.

MultiChain targets to solve the inherent problems public blockchain of mining, privacy, and openness via integrated management of user permissions. The core aim includes

- **Controlled access**: Limiting the functionality to ensure that the blockchain activity is only visible to chosen participant members.
- **Transaction visibility**: Having controls in place to ensure which transactions are permitted.
- **Effective mining**: To enable mining to take place securely without proof of work and its associated costs.

MultiChain uses public-key cryptography property to restrict blockchain access to a list of permitted users, by expanding the "handshaking" process that occurs when two blockchain nodes connect. The *handshaking* process is just a sequence of steps between two nodes of exchanging information and agreeing on to start information exchange with one another.

Mining in MultiChain follows Proof Of Work through with certain amendments to make sure that no single participant monopolizes the mining process. For this, MultiChain uses something called as mining diversity.

BigChainDB

Often termed as a blockchain database, it possesses both database and blockchain characteristics. It supports decentralization, immutability, and as well native support for assets. BigChainDB follows decentralization mode that is no one owns or controls everything, also there with no central node; there is no single point of failure. Each node in a BigChainDB network is generally owned and controlled by a different person or organization. Even in the case of the network that is existing within one organization, it's still the case to have every node to be controlled by a different entity, be it an individual or subdivision in an enterprise.

BigChainDB follows the concept of consortium in which a set of organizations run the network. As with any other consortium, it requires some form of governance to draft the policy around membership and access control rules. The consortium can work out the exact details of the governance process; however, this again remains decentralized.

BigChainDB can make blockchain data immutable in many ways precisely:
- There is no API for changing and deleting the data
- Data is replicated at different nodes, with an increasing degree of replication, immutability increases
- Use of cryptographic signature to check the integrity of messages
- Node owners can enforce strong security policies.
- Implementation of internal and external watchdog to monitor and audit data to check for irregularities

BigChainDB uses the Byzantine Fault Tolerant protocol for consensus, and for that, it uses Tendermint.

BigChainDB provided the full power of MongoDB's query engine to search and query all stored data, which includes all transactions, related assets, and metadata.

The above-given list of blockchain and its description is by no means exhaustive and is not the sole objective of this book. The idea of covering this section is to make readers aware that there are various platforms with different use cases to solve. Readers are expected to go through the detailed documentation of any platform that they wish to extend their knowledge in.

Use cases/examples

The successful adoption of any technological advancements can only be measured through its extent of use in the application of real-world use cases. Whereas public blockchain mostly (not all) been time and tested through the adoption of their native cryptocurrency, private/permissioned blockchain success can only be read by the help enterprising are realizing in removing the integrated business process friction. That is, how enterprises are putting these platforms into work to minimize the risk and challenges they usually face in working across different organizations.

While we have started seeing the positive outcome and adoption of permissioned blockchain platform across all industry segments, a couple of notable ones are:

- Supply Chain/Logistics
- Trade Finance
- Agriculture
- Health care
- Financial Services

In this section, I would just try to highlight a couple of uses cases that have been successful, and information is available in the public domain:

- **Honeywell Aerospace**: It has created an online marketplace using the Hyperledger Blockchain platform that caters to buying, and selling of aircraft parts online. In an estimated industry of $4 Billion, the transactions were still not online, < 3% of overall transactions were being done online rest still using the old way of closing transactions using a couple of phone calls and emails. Various sellers have tried doing this on popular e-commerce sites; however, due to regulations involved in the aerospace market, this was not doable till you have documentation of the entire history of ownership, use, and repair. A blockchain-based marketplace has helped removed all these obstacles, and now the 'GoDirect Trade' system developed by Honeywell is helping buyers and seller's coming online and do the transactions.

- **Walmart**: It is tracking the food supply chain through Hyperledger Fabric to bring transparency across. To isolate a food product, consumption of which could have resulted in the food-borne disease is a daunting task which could even take days to identify with the risk of that food item still being getting consumed. Walmart did face this issue, and that resulted in hefty losses, so they jointly developed a solution with IBM using Hyperledger Fabric that could help companies find the affected products and not impacting the entire ecosystem and jeopardizing the livelihood of people part of the ecosystem.

  Walmart started two initiatives in this direction, the first one was about tracing mangoes that were being sold in Walmart's US stores, and the second one was aimed to trace pork sold in its China stores. The Hyperledger Fabric blockchain-based food traceability system built for the two products has produced a desirable result. For pork in China, it allowed uploading certificates of authenticity to the blockchain, bringing more trust to a system where it was proving to be a grave issue. And then for mangoes, the time needed to trace their provenance drastically from 7 days to a couple of seconds.

- **TradeLens**: The TradeLens platform is a blockchain-based platform that has been jointly developed by Maersk and IBM. It is an open and neutral industry platform that has the support of major players across the global shipping industry. This platform promotes the efficient, transparent, and secure exchange of information to foster greater collaboration and trust across the global supply chain. TradeLens is using IBM Blockchain technology for this. TradeLens empowers multiple trading partners to collaborate and help them establishing a single shared view of transactions without compromising on details, privacy, or confidentiality. All significant partners of TradeLens such as shipping companies, freight carriers, port authorities, terminal operators, transporters, and customs authorities can interact more efficiently through real-time access to data and documents.

- **Everledger:** Everledger is a blockchain-based (Hyperledger Fabric) diamond Provenance Company, founded sometime in 2015. Everledger platform brings greater transparency to the open market places and global supply chain, and this it does by ensuring that the authenticity of the asset is secured and stored among all industry participants. This platform integrates and enhances data from miners, manufacturers, certification houses, and retailers. It also has a facility for consumers to view information like diamond characteristics and ownership. Blockchain has been adopted by several companies in the diamond industry to help to weed out 'blood diamonds' and fakes.

Again this list is not exhaustive, and readers are recommended to look for information that is available in the public domain to get a much better understanding of any industry-specific implementation that they might be looking for.

Conclusion

This chapter was there to focus on the need and use of blockchain in enterprises. The idea was to understand how blockchain adoption is going through in organizations. We first went through why there was a need for permissioned blockchain even to come up. We discussed several parameters that were required in any enterprise; however, we were not getting fulfilled by the available public blockchains. Consensus, throughput, controlled access were some of the reasons where technology fitment was not meant to be used by organizations as is and needed some way of change in the design thinking of the existing public blockchain platform to retrofit.

While on the one hand, there were some deviations needed from public blockchain; there were some enterprise needs that any application should comply with, such as regulatory and compliance, monitoring, logging, and so on, which were needed on top of initial deviations. With technology being available to achieve the inter-organization business process with lesser friction but then there was a strong need of a business driver for adoption of blockchain platforms. We did discuss that in one of the sections about business drivers.

We have been focussing on Hyperledger Fabric, but then we also looked into a couple of other platforms that are worth considering and may help achieve solve other business problems. We also devoted a small section on the prominent use cases that have been in production and saw how they are helping to solve different kinds of problems. In the next chapter, we will be covering the core concepts of Hyperledger Fabric.

## CHAPTER 6

Hyperledger Fabric

This chapter sets the tone for understanding Hyperledger Fabric. Before we delve into the understanding of how we can create a blockchain network using Hyperledger Fabric, we must understand the core concepts of Hyperledger Fabric. There are a lot of crucial components and moving parts of the fabric. This chapter would ensure that reader understands the basic concepts before applying them to make a practical application.

Structure

- Introducing Hyperledger Fabric
- Features
- Building blocks
  - o Nodes
    - ▪ Peer
    - ▪ Orderer (Ordering Service)
  - o Ledger
  - o Smart Contracts
  - o Channel
  - o Private Data

- o Identity
- o Membership Service Provider (MSP)
- Network view
- Important tools
  - o cryptogen
  - o configtxgen
  - o configxlator
- Conclusion

Objective

This chapter would help the reader understand Hyperledger Fabric at the conceptual level with all significant constituents that form the core building blocks of the fabric network. In the coming chapters, this understanding would help the reader realize the use and importance of these components when we set up actual Hyperledger Fabric and play around with it.

Introducing Hyperledger Fabric

Hyperledger Fabric is one of the most sought after and widely accepted permissioned blockchain platform across the industry. It is more so often called a Distributed Ledger Technology framework as well. It is an open-source, industry-grade, permissioned blockchain platform which has been developed with a view of enterprise considerations.

Hyperledger Fabric was conceptualized and conceived by the Linux Foundation somewhere around December 2015. The prime objective of creating the project was to develop blockchain and distributed ledger solution to advance cross-industry collaboration. The intention was to create a platform that could help in supporting global business transactions among major industry players across different verticals around the globe. Most of the initial code was contributed by IBM and Digital Asset, and now it has a thriving community of developers and an independent governing body.

The Linux Foundation origin goes back to the early 1990s when it initially started as 'Linux International,' mostly dealing around the use and promotion of Linux to gain wider acceptability. Somewhere around 2000, **Open Source Development Labs (OSDL)** was formed as a non-profit organization to *accelerate the deployment of Linux for enterprise computing;* it was backed by a global consortium. Then in 2007, Linux Foundation was formed resulting from the merger between OSDL and the Free Standards Group. The objective of the Linux Foundation is to support the creation and promotion of open source ecosystems for which they provide financial and intellectual resources. They also help provide non-core services for the development of new products in terms of infrastructure, services, and training. There is a long list of widely used products by Linux Foundation as of date, Jenkins, Kubernetes, NodeJS are a couple of examples from the long list.

Hyperledger, in general terms, is used as an umbrella for all the frameworks and tools that are being developed around blockchain capabilities. Notable frameworks are Fabric, Burrow, Sawtooth, Indy, and so on:

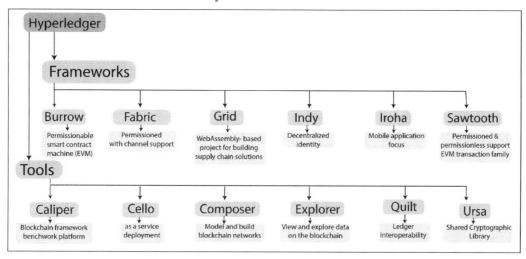

Figure 6.1: *Hyperledger Ecosystem*

Hyperledger Fabric is the first of the product out of Hyperledger Suite to get promoted from incubation to active state. More and more industry-wide players are joining the Hyperledger, and as of now, writing this book, a big chunk of $1bn+ companies are part of Hyperledger. With more players joining the rank, it enhances the open governance model that Linux Foundation encourages. At the same time, they gave a broader perspective to the platform to help them expand the platform in such a fashion that it tunes itself to address the industry-wide real-time issues.

While now we have started to understand Hyperledger Fabric (for the sake of brevity, I shall refer this now as fabric across the book) which is enterprise-grade, permissioned blockchain, we must get to know about the features of fabric as to how they fit into enterprise model and how are they different from widely known public and permissionless blockchains such as Bitcoin and Ethereum.

Features

I would use this section to list down the features that fabric provides and alongside would take the liberty to discuss the difference between fabric and other public networks.

No Native Cryptocurrency

In fabric, there is no inherent or implicit support of cryptocurrency, at least with version 1.4, which I am referring to at the time of writing this book. Cryptocurrencies are native mostly to the public blockchains specifically if we talk about Bitcoin, Ethereum, and many more that came after that. Fabric is supposed to be run as a private and permissioned blockchain, so it is mostly run in a closed environment. It is still worthwhile to understand that why we need cryptocurrency in a public blockchain; for private blockchain, it may or may not be needed basis the principle a private blockchain network is conceived. Public blockchain networks are decentralized that is without any central control, and yet thousands of nodes of a public blockchain are alive and kicking. There must be an inspiration, incentive to run a node in the public blockchain. Why would I run a node and be a part of the public blockchain network if there is no incentive for me?

Cryptocurrencies initially started as a store of value and as a medium of exchange so that people can transact among themselves without any intermediatory. People who were part of public blockchain needed to spend energy to be a part of the network, spending energy does have a monetary impact. The incentive for participating node was mining rewards; mining is the provision that can be used by nodes to validate transactions and help blockchain grow. As a result, a certain amount of cryptocurrency as a reward is given out to the miner who does help to validate the transactions. Another critical aspect of mining was security; there are rules laid out how consensus can be achieved or how transactions can be validated or how the problem would be solved and since all this requires a lot of energy and hence money, anyone who is being dishonest, that is not playing the rules may not be able to get to produce a validated block and hence would not be able to get rewards and so may end up losing money that any node would have spent on energy. With more and more nodes joining in, with the level of difficulty getting increased, the security of the entire network kept enhancing. So, we have the reason for native cryptocurrency support in the public blockchain.

Now coming back to Enterprise blockchain such as Hyperledger Fabric, we can consider all three aspects of having cryptocurrencies in the public blockchain of a medium of exchange, incentivization, and security.

The medium of exchange is not required in case of transactions between different participating nodes, which usually belong to different participating organizations of the network. The main motive is to do business transactions and record those transactions in such a manner that they don't have to trust anyone or need to do any kind of reconciliation.

Secondly, since a business network between companies established to achieve a common objective and the agreement of writing transactions on ledger could be achieved by consensus agreed by all of them than having **Proof of Work (PoW)** kind of consensus, so there is no need of giving out any reward in case of transaction finality

Lastly, game theory or problem-solving is required to achieve security in the public blockchain where members do not know each other and mostly anonymous to each other.however, in the case of fabric, all members are known to each other. Hyperledger fabric provided the concepts of identity management and signed transactions, which help control the access and content of the data to be written on the ledger.

Energy consumption

Energy consumption is one of the most talked-about points individually as a criticism that has been used in the context of blockchain. To achieve consensus, mining is done which is based on the game theory and mainly has a task to solve a problem with certain difficulty level, solving that problem is generally done by brute-force way that is hit and trial. There has been so much processing that needs to be done, and it ends up consuming a lot of energy. It is right in the case of public Blockchain, which works on the PoW consensus algorithm. Bitcoin and Ethereum both use the PoW consensus algorithm.

Again, in the case of Hyperledger Fabric, all participants are known to each other. There is no need to mining a slightly different set of rules to achieve consensus, so in the end, the limited infrastructure that has been employed by a group of participant parts of the fabric network may end up consuming electricity that otherwise would be required by any conventional system. So, while energy consumption has been talked about in public blockchain, which uses the PoW consensus algorithm, it is not a matter of much concern in private or permission blockchain such as Hyperledger Fabric.

Scripting

Scripting is a way that helps execute transactions in the blockchain. It is not a discriminatory feature among blockchain networks as most of the blockchain now have moved to smart contracts. However, Bitcoin, which was the first blockchain to come into existence, was using a scripting language. Bitcoin uses a Forth-like script that is simple, stack-based, and is processed from left to right. The initial intention of scripting was to provide a set of opcodes that could help validate transactions. Whereas, the script is easy to use, but it provides a minimal feature set for transactions. With the Ethereum coming into picture after Bitcoin, they looked for more control of transactions, and it was not intended only for exchange or transfer of cryptocurrency but more control around transactional rule through programmatically. Smart contracts are written in Turing complete language that simply means virtually you can program any condition for execution of business logic than simple transfer.

Permissioned

Blockchain initially started with the concept of a permissionless network where virtually anyone can join the network and do the transaction. Satoshi Nakamoto, who invented Bitcoin, released the whitepaper titled *A Peer-to-Peer Electronic Cash System*, and his sole intention was to enable peers to do the transaction without any intermediatory. Since this was meant to be joined by anyone, it was a permissionless network, and every participant was anonymous. There is no trust between participants, and there is always an agreed state of the blockchain that is reached through consensus.

Hyperledger Fabric, on the other hand, is a permissioned blockchain network intended to be run within a closed group of participants. They share common objectives and carry out transactions in that order. Permissioned networks are joined by known members, and generally, they would have an identity to establish themselves. All members need to agree to induct a new member of the group. All participating members agree on the consensus rule and a governance model for their operations. By members knowing each other even though they may not trust each other, there are very fewer chances of anyone doing any malicious activity such as changing the configuration or carrying out the illegal transaction is nil as all the steps are recorded on the blockchain, and the malicious node can easily be identified.

So, having a permissioned network, whereas it may not be viewed as a genuinely decentralized blockchain. However, still, it follows specific characteristics of blockchain, such as immutability, a level of decentralization, and so on, to bring this into a working model.

Smart contracts

The smart contract is what makes blockchain programmable. A smart contract is a decentralized code that runs on every node, and it contains the business rules as embedded code. Ethereum was the first blockchain platform to conceive this idea, and further blockchains have followed the notion. In Ethereum, every node contains the same copy of code, and a transaction done on any peer gets propagated on all the peers in the network and is visible to everyone. The vital point to consider here is most of the public, and permissionless blockchain follows what is called as **order-execute** architecture for validating and final writing transactions on the ledger.

Order-Execute is part of the consensus protocol that ensures:

- Validator node or miner validates the transactions, order them and then propagates to all peer nodes
- Each peer then execute the transactions sequentially so that the final state of the ledger is the same across all nodes

However, there is one catch, smart contracts that are executed in blockchain with order-execute architecture needs to follow deterministic behavior, that is peers may be executing the same transactions at different point of time so the output of the transaction should always be same so that consensus can be achieved. That is why solidity is a domain-specific language so that non-deterministic operations can be avoided.

While now comparing it with Hyperledger Fabric, we can write smart contracts in various languages such as Go Lang, Nodejs, and Java. Ability to write smart contracts in general-purpose language gives a primary reason for its wide-spread adoption as in most of the organization they would have these skills ready. The fabric uses the **execute-order-validate** approach to validate and for the finality of the transactions. This approach also ensures the elimination of non-deterministic behavior in the smart contract even with general-purpose language.

To achieve this behavior, the fabric has come up with altogether a different way of transaction validation and achieving consensus. This new architecture follows the **execute-order-validate** model.

The transaction flow consists of three steps

1. Peers upon receiving transaction request executes it against the data set available with them and then endorse it
2. Ordering service orders all the transactions and broadcast it to all peers
3. Finally, all peers validate the ordered transactions against an application-specific endorsement policy and then commit it in the ledger

We shall be elaborating more on these points when we discuss these steps in detail in the next chapter; however, the key take away is, Hyperledger Fabric uses general-purpose language and still ensures that the state of the ledger is maintained and thus eliminating non-deterministic behavior.

Modularity

Like in any other enterprise application, specific key characteristics are expected, modularity is one of them, where the final implementation of specific modules can be plugged with a custom implementation to bring more flexibility in the system. Similarly, ordering service, which is mainly delegated for the ordering of transactions and is logically decoupled from peer nodes, can employ different kind of mechanisms.

Similarly, all network entities have cryptographic identities in the network, which can be provided by the membership service provider of choice.

The fabric also gives the flexibility to choose the persistent store that can be used to configure ledger data. They also have the option of having a pluggable endorsement and validation policy.

Privacy and confidentiality

In a permissionless blockchain, every data and code is present on all the nodes and, at the same time, is visible to anyone and everyone. It merely means that there is no confidentiality of the transaction rules by a visible smart contract on all the nodes as well, not the privacy of transactional data itself. It is a trade-off between the confidentiality and security of the public blockchain, which employs the PoW mechanism to ensure the validation of data truly and to be able to validate transaction data needs to be visible for that node.

However, in the case of the closed network of participants who know each other but do not trust each other, confidentiality could be a concern. In a permissioned blockchain business network, there could be a network of suppliers or buyers who may want the transaction among each other. Still, at the same time, they might be competing among themselves and would want not to disclose their transaction between a set of participants. Hyperledger Fabric addresses this issue by a notion call channel. The channel gives an additional layer of privacy and confidentiality among partners. Even though there might be a large number of participants in a business network however chosen partners can opt to establish a channel among themselves, and the data moving in this channel shall be restricted between participating members of the channel only.

Hyperledger Fabric is also exploring other means to ensure confidentiality other than using the channel. One of the examples is Zero-Knowledge Proof; it's a protocol in cryptography in which a party can prove something to another party without revealing the actual value which the first party is trying to prove. We shall not delve much into Zero-Knowledge Proof as this is still something being explored in the fabric; however, I would still recommend doing a reading about this as there are a lot of blockchain systems that are actively using this.

Building blocks

With a better understanding of Hyperledger Fabric as permissioned blockchain, its features, and how it differs from prominent public blockchain, now we shall start getting an understanding of the critical concepts of the fabric. We shall be individually getting to know all these concepts, and finally, we would bring all together to see how they knit together to create a permissioned blockchain network.

Peer (Node)

A blockchain network is a decentralized network of peers or sometimes called nodes. A node by itself is a self-sufficient unit that forms an integral part of the blockchain network. It's a group of nodes that can do peer to peer communication among each other and make a full functioning blockchain network. A simple way to connect to a blockchain network is to bring up a node and connect to a blockchain network. For instance, in Ethereum, a very popular Ethereum node 'Geth' can be installed and then instantiated to join the Ethereum network. Then it becomes a node in the Ethereum blockchain network. The same goes for Bitcoin, where 'Bitcoind' client is installed and instantiated. A node is essentially a software client that has all the modules of communicating with peers, validating the transaction, performing the role of the miner, helping validate the transaction, and follow the rules of the network that are there in the software unit.

Likewise, Hyperledger Fabric is also a network of nodes, which are specifically called Peers in fabric network, these peers carry out almost all the functionalities as any other node does in other blockchain networks, such as transaction validation, gossiping with other peer nodes, executing smart contracts, writing data into the ledger, and so on. They are considered to be the fundamental unit of the network. The best way to visualize the peer is a unit of the network that holds the ledger and hosts a smart contract that it uses to write transactions on the ledger. We shall be discussing more ledgers and smart contracts in detail shortly.

Below is the simplest of the diagram that shows a set of peers that constitutes a Hyperledger based blockchain network. This network is having three peers Peer **1, Peer 2, and Peer 3.** Every peer maintains a ledger and a smart contract. Ledger is more of the data store of all the transactions, and smart contracts are the rules that help write transactions on the ledger. As we can see in the diagram, **S1** smart contract is deployed on each node, that is, the same business rule codified and deployed on different peers. Each peer would have a ledger to maintain the state of objects, which can only be updated by smart contracts:

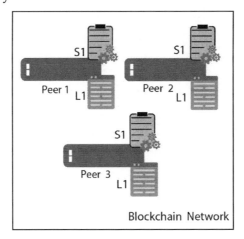

Figure 6.2: Blockchain network

Note: In Public, permissionless blockchain network, all nodes are equal; they are anonymous to each other and do have a pair of public/ private keys to carry out transactions. In the case of Hyperledger Fabric, nodes are at times different from each other to what operations they can do based on the access level assigned to them. Each node in the network would have an identity by way of the certificate issued to them, so all member peers are known to each other.

While we have been discussing the peer, its role in the network, it is worthwhile to look at how closely it works with the ledger, channel, smart contract, and how it relates to organizations and how identities are managed. All this would set us up for a detailed understanding at the more granular level.

Peer and ledger

A ledger is a collection of records or transaction events that are updated by the peer through smart contracts. Every peer maintains a copy of the ledger that belongs to this peer only. Each ledger does have two components or two ways by which it stores and maintains the data. The first part is the **Transaction Log** and another one in the **State**. Both transaction log and state come with in-process LevelDB, though with the state, we have the option to use CouchDB instead of LevelDB.

Below is a simplistic view of how ledger looks like:

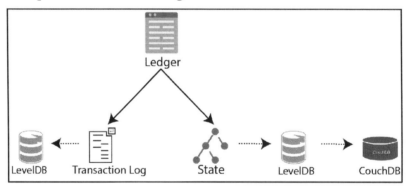

Figure 6.3: Ledger

The option of changing state storage mechanism from **LevelDB** to **CouchDB** can be easily achieved through configuration. **Transaction Log** maintains all the transaction events, and it is immutable; immutability is the key feature of the blockchain network. State DB is something that represents a world state that is a snapshot of the data at any particular point of time. It holds good for productive queries and serves a great purpose to the applications connecting to the blockchain network and used by application users built on top of the fabric blockchain network.

As design flexibility provided by the fabric, any peer node can hold multiple ledgers. To access and change (write) the ledger, smart contracts (called chaincode in fabric) are used. For all practical purposes, there shall be one or more chaincode that can access the ledger, although there is a way by which peer can access the ledger even without having chaincode, which is a rare case so we would not be discussing much that.

In the following figure, it is evident that **Peer 1** is having access to two ledgers **L1** and **L2**. Ledger L1 can be accessed by chaincode S1, and Ledger L2 can be accessed by chain codes **S1** and **S2**. A peer hosting multiple ledgers is possible only because the peer is participating in multiple channels. We will cover channels shortly, and chain codes are deployed to the channel and not on the network. Channels help maintain transaction privacy as they maintain separate ledgers per channel:

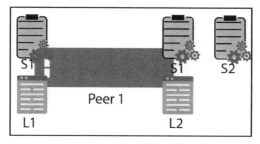

Figure 6.4: Peer with multiple ledgers

Peer and smart contract (chaincode)

In Hyperledger Fabric, smart contracts are called as chaincode so that we might be using the term smart contract and chaincode interchangeably in the context of fabric. A peer can have multiple ledgers and multiple chain codes accessing it. There has not been any given number of fixed relations between ledger to chaincode and for that matter between peer to chaincode or ledger to the smart contract:

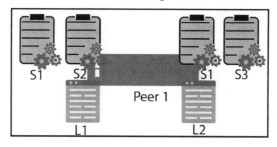

Figure 6.5: Peer with multiple smart contracts

In the above figure, it's notable that multiple chain codes can access multiple ledgers. However, **L1** and **L2** are on different channels, and chain codes deployed on specific channels can access ledger present in the channel. Also, as we could see, the S1 can access both **L1** and **L2**, but both **S1** are separate instances of the same chaincode and deployed on different channels.

Peer and channel

A channel is a mechanism by which interested peers within a blockchain network can collaborate, communicate, and do transactions among themselves securely and privately. A peer can be part of multiple channels having different participants in the channel, yet fabric ensures that there is no cross transaction is happening between the channels. We probably can think of channels as a group where only joining members can communicate with each other and see each other's messages. A member can be part of different groups, and group messages are mutually exclusive of each other. In a bigger context, group members go beyond just peers, and orderer nodes; client applications can join a channel and share and collaborate on managing the identical copy of ledger among themselves.

The following are the couple of examples that would help us understand the concept of channel, peer, and chaincode once working together. Channel works as a communication medium with boundaries and known participants who are a member of the group in that boundary.

The below-given figure is the simplest way of demonstrating a channel, assuming there are multiple participants, and they share a common business objective. They all come together and become part of a blockchain network to achieve that objective among themselves without the need of a mediatory and without having to trust each other. Party A, B, C, D, and E in the image are part of a single channel:

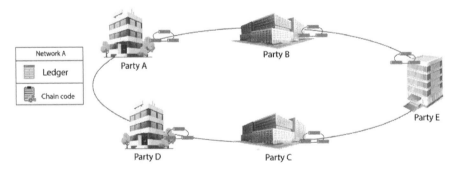

Figure 6.6: Simple Channel

Since they all are part of one channel, they maintain their copy of the shared and consistent immutable ledger with the chaincode deployed on the channel that helps access the ledger. It is more of an illustration; however, in real life, there shall be other components as well which takes part, one of the vital components is orderer service and may also have the **Certificate Authority (CA)** server that can be used to issue and manage identities for the participating nodes. As well, there shall be a client, which interacts with the blockchain network; however, the foundation of the network principle remains the same where one channel does have a corresponding ledger that can be accessed using chaincode deployed on the network.

Following the above example and improvising it to make a more real-world use case, think of a network having multiple participants sharing a common channel and ledger then there is a requirement of a couple of participants among the network may want to have some other transactions which are visible to them and not to the other participants of the network. In the below-given figure where five parties A, B, C, D, and E are already part of a blockchain network and doing the transactions which are visible to all of them then party C and E decide to open up another channel between the two where transactions are visible to only both of them and not to anybody else. For this, they create a separate channel exclusively for both of them, resulting in another ledger copy with the different transaction set and having a different chaincode deployed on that network, which can be accessed by only both of them to view and update the data of the ledger. In this complete process, their earlier ledger, chaincode, and channel network remain intact, and business is as usual on that channel.

It is unique flexibility that fabric provides as these maps to the real world transaction, imagine a supply chain network where a lot of participants are working together. Still, yet a seller may want to offer some exclusive deals to another member, and they can form a separate channel to achieve this:

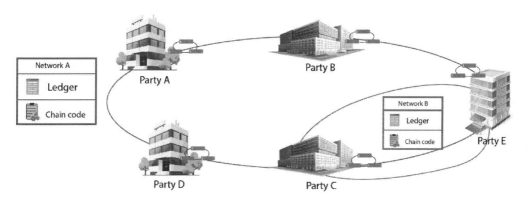

Figure 6.7: Multiple Channels

Let us consider one more example, where not all participants are in the first channel network. In the following figure, party A, B, C, and D are part of a channel where they share a shared ledger and have the corresponding chaincode. There is another network B, C, and E where 'E' was not part of the initial network, so channel gives us the flexibility of having private transactions among a selected group of participants regardless if those participants are part of any other channel or not. The second takeaway is that every channel would have its ledger and at least a chaincode instance to access that:

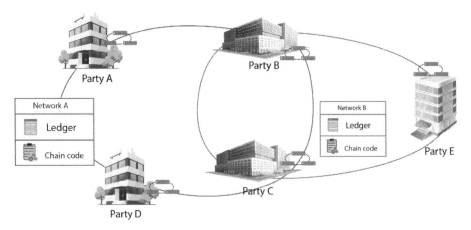

Figure 6.8: *Multiple channels*

Peer and organization

Hyperledger fabric-based business network is intended to be established between legally separate entities who may not trust each other but still have come together to achieve a common business objective without any intermediatiory to save on transaction cost and time. To be part of the network, organizations need to bring up their peer and join the specified channel on the network.

As with any other enterprise solution, business continuity, security is an essential aspect of the solution. So, organizations would come up with a set of peers so that there is no single point of failure. Also, to secure the peer setup, organizations may choose to expose only a single peer out of a cluster of peer nodes. The peer that is exposed to the other entities is known as anchor peer. Anchor peers act as connections points between the organizations.

A simplistic view of peers connecting is shown below. Assuming it's a network between two organizations, they have a couple of peers that have been set up and form a network, but then they have unique peers configured as Anchor peers that communicate with each other. The protocol that is used to communicate between peers is Gossip protocol; we shall have a section on Gossip protocol in detail later in the book. Anchor peers are the only discoverable entities in the blockchain network, and they become the interface for the entire peer network they are part of:

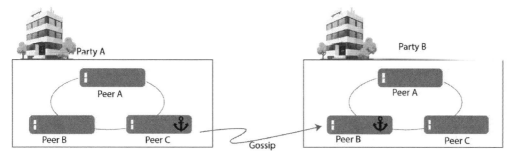

***Figure 6.9**: Anchor Peer*

Below is a more exhaustive setup of a network; this setup is established between four organizations, and the channel is set up only between five nodes, and the rest of the nodes could be there for different channels. Fabric does also gives the flexibility to add or remove any organization to the network. Similarly, any organization can also add or remove any peer node in their side, depending on the requirement that has to the address:

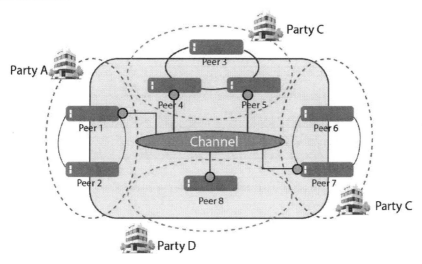

***Figure 6.10**: Hyperledger Fabric Network*

Another essential concept is the application; any organization would want to have a user interface based applications that can help organizational based users to see the ledger data in different forms and shapes as they would wish to see. The organization can develop the applications based on their specific requirements, which means the presentation layer and business logic would be different even though having been on the same channel means having the same ledger data.

Peer and identity

In public and permissionless blockchain, any node that becomes part of the network is anonymous; it doesn't have to reveal its identity, a node still carries out transactions and have access to its assets. It is possible because of the public/private key that node holds, the node uses pair of keys to create a transaction, sign it, send it, and receive it and prove the ownership of the assets finally. However, in the case of permissioned blockchain, all members are known to each other as they have come together to achieve a mutual objective. Identity is essential in the case of a private blockchain, and it is essential to know who is who and who can do\has done what.

In Hyperledger Fabric, there is a concept of identity, any node or application who wants to interact with the blockchain network needs to have an identity. In Fabric, identity is made available to every participating node or application in the form of a digital certificate that gets issued from a certificate authority. The certificates issued in the fabric network are X.509 digital certificates, which works as an identity for the holder, and it does have a lot of valid information about the holder. Every organization administrator would issue a digital certificate to all peers and participants who want to access the blockchain network.

Membership Service Provider (MSP) is an essential concept in Hyperledger Fabric, which is known to provide details about the identity of a participating entity in the network, be it peer, orderer, or client. We shall discuss this in detail in a separate section, however just to set the foundation, a channel in a blockchain network maintains a channel policy; it is the configuration that helps determine the rights and access of a peer-based on its identity.

In the below-given image, all peers have a digital identity in the form the certificates such as D1, D2, and so on, which are issued to them by the respective organization's Certificate Authority. A peer ideally should be linked to an organization as it would have been set up and made to join the network by an organization. Peer when connects to the blockchain network using the channel, they interact with an identity which is called the **principal**. Channel than refers to the channel policy, which refers to MSP defined as part of channel configuration and figures out the organization of the peer and also the access right as defined:

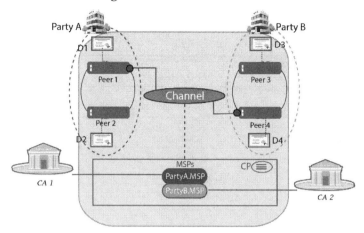

Figure 6.11: *Identity in Blockchain Network*

Peer types

In a Hyperledger based blockchain network, there shall be many organizations that would collaborate. Every organization is supposed to bring up its peer nodes as in truly decentralized fashion. Hyperledger Fabric, to bring more granularity in the network and to have concrete responsibilities of peers, gives the flexibility to use peers in three different modes:

- **Anchor peer**: To bring security in the system, where organizations may come up with a cluster of peers, they shall designate one peer as an anchor peer, which generally interfaces the outer world. So, anchor peer is the one that is discoverable and connects to other discoverable peers in the blockchain network as well with the non-discoverable peers of the parent organization.

- **Leader peer**: Orderer is responsible for sending the blocks of ordered transactions to all the peers, likewise an anchor peer, leader peer is the one, which gets blocks from the orderer, and not all the peers in the organization are required to get connected to **Orderer**. Once a leader peer gets the block from the orderer, it sends the block to other peers:

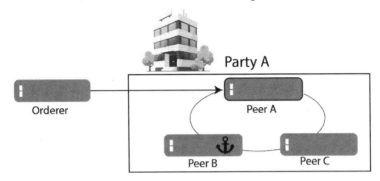

Figure 6.12: Leader peer

- **Peer**: Peer or regular peers are the ones other than Leader or Anchor Peer. From the software perspective, all peers are the same; however, based on the configuration at times, they place the role of Anchor or Leader. We would get to see all of the action in later chapters when we set up the network.

Comprehensive view

A peer is a fundamental unit in the blockchain network and probably the most important as it executes chaincode, maintains the ledger, and interacts with other entities in the network. Below is the comprehensive high-level view of a peer, which exposes services as well for other participants and talks to them through gossip protocol:

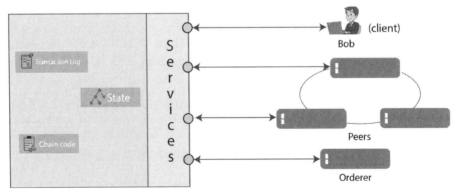

Figure 6.13: Peer

Ordering service

Ordering service or orderer as it is called many times is an essential constituent in the Hyperledger fabric-based blockchain network. The consensus is an essential aspect of the blockchain network that helps determine what needs to go into the ledger. In what order, the consensus is a process of reaching an agreement between various participating nodes of the network so that there is a consistent state between the ledgers at nodes.

In public or permissionless network, transactions are ordered and collated in a block, and that could be done by any node and once that block is distributed among the peers they determine the validation of transactions in the block along with the proof which is generally a mathematical problem solved by the proposer node. These systems are based on a probabilistic consensus algorithm such that once an approved blocked is added into the blockchain, all validated transactions in an order shall be added to the ledger. However, at the time, this ends up having a condition called 'Fork,' which is getting two different ordered blocks with validated transactions and proof of the solution of a mathematical problem. It results in two blockchains in progress. However, there are ways by which this is solved at the blockchain level, and eventually, the longer chain exists.

In the case of fabric, there is no concept of Fork as at any point in time, there should exist only one blockchain, and that is the source of truth for participating members. Orderer is the one that facilitates this. Fabric works on a deterministic consensus algorithm, which simply means at any point in time when a peer receives a block of ordered transactions, and when it validates the transactions and writes them down into ledger, order and finality is guaranteed. All this happens as the orderer plays an essential role in transaction processing in fabric.

In the fabric network, every participating member has an identity; similarly, an orderer does also have an identity which is issued by Certificate Authority and is stored in orderer MSP.

To achieve ordering functionality, Hyperledger Fabric has given multiple implementations:

- **Solo**: This is the default implementation of ordering service; it is a single ordering service that can be used in the fabric network to help reach consensus and ordering of transactions in the block. As the name suggests, it's solo that means a single instance, and so there is no way of avoiding Single Point of Failure while deploying ordering service as a solo. Solo is mainly intended to be used in development and Proof of Concept and is no way recommended for production. An orderer node is set up exclusively as we do set up a peer node, and it derives a lot of its configurations from a YAML file. **YAML** stands for **YAML Ain't Markup Language,** and it's a kind of configuration file. It is used extensively in providing configuration parameters and values in setting up the various constituents of the fabric network. We shall go in detail about the different YAML files in the *Setup* section.

- **Kafka**: To promote the architectural principle of modularity and be able to set up an enterprise-grade ready blockchain network, the fabric does support ordering service to be set up as a Kafka cluster. Kafka setup is **Crash Fault Tolerant (CFT)** system; there is no single point of failure in the Kafka cluster. Kafka uses the "leader and follower" configuration mode, where transactions, also known as messages in 'Kafka,' are replicated from the leader node to the follower nodes. In the event the leader node goes down, one of the followers becomes the leader, and ordering can continue, thus ensuring fault tolerance.

The entire coordination and management of the Kafka cluster, such as task handling, access control, and controller election, and others, is managed by a Zookeeper and its related APIs.

Whereas, Kafka and zookeeper setup as CFT Ordering service gives the flexibility of resilient ordering system and much of that is achievable through template configuration files provided with the setup of Hyperledger Fabric, at the same time it is tricky sometime to go through all that and come up with a running system

- **Raft**: Raft is a new addition in Hyperledger Fabric v 1.4.1. The raft is again a Crash Fault Tolerant ordering service implementation based on Raft protocol. The raft is a distributed consensus algorithm; it helps multiple servers agree on a shared state or consensus even in case there are failures. Raft follows a "leader and follower" model, where a leader node is elected, and its decisions are replicated by the followers. Raft maintains shared status, which is a data structure backed up by logs that are replicated all over. In this setup, the leader accepts client requests and manages the replication of the log to other servers.

  The raft is proving to be the choice of selection for ordering service implementation in a production-ready Fabric network. Since it follows the leader and follower model, a leader is chosen dynamically among the ordering nodes in the channel. The leader is responsible for replicating the message to follower nodes. Raft based ordering system is truly CFT as it can sustain the loss of nodes as long as the majority of nodes are up and running.

There are few noticeable changes between putting up Kafka based or Raft based ordering service, and they are worthwhile to note.

1. Easy Setup: those who have worked with Kafka would appreciate the fact that setting up the Kafka cluster is not a straight forward job. It requires the right amount of expertise in setting up a Kafka based infrastructure. Additionally, setting up the Kafka cluster need the Zookeeper setup as well, and then there are tricky configurations in the YAML file that needs to be done. Version match between orderer node and Kafka is something that also needs to be taken care of. The good point of using Raft as an ordering service is that it comes embedded in the ordering node.

2. Kafka and Zookeeper cluster cannot be run in a truly decentralized fashion, which would mean that any one organization in the network shall own and run this cluster, and hence ordering service which needs to be running on one cluster shall be under the control of one organization. It somehow moves control from decentralized fashion to one single organization. Using Raft, each organization can employ its ordering nodes, can participate in the ordering service, which leads to a more decentralized system.

3. While Kafka and Zookeeper based ordering service provide CFT and are compatible with fabric. Yet, they come under Apache License, so compatible images are required to be arranged separately, and version matching needs to be considered very carefully. On the other side, Raft is being developed and maintained by the Hyperledger community itself, so compatibility is never an issue.

Ledger

A ledger, as in the conventional world, is a way of bookkeeping transactions that have happened over some time. At any point in time, it can be used to view the current state of any asset, and entries of credits and debits help us understand the transactions over some time. The concept of ledger goes back thousands of years; however, in recent times, the most common example is a bank account where available balance tells the current state of the account, and looking at the debits and credits tells us about the transaction summary over some time.

Similarly, the ledger in Hyperledger fabric as well in other blockchain systems is an essential constituent of the complete blockchain ecosystem. Hyperledger Fabric is primarily addressing these two concerns—to be able to show the current value of a set of ledger states and to preserve and maintain the history of the transactions that eventually lead to these states.

In the Hyperledger Fabric blockchain network, we primarily deal with transactions, and these transactions generally represent the event of a change of a state of an asset, for example, changing the ownership of the car. Along with ledger and states, there is a critical phenomenon of *facts*. In the ledger, we are not storing any specific business object rather facts about the object, following up the example of cars; it could be the owner of the car. In doing transactions, we are recording the facts about the current state of an object, and the facts about the history of transactions that led to the current state. Ledger is responsible for holding the state of the asset blockchain network.

A silly question might arise at this point, what is so different that we are doing at this point of time by just recording transactions and glorifying state at this point. However, while the facts about the current state of an entity or business object may change as a result of the transaction, the history of facts is immutable; it is the permanent state of a transaction event. It cannot be retrospectively changed though new records can always be appended on top of it.

In one of our earlier sections, we did briefly touched upon ledger. A ledger consists of two parts, state and transaction log:

- World state: In fabric, a state is generally termed as a world state. A world state is a database of the cache of the current values of a set of ledger states. The world state comes handy for a client program that can directly access the current value of a state rather than calculating it by traversing through the entire set of the transaction log. In Hyperledger Fabric, ledger states are, stored and retrieved as key-value pairs, and that helps giving out a lot of flexibility to the client programs who may choose to represent the world state in a different format as required by the organization or serving application. Like any other entity which gets affected by the transaction, the world state can frequently change, as states can be created, updated, and deleted.

- Transaction log: Transaction log is another essential part of the ledger. It records all the changes that have happened over an asset as a result of a transactional event. Transactions are ordered and collected in the block, and upon transaction commit this block get appended to the blockchain, this results in the understanding of the events that have taken place and resulted in the current state. The blockchain data structure is different from the world state because it is persisted permanently, and once written; it cannot be modified; it is immutable.

Below diagram on high level depicts that ledger consists of two parts, world state, and blockchain, which is nothing but transaction log. An important point here to consider is that it's the transaction log entries that eventually determine the world state. Though we have talked about the ledger in general, as a principle of decentralization, there shall be multiple copies of ledger being maintained by peers of the network. They are entitled to be part of the channel that holds this ledger. Also, it is through a consensus process that entries in the ledger are updated so that any point of time there is a single version of the truth and consistent state that is available at the ledger level:

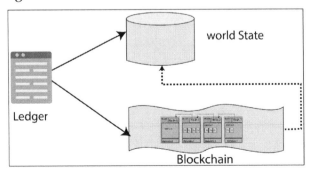

Figure 6.14: Ledger Composition

Having covered a high-level detail of world state and transaction log, we will go bit deeper into these concepts to get familiar with how this works at ground level.

World state

While the blockchain network helps different organizations collaborate and do transactions among themselves to save themselves from intermediaries, time-saving, and cost-saving were resulting from not having to do expensive tasks such as reconciliation. However, as an organization or a user, all this can be done through the application that can access data from the blockchain network. Data being a vital ingredient here that needs to be made available to the client applications to view and prepare for the next actions. In a traditional application, this data sits on a database that can be fetched, applied certain business logic, and can be presented to the users. To facilitate the same, client applications can access the data from the world state, which otherwise might be difficult to access and recreate from the transaction log. The world state here is implemented as a database. It helps a lot because a database provides a rich set of operators for the efficient storage and retrieval of states from the world state.

The world state helps to provide the current state of the attribute of a business object. Considering the below figure, the current state of an asset such as a car. The following figure shows ledger states for two cars of different brands, BMW and MERC, each having a key and a value. The client application program can make use of smart contracts (chaincode) and invoke them, which in turns uses simple ledger APIs to operate, such as to get, put, and delete states:

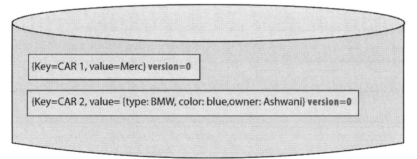

Figure 6.15: World state

One of the vital aspects here is to consider that it is not as simple as it looks to retrieve and put the data. In Hyperledger Fabric, everything that goes into the blockchain network is a set of transactions which involves creating transaction proposal, execution, ordering, commit, and so on. It also requires various endorsement policies coming into effect. Still, the good part is fabric has insulated developers from this by providing various SDK that can be used to develop client applications and then interacting with the blockchain network. We shall be discussing this in detail in later chapters.

You also must have noticed world state does maintain version number with the state, and in the diagram above, states CAR 1 and CAR 2 have versions, 0. Hyperledger Fabric internally maintains the version, and increments the version number every time there is a state change. The version checking is done to ensure that the version matches the version that was there at the time of endorsement. It is done to make sure that the world state changes are done in accordance, that there has not been a concurrent update and the current update is the expected.

World state options

Since Hyperledger Fabric gives the flexibility to store world state in the database, to help client application to store and retrieve data quickly, it will take a quick look at the database support that it provides. As of now, LevelDB and CouchDB are the databases that can be used to support the world state. LevelDB is something that comes as by default with the peer configuration. If the records being persisted are of simple Key-Value pair, then LevelDB could be an appropriate choice as it is co-located with the peer itself and is embedded in the same process.

However, if we intended to store JSON documents and as well have the need to use productive queries for the client application, then CouchDB is the right choice. A CouchDB instance can be run separately from the peer node, and generally, there shall be a single instance of CouchDB mapping to the peer node. Switching of LevelDB and CouchDB is another example of an enterprise architecture principle that Hyperledger Fabric follows with pluggable being supported. The change is usually straightforward, and with a couple of configuration changes, a peer node can be made connect to CouchDB instead of LevelDB; we need to bring up an instance of CouchDB in the network whose particulars need to be given to node. We have an example to showcase the change fo configuration for switching the world state DB from LevelDB to CouchDB in a later chapter. Also, from a smart contract perspective, there is no need for making any special consideration or change when we are writing a chaincode to persist and retrieve values. It has been isolated for the developers.

Transaction log (Blockchain)

The second part of the ledger is the transaction log or blockchain. Whereas the world state gives the current state of the attributes of business object representation of an asset, blockchain would record all the transactions leading to the current state. It is the historical recording of the transactional event on business objects. In an earlier chapter, we have discussed in detail about blockchain as a data structure; blockchain is connected linked list of blocks where each block contains several transactions.

In Bitcoin, we saw how the concept of transaction works with the UTXO model and script notations, but in the case of fabric, each transaction represents a query or update to the world state.

Like in the case of bitcoin or for that matter in Ethereum or most blockchain system, a block's header includes a cumulative hash of the transactions present in the block. The header also includes a copy of the hash of the previous block's header. It ensures that all transactions on the ledger are sequenced and cryptographically linked together. The linking through cryptographic hashing makes the blockchain data very secure. In the event of any malicious node hosting the ledger tampers, the data to its benefit, would not be able to prove all the other nodes that it has the correct blockchain as the ledger is shared and distributed between the network of independent nodes.

Whereas the world state uses a database, which primarily intended for the client application, blockchain is implemented as a file system in Hyperledger fabric. The sole reason of keeping the design simple as appending of data in the blockchain is the primary operation, and querying directly from the blockchain is seen as a relatively not so frequent operation.

Below is the pure representation of blockchain, where all blocks are linked together with a hash value of the previous block, which is stored in the header of the current block. The first block in the blockchain is the genesis block, and we would see in later chapters how we generate genesis block:

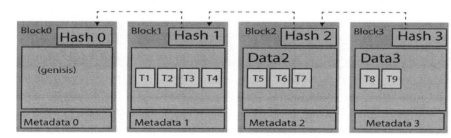

Figure 6.16: Blockchain

We shall also have a look at the individual block as to how it looks like; a block consists of the block header, block data, and block metadata:

- **Block header:** Block header contains block number, current block hash, and previous block hash.

- **Block number**: This is a simple incremental number, which starts from 0 for genesis block and then increases by one every time there is an addition of a new block in the blockchain. A Block number can help identify the depth of blockchain.

- **Current block hash**: Current block hash is the hash of all the transactions contained in the current block. In most other blockchains such as bitcoin and

Ethereum, we would not see the current block hash being saved in the same block.

- **Previous block hash**: This is an essential ingredient in the block header as it helps to secure the immutability. It is a copy of the hash from the previous block in the blockchain.

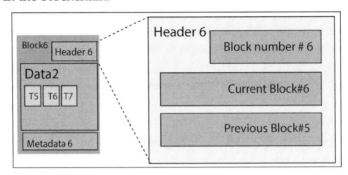

Figure 6.17: Block Header

A quick reference would be to have a look back as to how bitcoin's header looks like:

Field	Description
Version	Version number to track software upgrade
Previous block hash	Reference to the hash of the previous block
Merkle root	Hash of the root of the Merkle tree of current block's transactions
Timestamp	Approximate creation time of the block
Difficulty target	Proof-of-Work algorithm difficulty for the block
Nonce	Counter used for PoW algorithm

Table 6.1

There are no fields such as difficulty target and nonce, which are extensively used in the blockchain where Proof of Work is used as a consensus algorithm. Since Bitcoin uses PoW, these fields make sense there, but in the case of fabric, there is no concept of mining, and the consensus is achieved through the help of ordering service.

Block metadata

This section contains:

- The timestamp of block creation
- Certificate, public key, and signature of the block writer

Subsequently, the block committer also adds a valid/invalid indicator for every transaction. However, this information is not included in the hash, as that is created when the block is created.

Block data: Block data contains a set of transactions.

Transaction

The transaction, as in other blockchain becomes a fundamental unit in the blockchain. A transaction represents the change of state of an attribute of a business object. Like in Bitcoin, a transaction in fabric represents a container that holds multiple attributes. In the below-given figure, an extrapolated view of transaction is shown:

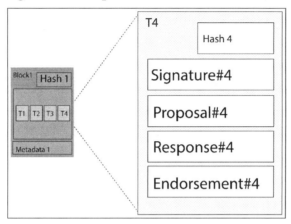

Figure 6.18: Transaction

Following are the fields in the transaction:

- **Header:** The header is responsible for carrying the metadata information of the transaction, such as the chaincode name and its version.

- **Signature**: Signatures are a cryptographic signature, and they are created by client applications using their private key who are responsible for generating the transaction. This field helps to check that the transaction details have not been tampered with.

- **Proposal**: Proposal is the set of input parameters that are supplied by the client application to the smart contract with the intent to update the ledger data. The proposal is an integral part of the transaction process, which provides a set of input parameters. When an essential operation is performed, then with the current world state, a new state comes into existence.

- **Response:** Upon successful execution of the smart contract with the input provided in the proposal, a Read Write Set is created that contains before and after values of the world state. This RW-Set is called the response. After ordering and successful validation of the transaction, this is applied to the ledger, which results in an update of the world state.

- **Endorsements:** Endorsement is the affiliation of the different organizations of the blockchain network to agree on a transaction response. For a transaction proposal, there could be a single response but could have multiple endorsements which get resulted from the endorsement policy. If a particular transaction does not include the required number of endorsements as required by the policy, then this transaction would not go through updating the ledger and hence shall be rejected.

All these attributes shall be discussed in detail when we would go through the transaction process in Hyperledger Fabric. The objective of describing them here is to get a high-level understanding of transaction objects, and soon we will see all of them in action.

Smart contracts

Organizations that do take part in a Hyperledger Fabric blockchain network do have the purpose of being a part of the network that is to carry out transactions. In the real world, whenever two organizations do the transaction, they do under the preview of rules or a contract. Similarly, to enable companies to be able to do business on a blockchain network, the rules are followed in the form of executable logic, which is called a smart contract. The notion of the smart contract came with the Ethereum as they wanted to create a programmable blockchain which can carry out a transaction of any kind than directly transferring of cryptocurrency.

While the ledger is used to hold the business objects history and state, smart contracts are the agreed rule of the game that executes the logic and update the ledger. In Fabric, a notion of chaincode is used interchangeably with the smart contract; however, it is essential to understand that there is a subtle difference between the two. Generally, a smart contract contains the agreed transaction logic that gets executed and controls the transaction lifecycle update of the associated business object. Chaincode, on the other hand, is mostly related to administrative aspects of smart contracts. Smart Contracts are packaged in a chaincode and then deployed on the network. Chaincode rules how smart contracts are packaged and deployed. Below figure gives a high-level view of chaincode and smart contract:

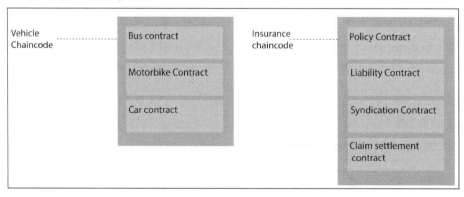

Figure 6.19: *Smart Contract*

In the given image, for a vehicle chaincode, there are three smart contracts. So, a smart contract is defined within a chaincode, and there could be multiple chain codes. A chaincode is something that gets deployed on the network, and once a chaincode is deployed, all smart contracts included in the chaincode shall be deployed at once.

A chaincode can be thought of as a technical container of a co-related set of smart contracts that are used for smart contracts installation and instantiation.

Anatomy of smart contract

While in the end, the smart contract is a technical program written in a language and deployed on the network to do the transactions. Even before two or multiple organizations can start working together, they need to agree on the data set, rules of execution, and any other processes that are vital for carrying out the business transaction.

For example, below given is the simplest example of a smart contract, which defines certain operations related to a business object, that is, car. The good part in the fabric is for developing smart contract developers do not need to learn a new language as in Ethereum, people need to know solidity. As of now, fabric supports chaincode development in Go Lang, NodeJS, and Java. Support for other popular languages may be included in further releases:

```
car contract:

query(car):
    get(car);
    return car;

transfer(car, buyer,seller):
    get(car);
    car.owner = buyer;
    put(car);
    return car;

update(car,properties):
    get(car);
    car.colour = properties.colour;
    put(car);
    return car;
```

Figure 6.20: *Car Contract*

In the above-given pseudocode of car contract, it is prevalent that query, transfer, and update are the operations that can be called on car business objects. As a result of any operation, the state of the car shall be updated in the ledger. So, the smart contract here helps the organization carry out the transaction with a predefined rule, and once written in the ledger; it becomes permanent.

The sole purpose of the smart contract is to update the transaction logic and accordingly update the ledger, Smart contracts primarily put, get and delete states in the world state, and can also query the immutable blockchain record of transactions:

- A get as the name suggests helps to fire a query to fetch the information about the current state of a business object
- A put would help create a new business object or modifies an existing one in the ledger world state
- A delete would remove the business object from the current state of the ledger, but not its history

Whereas the developer writes smart contracts, there are APIs available known as SHIM API for developers that can help them interact with ledgers. We shall have a great look at smart contracts and SHIM API in the later chapter.

Intercommunication is possible between smart contracts; that is, smart contracts can call each other within the same channel or across different channels. A smart contract deployed on a channel can only access its ledger and no other channel's ledger. Intercommunication is a way by which one smart contract can query another channel's ledger. There are different APIs available to accomplish this, and there are specific considerations that we need to keep in mind;

Peek into system chaincode

Smart contracts defined within chaincode have the primary purpose of creating an agreed, and domain-specific business rules that help solve the transaction between the participating members of the fabric network. In Hyperledger, domain-independent low-level chaincode have been created that help in various aspects of smart contract processing.

Following are the different system chain codes; these are just for information, and we shall have a detailed discussion on them in a later chapter:

- **Lifecycle system chaincode (LSCC):** This chaincode runs in all peers, and its primary purpose if to handle the life cycle of chaincode, that is, package signing, installation, instantiation, and handling chaincode upgrades
- **Configuration system chaincode (CSCC):** Again, this chaincode runs on all peers, and its responsibility is to handle changes to a channel configuration, as a policy update.
- **Query system chaincode (QSCC):** This also runs in all peers, and it provides APIs for leger that helps to query block and transaction info

- **Endorsement system chaincode (ESCC):** A transaction response is required to be signed, and ESCC helps to do that
- **Validation system chaincode (VSCC):** This helps to validate a transaction, including checking endorsement policy and read-write set versioning.

Channel

In most straightforward words, the channel is the mode of communication between a specific set of entities that are part of a channel. In a blockchain network, participants are peer nodes from different organizations, ordering service, client applications, and so on, and the channel is the way to communicate between all entities. Channel paves a way to carry out business agreed and defined transactions between participants that could be between two participants, between three participants or even between multiple participants. Channel gives the flexibility to establish a connection for exchanging transaction objects between any numbers of participants.

Likewise, a channel can have multiple participants; a participant can join multiple channels. Channel then works as a closed and private network or subnet of participating nodes where they can carry out private and confidential transactions, which is only meant to be between the members of channels. A channel does have its ledger that is shared between member peers. Chaincode that is required to query and update the ledger is also deployed on the channel.

Each peer that is willing to join a channel has to have its own identity that is provided by a **membership services provider (MSP),** which authenticates each peer to its channel peers and services. Channel also provides the flexibility of designing a network with a controlled level of access to a particular group and, at the same time, if required, can enable full access to participants.

It is the notion of the channel that helps the same organization take part in various blockchain networks at the same time, still ensuring the data between channels remain independent of each other. In the ability of peers joining multiple channels, it is often referred to as participating in the network of networks. Channels provide a way of the optimized collaboration of underlying infrastructure while guaranteeing data and communications privacy. Peers are mutually exclusive enough to have organizations separate their business transaction traffic with different counterparties, but still integrated into such a fashion to be able to coordinate independent activities when necessary.

As shown in the below picture, a channel is providing a completely separate communication way between different participating organizations. **Org1** in the picture is part of two channels, in one with **Org2** and another with **Org3.** Different chain codes shall be instantiated on different channels, and participating Org can use the chaincode to update the ledger between the two. Endorsement policy also plays an essential role in the channel as any transaction taking effect on that channel follows an endorsement policy:

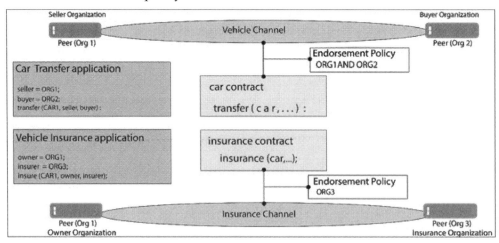

Figure 6.21: *Channels*

Whereas writing a smart contract is something that is the responsibility of the developer, an administrator is responsible for deploying chaincode on a channel. The administrator would define an endorsement policy for a chaincode when it is instantiated on a channel and can change it when the chaincode is upgraded. The endorsement policy is at a chaincode level and hence gets applied equally to all smart contracts defined in that chaincode, which is deployed to a channel. It gives great flexibility in terms of having a single, smart contract that is deployed to different channels can have different endorsement policies.

In the above figure, a car contract has been deployed to the **Vehicle** channel, and at the same time, an insurance contract is deployed to the **Insurance** channel. Endorsement policy defined for car contract on vehicle channel requires both **ORG1** and **ORG2** to sign transactions before they are considered valid and can be written on the ledger. In contrast, in the case of the insurance channel, the insurance contract is following an endorsement policy that requires only organization **ORG3** to sign valid transactions. Here, **ORG1** is participating in two networks, the **Vehicle** channel, and the **Insurance** channel, and can coordinate activity across these two networks with **ORG2** and **ORG3** respectively without having to share any transactional data between these two networks.

In the later chapter, when we would set up the networks, we shall look deeper into how the channel works, how to create a channel, and what all configurations that take part in the channel and how we can tweak them to see different behavior of the network.

Private data

Whereas a channel has got its fair share of benefits, which gives the flexibility of establishing communication medium between choices of participants, and then this gets enhanced with a peer node joining multiple channels. Peer joining multiple channels can transact securely and privately without having to share between the channels. Essentially, if there is a need to have more private communication for a set of organizations out of the entire organization in the network, there is an option of creating a new channel only comprising of the organization that needs to access the data.

However, creating separate channels have a couple of issues:

- To create a separate channel, there are additional administrative overheads that need to be addressed, such as having separate policies, maintaining separate chaincode versions and deployment, managing MSP, and so on

- There is no provision in channel setup, where a portion of data could be kept private for specific organizations while having all organizations accessing the complete data

To overcome these issues and to provide flexibility for the use cases where specific organizations can still the controlled data among a set of participants out of the complete network without creating an entirely new channel. The fabric came up with the idea of private data collections, starting version 1.2.

Private data collection

A private data collection has two constituents:

1. **Actual private data:** This is the set of data that is private and shared between authorized nodes through gossip protocol as opposed to data being sent by orderer in blocks. This private data is stored only in the private state databases of the authorized organizations. Similarly, this private data collection can only be accessed from chaincode on these authorized organizations. Think of these authorized organizations is the organizations out of the channel who have agreed to share some private data among themselves without creating a new channel and still be part of the original main channel.

    The data is shared between authorized peers through gossip protocol, and hence ordering service is not involved there and doesn't get to see the actual data as in the case of a regular transaction where it orders the transaction.

2. **Hash of data**: In a blockchain network, all peers have the same ledger however with private data collection, set of data is being maintained separately on a couple of nodes out of the network, so still to keep the ledger sync throughout the network, the hash of the private data is endorsed, ordered and persisted on all the peer's ledger on that channel. The hash of the private data serves

as evidence of the transaction and is used for state validation at a later point of time and can be used for audit purposes:

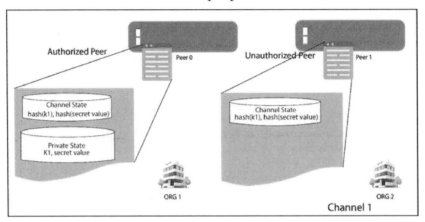

Figure 6.22: Private Data Collection

As given in the above diagram, there are two organizations in a channel, one authorized and another one unauthorized. Whereas, both the peer nodes maintain a set of data that is available for all the nodes on the channel, other than that authorized peer store an individual state of data. Additionally, the hash value of the data is stored both at the authorized and unauthorized peer ledger.

It is helpful in regards to being able to prove that a particular data set existed on the individual state, in which case any other party can compute the hash of private data and compare it with the hash stored in their ledger.

Likewise, a peer can be a participant in multiple channels, the same way a peer can have multiple private data collection, and this gives more level of granularity and the option of establishing more relationships among participants with varied interests. For example, in the below-given diagram, a peer on a channel can maintain multiple **private data collection (PDC):**

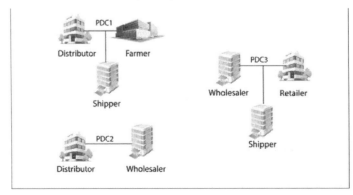

Figure 6.23: PDC

Because these databases are kept separate from the database that holds the channel ledger, private data is sometimes referred to as **SideDB**. As shown in the below diagram, the separate private state is maintained between different participants depending on the use case:

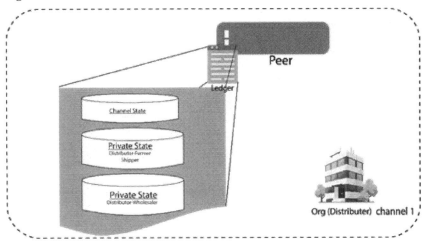

Figure 6.24: PDC

We shall have a more detailed discussion on the private data collection architecture and a sample program set up in the latter part of the book.

Identity

In a blockchain network, many participants come together to achieve a standard business functionality. Hyperledger Fabric network has many organizations that join as participants by way of setting up peer nodes. We have ordering service as well in the network that orders the transaction, creates the blocks, and disseminates them to participating peers. We do have client applications that many organizations would set up to make blockchain network data available to end-user and systems to carry out business functionalities. All of these participants are known to each other as opposed to being anonymous, as we have seen in public blockchains.

Whereas on the one hand, members are known to each other; on the other side, every member does have an associated privilege or access right as to what information or operation they can perform on the fabric blockchain network. Each participant due to above mentioned both reasons are provided with an identity. This digital identity is issued to participants in the form of an X.509 digital certificate. These identities help determine the correct permissions over resources and access to information that participants have in the fabric blockchain network. An identity where helps establish who the participant is, it also provides additional attributes that help to determine the permission (what can it do) to the identity holder. In Hyperledger

Fabric, there is a concept of principal, which is a union of identity and its associated attributes related to permissions.

In the traditional world, identities are issued generally by **Public Key Infrastructure (PKI)** in the form of digital certificate, public /private key. These PKI should be trusted authority, and we have established organizations that play the role of trusted authorities. Now, by merely having an identity from a trusted authority alone doesn't solve the problem as they issue generic digital identities. Still, it's the role of **Membership Ship Provider (MSP)** in the fabric that defines the rules that govern the strong identities applicable for a given fabric blockchain network. MSPs turn verifiable identities into the members of a blockchain network.

A simple analogy could be having a valid Credit Card from an issuing authority such as VISA, Master or AMEX, and so on. Still, in a given supermarket, they would outline which credit card they accept. So, while you have a valid Master card issued by a valid issuing authority but yet you cannot use it in a specific supermarket as they might not be accepting Master card.

Fabric CA is provided by the Hyperledger fabric as an option to help generate certificates. Fabric CA is a private root CA provider capable of managing digital identities of Fabric participants that have the form of X.509 certificates. Fabric CA, along with MSP in the blockchain network, helps to validate the identities as well as restricting the participating members to access the blockchain resources as defined by the access control list of the member.

Membership Service Provider

We noticed in the Identity section that PKI helps to provide verifiable identities; however, to make these identities work in the fabric blockchain network as per the access granted to them is something that an MSP helps with. An MSP helps identify access rights that a participating member does have within the ambit of the organization the MSP represents. The access role could be of admin or members of a sub-organization group. MSP sets the ground for defining access privileges in the context of a network and channel as to if the participating member is a channel admin, reader, or writer.

MSP is attached to an organization or its groups and is notified by way of configurations. There are two kinds of MSP, Channel MSP, and Local MSP. The channel MSP is published to all the channels where members of the corresponding organization can take part. Local MSP is meant for peers, orderers, and clients who maintain their MSP configuration that defines their permission over a particular component.

Generally, an MSP is defined at an organization level; for instance, for an organization ORG1, there could be an MSP defined as ORG1-MSP. The org level MSP is usually used at channel level. This MSP at the channel level would help identify the transaction coming from the members of the organizations. However, there are use cases when a single organization might have different departments or business divisions that carry out functionally different business, and so it makes sense for them to join different channels; in that case, a group level MSP can also be defined to facilitate it better. An example figure showcasing that could look like:

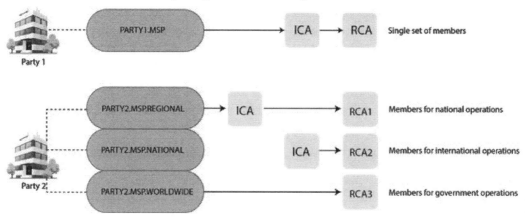

Figure 6.25: MSP at the Org level

Local MSP

While MSP is a relatively tricky concept and takes time to understand, we would cover some aspects of Local MSP here. These concepts would become more evident as we dive deep into setting up the actual business network, which we would cover soon.

Participating members of the network are peer, orderer, and client. Local MSP is defined for them. Local MSP defines the certificate authority and permissions for that specific node. The local MSPs of the member allow its side to authenticate itself in its transactions against specific permission such as a member of a channel able to do chaincode transactions, or as the owner of a specific role into the system such as org admin who can carry out a more specific task such as configuration transactions. Every participating member should have local MSP configured to take part in the network either as administrative rights or as participatory rights.

In the end, local MSPs are set of files residing on the file system of the participating member to which they apply. Henceforth, physically and logically, there is only one local MSP per node or user.

Channel MSP

Channel MSP is way higher than Local MSP, and it is defined at the channel level. It defines participatory and administrative rights at the channel level. Every participating organization should have an MSP defined for all the channels it is supposed to take part it. Peers and orderer on a channel will all share the same view of channel MSPs, and will, therefore, be able to authenticate the channel participants correctly. It merely means that if an organization wishes to be part of a channel, an MSP containing the entire chain of trust for the organization's members would require to be included in the channel configuration. Not having channel MSP of participating organizations would result in the rejection of transactions originating from this organization's identities.

The trust domain (for example, the organization) of each peer is defined by the peer's local MSP, for example, ORG1 or ORG2. Representation of an organization on a channel is achieved by adding the organization's MSP to the channel configuration.

A channel MSP unlike local MSP is instantiated on the file system of every member in the channel and kept synchronized via consensus. So while there is a copy of each channel MSP on the local file system of every node, logically a channel MSP resides on and is maintained by the channel or the network.

MSP structure

While we have tried to understand the concept of MSP at Local and at Channel MSP level, in this section, we would have just had a high level look into as to how MSP looks like, in the end, it's just a file structure from configuration perspective with different files in different folders. It is picked up relevant members at the required time. The below-given figure gives a high level of the MSP directory structure. Every folder is self-explanatory and has a relevance that gives different input:

Figure 6.26: MSP structure

There are nine directories in the root MSP folder, the root folder is MSP name, and subsequent subfolders represent different MSP configurations. This structure holds good for local MSP, and channel MSP differs from this. We shall cover a brief description of al subfolders:

- **Root CAs:** In this folder, there shall be a list of self-signed X.509 certificates of the Root CAs which are trusted by the organization that is being represented by this MSP. There must be at least one Root CA X.509 certificate in this MSP folder.

- **Intermediate CAs:** This is an optional folder; it contains a list of X.509 certificates of the Intermediate CAs trusted by this organization. Each certificate must be signed by one of the Root CAs in the MSP or by an Intermediate CA whose issuing CA chain ultimately leads back to a trusted root CA. It is useful when organizations wish to have a separate MSP for their divisions. As this is an optional folder, in case there are no intermediate CAs, then this folder would be empty.

- **Organizational units:** This is also an optional folder and could be empty if not required. It has been provided to give additional flexibility in terms of restricting the member of an organization.

- **Administrators**: As the name suggests, this folder contains a list of identities that can play the role of administrators for this organization. In a standard MSP, there shall be at least one X.509 certificate in this list.

Note that just because an actor has the role of an administrator, it doesn't mean that they can administer particular resources. The actual power a given identity has to administer the system is determined by the policies that manage system resources. For instance, a channel policy might specify that ORG1 administrators have the right to add new organizations to the channel, whereas the ORG2 administrators do not have such rights.

- **Revoked certificates:** This folder contains identifying information about a member identity whose access has been revoked. This list is more or less the same as a CA's **Certificate Revocation List (CRL),** but more importantly, it also relates to the revocation of membership from the organization. The administrator of an MSP, be it local or channel, can revoke participating members from an organization by advertising the updated CRL of the CA.

- **Node Identity**: This folder contains the identity of the node; it's more of an X.509 certificate for that specific node. It is mandatory for local MSP.

- **Keystore:** In simplest terms, this contains the private key for the participating member, its also known as signing key, and it works in conjunction with the identity included in the Node Identity folder. It is a mandatory folder, and it must contain exactly one private key of the node it belongs to. It is not applicable for Channel MSP as channel MSP offers validation functionalities and not signing abilities.

- **TLS Root CA**: This folder contains a list of self-signed X.509 certificates of the Root CAs trusted by this organization for TLS communications. It is more like the Root CA folder but having the additional capability to do TLS communication.

- **TLS Intermediate CA:** This is an optional folder, and it contains a list of intermediate CA certificates of CAs that are trusted by the organization that is being represented by this MSP for TLS communications.

Hyperledger Fabric Blockchain Network View

Having gone through in detail of all the critical constituent of Hyperledger Fabric, it now makes sense to see how all of them come together to make a complete blockchain network and what importance does one have in the network. First thing first, a blockchain network is a technical infrastructure of nodes, ordering service, client applications connecting through channel driven by policies that provide shared ledger across all nodes that can be queried and updated by the chaincode deployed on the channel.

It all starts with a set of an organization aiming to achieve a business purpose come together as a consortium to form a business network. With the configuration of the network, all organizations agree on the permissions defined by policies.

Below is a high-level network diagram of a consortium blockchain that has been set up between Org 1, Org 2, Org 3, and Org 4. Following are the high-level points of the network:

- There is an ordering service O4 which has been initiated by organization Org4 that services as a network administration point for N, and uses the system channel.

- Each of the four organizations has a preferred Certificate Authority, such as Certificate Authority 1, Certificate Authority 2, Certificate Authority 3, and Certificate Authority 4.

- Channel C1 is governed according to the policy rules specified in channel configuration 1; the channel is under the control of organizations Org 1 and Org 2.

- Channel C2 is governed according to the policy rules specified in channel configuration 2; the channel is under the control of organizations Org 2 and Org 3.

- Peer node Peer 1 maintains a copy of the ledger L1 associated with C1.

- Peer node Peer 2 maintains a copy of the ledger L1 associated with C1 and a copy of ledger L2 associated with C2.

- Peer node Peer 3 maintains a copy of the ledger L2 associated with C2.

- Org 1 and Org 2 need private communication within the overall network, as do Org 2 and Org 3.

- The ordering service also supports application channels C1 and C2, for transaction ordering into blocks for distribution.

- Organization Org 1 has a client application (App 1) that can perform business transactions within channel C1.

- Organization Org 2 has a client application (App 2) that can do similar work both in channel C1 and C2.

- Organization Org 3 has a client application that can do this on channel C2:

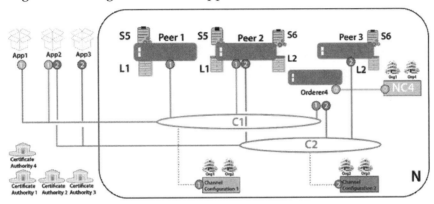

Figure 6.27: Hyperledger Network View

The objective of this diagram is to come up with a comprehensive view of a blockchain network. As could be seen, there are multiple organizations; then, by business requirements, multiple organizations can take part in separate channels. Also, the organization's peers have ledgers and corresponding chaincode that can update the ledger.

Similarly, peers like P2 is part of multiple channels such as C1 and C2 and has two ledgers and respective chaincode for the corresponding channel. Both the channels are connected to the same ordering service, so whenever ordering service delivers a block, it sends it to the peer of the appropriate channel.

Other than that, there are client applications A1, A2, and A3, which connects to corresponding channels, and the transaction submitted by these applications goes to peer on that channel only. Then in the same context, we have set of Certificate Authorities corresponding to each organization that issues certificates that provide them an identity. With the help of MSP, participating members exercise their access right as well. So, there are a lot of moving parts in the fabric network, and every component has a role to play in it. We have seen a detailed view of individual components and then how they interact when they come together.

So far, it might be too theoretical and maybe more than what we can digest, however when we move into the Setting up Network chapter, these details would come handy for us, and referring back to these details would help more in understanding.

Important tools

In this section, we would talk about the essential tools that do not take a direct part in the blockchain network but are crucial for generating the various artifacts and configuration that is required to create a network.

cryptogen

In the Hyperledger Fabric blockchain network, all participating members would have an identity; this is issued by PKI, which results in every member having a digital certificate and a private key. All organizations that are taking part in the network would get their identities from any Certificate Authority of their choice.

During development and testing, it is generally cumbersome and time-consuming activity to get certificates from the Certificate Authority. So, to cut the time for setting up a network without relying on cryptogen for the time being, Hyperledger Fabric did provide a utility for creating crypto material.

In this case, developers would provide all the participant details such as peer, orderer, and client application through a YAML file to cryptogen tool, which in turn would generate required crypto material for all participant defined in the config YAML file:

Figure 6.28

Cryptogen is a command-line tool, and running this on config YAML would result in multiple MSP folders (assuming we are setting up a network with multiple participants) having a structure more or less as we saw in MSP structure section. The result is more of a sample crypto material yet enough to set up a network.

We would go into more detail later on this.

configtxgen

Likewise, cryptogen, `configtxgen`, is also a command-line utility that is used to generate configuration artifacts. These artifacts again provide essential configurations and other required information to bootstrap the network. The artifacts are as below:

1.   Genesis block
2.   ChannelTx
3.   Anchor Peer Tx

configtxlator

configtxlator is one of the command-line utility tools; however, it is not required to do anything from network bootstrapping purposes. This tool is used more for reconfiguration purposes. This tool derived its name from configtx and translator and became configtxlator. Its sole purpose is to translate configtx generated artifacts into various formats, one is which is required by the network, and the second is which can be worked upon by the developer. Once a network has been set up, there could be a need for adding new organization into the network or adding a new member, and this requires configuration updates at any level. Configtxlator helps to do all the configuration updates.

The standard usage is expected to be:

- Retrieving latest configurations
- Using configtxlator to produce a readable version of config for the developer's help
- The developer would then edit or update the config
- configtxlator then helps compute config update representation of changes to the config
- developer/ administrator uses SDK to sign and submit the config

Conclusion

This chapter is primarily the core of the book intended to cover the fundamentals of Hyperledger Fabric and set the ground for a more complex and working set of fabric-based business network. Hyperledger Fabric is way more than a node running on this own as with the case of other blockchains, so it is essential to understand the platform in its entirety, and every component plays an essential role in establishing the network.

We started with the introduction of Fabric and covered a bit of history to give an understanding of the kind of workforce behind the development of Fabric. The kind of ecosystem is being planned to develop. We did try to cover an exhaustive list of features of permissioned blockchain, and at the same time, we tried to cover the difference with public blockchain at times taking examples from Bitcoin and Ethereum.

Then on we delved into the vital core concepts of the Fabric, discussing and detailing out every module, concept to make a better foundation for ourselves as we would get into more hands-on the exercise of creating a network, defining policies, establishing identities and working on the smart contract.

We did have a detailed look at the peer as a fundamental unit of network and how peer relates with the ledger, chaincode, identities, and so on, and type of peer. It was a relevant section as it covers a lot of ground and helps us understand the various moving parts of the network, specifically around peers. A peer in fabric plays almost the similar role as Ethereum node in the Ethereum network.

After that, we covered ordering service, its role, and what are the options by which ordering can be deployed on the blockchain network.

Peer and Orderer are the core components of the fabric blockchain network, and at the same time there are other essential components that we discussed, we covered ledger and its internals in detail at the same time we did focus on blockchain and covered a bot if its difference with Bitcoin blockchain data structure. The concept of smart contract and chaincode was also discussed such that we understand the difference and use chaincode and smart contract reasonably with having a clear difference between both of them in mind.

We moved on to the limitations of channels, and private data collections have helped overcome that. Then we had a look at one of the essential aspect of identities and how Membership Service provider plays an essential role in identities.

With the core concepts, we also had a look at general-purpose command-line utility tools that help set up the configuration and other artifacts of the blockchain network.

In the next chapter, we would bring all these components together to understand how they all work together, how transactions are sent, and persisted on the network is an exact blockchain way.

CHAPTER 7

Hyperledger Fabric Architecture and Transaction Flow

Following up on understanding the fundamental units and core concepts of the Hyperledger Fabric, we would now dive into understanding the architectural considerations of the fabric. This chapter, on the one hand, would help us gain deep architectural insights and exciting design choices. At the same time, we would also understand how the transaction works right from the start of submission to getting persisted in the ledger.

Structure

- Introduction
- System architecture
- Transaction workflow
- Endorsement policies
- Conclusion

Objective

It is more of a technical chapter that would help the reader understand how the foundational building block components of Hyperledger Fabric come together to help transaction flow.

Introduction

Hyperledger Fabric, by design, to become an enterprise-grade blockchain platform solution, has always emphasized on modularity and extendibility. The idea was to be able to handle case basis requirements such that it should be able to support pluggable consensus protocols that can be retrofitted based on the agreement and ease of joining members of the network. As seen in earlier chapters, a series of informed design decisions were taken to move away from certain restrictions that are inherent in established and prominent blockchains such as Ethereum.

Fabric is the first blockchain that supports the writing of smart contracts in general-purpose languages such as Java, NodeJS, and Go Lang as compared to domain-specific language such as Solidity in Ethereum. Given all peers may execute smart contracts for validation of transactions at a different time. So there are higher chances of getting non-deterministic results, which may end up having peer ledgers going out of synchronization, fabric handles this through the carefully designed transaction process and use of ordering service. Secondly, public blockchains see the implicit requirement of incentivization through cryptocurrency; the fabric does not have any native cryptocurrency and yet able to keep the network secure. Fabric does this through the notion of the membership service provider, which again can be integrated with the industry-wide identity management system. This way, it gives the flexibility of having joining members choose and work with the identity management system of their own choice and comfort.

Hyperledger Fabric is an outcome of well thought through decisions around design choices that have helped fabric grow and mature such that it can deal with the challenges around non-deterministic execution, high resource consumption, and denial attacks.

In this chapter, we would also go through some of the limitations that public blockchain poses and how Hyperledger Fabric has come up with a specific design and implementation considerations to overcome that.

Setting up context

In this section, we would cover a fundamental ground of how public or permissionless blockchain work and what are the fundamentals they follow, how they are different from permissioned network and then how Fabric came up with the ideas to manage the challenges that public blockchain provides in the context of setting up same in an enterprise environment.

Starting with the refresher, blockchain is a peer to peer distributed system with every peer maintaining an immutable copy of its ledger and recording transactions happened over the network. Peer does contribute to achieving consensus by validating transactions, grouping all transactions in a block, and then linking the blocks by using a hash chain over the blocks. The result of this is a consistent ledger residing with all the peers that can act as a single source of truth. Interestingly, peers taking part in the distributed network are mutually trustless; no peer trust each other, yet they carry out transactions with the agreement.

Most of the public blockchain, such as Ethereum and, to an extent, some of the permissioned blockchain such as Tendermint follows an order-execute architecture approach for transaction processing. In order-execute approach:

- Every participating node or peer in the network collects and arranges all the valid transactions into a block and confirms the validity of all transactions by pre-executing those transactions

- The peer work towards and tries to solve a complex mathematical problem according to difficulty level as defined by the network

- Once the peer has been able to solve the mathematical problem puzzle and has come up with desired result also known as a nonce value, then it spreads out the block to all the peers in the network via peer to peer gossip protocol

- When a peer receives the block, then it shall independently validate the solution of the puzzle provided and, alongside, would validate all the transactions in the block. In essence, every peer would then repeat the execution of the originator peer from its first step

A shown in the image below, an *Order-Execute* approach is followed in most permissionless blockchains:

Figure 7.1: Order - Execute

During the entire process, all transaction execution results need to be deterministic to have all peer ending up with the consistent state of the ledger. Whereas, the order-execute architecture has been proven in public blockchain systems; however, considering this approach for permissioned blockchain such as fabric had certain limitations that were required to be addressed.

The following section talks about a list, though not exhaustive, of specific high-level issues that the Order-Execute approach has and how Hyperledger Fabric overcome that.

Limitations of Order-Execute

The order-execute architecture is conceptually simple and is proven to be successful and, therefore, been used widely. Even then, there have been several limitations, which we briefly touched upon in the last section; in this section, we would go over on most prominent ones.

- **Sequential Execution:** In a public blockchain, once all peer gets a validated block provided by another peer in the network. They then would execute transactions sequentially; this could be prone to malicious code attack through untrusted smart contracts. Blockchains are generally termed as a universal computer, and anyone can deploy a smart contract on any node which eventually gets propagated to all the peers. All peers then execute the same smart contract giving it is a notion as it is happening on one engine. As an example, Ethereum is often called **World Computer.** As a result of the same code being executed on every peer, this allows an adversary to deploy malicious code and initiate **Denial of Service (DoS)** attack, such as an infinite loop that can bring down the entire network down.

  To avoid these incidents occurring and in a way to increase the security of the blockchain network, for instance, Ethereum came out with the concept of execution cost. They introduced the concept of gas, which is essentially a unit for operations, and then there shall be a gas price for every unit of gas corresponding to the operation. The submitter of the transaction on the network shall be charged for the cumulative sum of all operation units as per the prevailing gas price at the moment. Every block that gets formed in an Ethereum network then gets limited by the gas that it can consume.

  So, sequential execution was an inherent part of the order-execute architecture, which could have consequences because of malicious code, and that was controlled by implementing fees to the submitter of the transaction. Whereas this probably looks good for public blockchain as it has native support for cryptocurrency that can be used for paying the gas prices but given permissioned blockchain came up without any native support of cryptocurrency it could have been difficult situation to handle with sequential transaction execution.

- **Non-deterministic code**: Non-deterministic code execution is another challenge that comes with the order-execute approach. It is expected that once peer they received validated block, then output produced as a result of executing transactions should result in a consistent state across all peers. Having different outputs from transaction execution would have resulted in an inconsistent state of the ledger across the peer that goes against the basic premise of the blockchain of having the same ledger state across all the peers.

  It has been addressed by enabling smart contracts to be developed in the domain-specific language, which is expressive enough for developers to write business transaction rules but yet could be controlled by deterministic execution. It resulted in coming up with new domain-specific languages such as Solidity for Ethereum. The downside of this is, it requires developers of smart contracts to learn new languages.

Universal languages could not be used for blockchain programming because even if a developer doesn't try to create malicious code implicitly, some of the native implementations could result in non-deterministic behavior and hence impact the blockchain network.

So, while making design choices for Hyperledger Fabric, a decision had to be made if the general-purpose language could be used there.

- **Confidentiality of execution**: In a public blockchain, smart contracts upon deployment get propagated on all peers, and the smart contract code can be seen by anyone. Whereas this is okay in case of a public blockchain network, it may not hold good for a permissioned blockchain network where competitors or peers not trusting each other could be part of the network.

  Confidentiality is an essential aspect in enterprise blockchain, where transaction rules are encoded in the smart contract, and they should be visible only to intended participants; ledger states should also be restricted between participating members.

- **Hard-coded consensus:** Consensus is generally hard-coded with most of the blockchain platform, that is, it is natively written in the code; however, this was realized that there is no single consensus algorithm that can serve the purpose for all, the participating members may have different choices as to how they would want to reach the agreement. In fabric, this was achieved through a pluggable consensus. Other than business agreement, this has been observed that **Byzantine Fault Tolerant (BFT)** protocol varies in their performance when deployed in varied network conditions. Permissioned blockchain where would want to have different BFT algorithm and same time having the option of the alternative consensus model.

- **Static trust model:** In a public blockchain, the trust model is also inbuilt with the consensus protocol as to how transaction validation should be done, this cannot be adapted to the requirement of the smart contract. In fabric, the approach of endorsement policies has been taken to control the operation execution of the smart contracts by defining who can participate in transaction validation. In a flexible system, trust at the application level should not be at the protocol level.

Execute-Order-Validate architecture

To overcome the limitations of order-execute architecture and to be able to address the enterprise requirements of doing transactions, the fabric came up with the execute-order-validate architecture.

We shall discuss each phase separately, and that would give us an understanding of how different components of this architecture approach work together. Before we jump into the detailing of each phase, we would briefly refresh and try to grasp essential concepts:

1. **Smart contract:** A smart contract, also known as chaincode, is essentially a business agreed on transaction execution logic that runs in the execution phase as part of the transaction submitted by the client. A client, in this case, is usually an application layer code that provides a user interface for the user to initiate and submit a transaction. Chaincode is developed by developers who are often untrusted and may induce malicious code knowingly or unknowingly.

2. **Endorsement policy**: Another vital aspect is the endorsement policy, which gets evaluated in the validation phase. Whereas developers are responsible for designing and developing the chaincode as per business needs, system administrators are responsible for or have permissions to modify endorsement policies through available system management functions. An endorsement policy works as a static library that helps in the validation of submitted transactions in fabric, which only can be parameterized by the chaincode. Endorsement policy lets the chaincode specify that who all peers can endorse the specific transaction. It follows logic expression language to specify endorsers and their combinations. Such as Peer A and Peer B must endorse the transaction; another example could be either of Peer A or Peer B and Peer C.

The below image represents a typical execute-order-validate approach and various steps involved at each level:

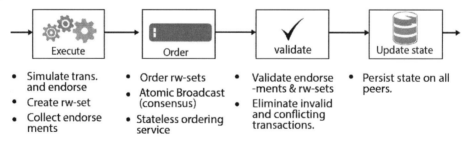

Figure 7.2: Execute-Order-Validate

In a nutshell, a client would create and send a transaction proposal using various provided SDK to various peers as specified in endorsement policy. Each transaction is then executed by required peers, and output would be produced and recorded; this is known as an endorsement. After execution, transactions enter into the ordering phase, which ends up producing an ordered sequence of endorsed transactions and then group them in blocks. After this, these blocks would be broadcasted to all the peers; every peer then would validate the changes from endorsed transactions while complying with endorsement policy and maintaining the consistency of the execution in the validation phase. Since all peers validate the transactions in the same order as presented in the ordered block, the validation is deterministic.

In the following section, we would go into detail of each aspect of execute-order-validate architecture:

- **Execution phase**: In the execution phase, a client would create, sign, and send the transaction proposal or only a proposal to designated endorsers (one or more) for execution. Think of a transaction proposal as a request for changing the state of an asset through execution of business logic that shall result in the change in the state of ledger permanently. Also, as we saw in the last section of endorsement policy that every chaincode shall have rules defined for endorsement of transactions that it can execute.

Transaction proposal would have:

- Identity of the submitting client acquired by Membership Service Provider
- Transaction payload
  - o Operation to execute
  - o Parameters
  - o Chaincode identifier
- Nonce
- The transaction identifier (derived from nonce and client identifier)

Once endorsers receive a transaction proposal, they would execute the corresponding operation on the designated chaincode as part of the proposal simulation. Simulating a transaction proposal means that transaction is simulated\pseudo executed on endorser (peer) local blockchain state without any synchronization with other peers. At this point, no state change is taking effect, and endorsers do not persist the result of simulation to the ledger.

As an output of this exercise of simulation, each endorser produces:

- **readset**: All keys (that are supposed to be updated) read during simulation along with their corresponding version numbers
- **writeset**: This is a set of state updates produced after the simulation (operation execution), that is, all modified keys along with their values

After this simulation, the endorsers would create a proposal response, which is then sent back to the client as a response to the transaction proposal. This proposal response is a result of cryptographically signing of a message called an endorsement, which contains earlier generated readset and writeset along with metadata information such as transaction ID, endorser ID, and endorser signature.

The last step of the execution phase is endorsement collection, which would come from all peers who received a transaction proposal and have simulated the transaction; this step is performed at the client-side. The client collects endorsements to make sure that to be able to transaction to go through finality, it should satisfy the endorsement policy of the chaincode.

- **Ordering phase**: Ordering phase is the next step following the execution phase. In this phase, the client receives and accumulates required endorsements on the transaction proposal that it sent. The client would then assemble, organize the complete transaction, and send it to ordering service. Ordering service now would order all submitted transactions; ordering happens for transactions that pertain to a channel, to ensure confidentiality, and then would atomically broadcast endorsements to all the peers, again of the specific channel.

  In due course, the ordering service job is to batch multiple transactions into blocks and produce an output of a hash-chained sequence of blocks containing transactions. The grouping/batching of transactions into blocks improves the throughput of the broadcast protocol, as network calls can be contained in that way.

  One of the essential design considerations with fabric architecture having ordering as a separate phase altogether is that it doesn't get involved in the validation/execution of transactions. This way of ordering service being separate from execution and validation phases gives the flexibility of having consensus as modular as possible. It also gives the option of using case fit consensus algorithm protocols for implementation of the ordering service; this way, the fabric moves away from the limitation of the hard code consensus algorithm. The hash chain integrity property and the chaining of blocks help make the integrity verification of the block sequence at the peer level more efficient.

- **Validation phase**: This is the last step in the execute-order-validate architecture; this gets triggered off when ordering service delivers blocks back to the peers.

  This phase has three steps that the peer needs to perform:

  1. **Endorsement policy evaluation**: Endorsement policy evaluation for all the transactions in the block happens in this step of the validation phase. Validation system chaincode or VCSS is a system-level chaincode, a part of blockchain configuration which validates the endorsement as per chaincode configuration. If the endorsement is not found to be valid, then those transactions would be disregarded, and those changes would not take effect on the ledger.

  2. **Read-write conflict check**: This is the second step of the validation phase, is performed sequentially for all the transactions in the block. All transactions are picked up one by one, and a comparison of the versions of the keys in the readset field to those in the current state of

the ledger, as stored locally by the peer, is carried out, to ensure that they are still the same. If there is a discrepancy in the version, then the transaction is marked as invalid, and its effects are disregarded.

3. **Ledger update**: This is the last step in the validation phase in the entire process. In this step, the block is finally appended to the locally stored ledger, and the blockchain status is updated. Interestingly, along with updating the state data into the ledger, validity check results from the first initial two steps of the validation phase are also persisted. It is done in the form of a bitmask, which denotes the valid transactions within the block. In this step, all state updates are applied by writing all key-value pairs in writeset to the local state.

One of the essential differences between the order-execute and execute-order-validate approach is that in the public blockchain, only transactions that are deemed valid get appended to the ledger; however, in the case of fabric, it contains all the transactions even if they are invalid. It happens because ordering service is chaincode logic agnostic, and its primary approach is to order the transactions and produce the block. Since validation happens at a later level, there is no way that it can remove the invalid transactions. As an enterprise, having multiple untrusted organizations transacting together, this proves to be an essential aspect to keep the invalid transaction as well for audit purposes as well it helps isolate the client who might be trying to mount DoS attack by flooding the network with invalid transactions.

With the understanding of execute-order-validate architecture at a granular level and reasonable understanding of the difference between this approach and order-execute, we would now look into how the transaction workflow works in Hyperledger Fabric using this approach.

Transaction workflow

This section outlines the transaction workflow in the Hyperledger Fabric blockchain network that starts from the client proposing a transaction, getting transaction persisted into the blockchain ledger, and then notifying back to the client about a successful transaction. This complete workflow follows the execute-order-validate architecture that we have just discussed in the last section. It would be a more elaborative version of the transaction workflow and Hyperledger Fabric architectural approach.

For the sake of simplicity, it is assumed that the network has been set up, channels are up and running, and the various client and peers have registered and enrolled themselves with valid Certification Authority and have cryptographic materials such as certificates and keys. It is also assumed that chaincode is also deployed, and endorsement policies are into place.

The entire transaction workflow is broken down into seven steps.

Propose transaction

In the given setup, where we would be talking about transaction workflow, the complete network is the set-up of five peers, out of five peers, three are endorser peers (shown as dotted boundary nodes), and rest of the two are committing peers (shown as a regular peer), that is, both of committing peers are not part of endorsement policy. Chaincode A and Chaincode B are deployed on endorser peers, and they maintain a ledger. Committing peers also do have a ledger, which is required to maintain the state, and chaincode is deployed only on one peer (Peer 3) and not on another (Peer 4).

To access the Hyperledger Fabric blockchain network, chaincode deployed on peer needs to be invoked. For that, the fabric has provided specific SDK such as for Java, Python, and NodeJS client. The client developed in Java, Python, and NodeJS need to have fabric provided SDK included in their programming model, and it provides them with constructs and libraries that help interact with chaincode, which is necessary to invoke various business logic.

Now, the first step in the transaction workflow is to construct a transaction proposal. Client application by leveraging SDK provided API generates a transaction proposal. The transaction proposal is a request to invoke a chaincode function (business transaction logic) with specific input parameters, with the motive of reading and/or updating the state ledger.

The fabric provided client language-specific SDK helps to create the transaction proposal into the required format, and along with the transaction proposal, it carries cryptographic credentials of the requesting user that produces a signature set for this transaction proposal, which is unique.

Technically, a client sends a PROPOSE message. However, it could send a transaction proposal message to a subset of endorsing peers depending on endorsement policy, assuming out of two, even if one peer can endorse the transaction for the fulfillment of endorsement policy, then in that case client can choose it to send it to anyone of them. However, in the real-world, endorsement policies could be more comprehensive, and some endorsers might be from different organizations or could be offline, so the client could choose to send it to a broader group in anticipation of getting valid endorsements.

The message structure of PROPOSE looks like `<PROPOSE, tx, [anchor]>` where `tx` is mandatory and anchor is optional:

```
tx structure is like tx=<clientID, chaincodeID, txPayload, timestamp,
clientSig>
```

The parameters are described as follows:

- `clientID` is the ID of submitting a client who is sending the PROPOSE message.
- `chaincodeID` is the identification of chaincode for which transaction needs to be executed
- `txPayload` is the actual transaction payload.
- `timestamp`
- `clientSig` is the signature of the client

Now, `txPayload` are of two types:

- **Invoke transactions**: Used most of the time and referred to the actual invocation of the chaincode functions:

  `txPayload = <operation, metadata>`
  The parameters are described as follows:

  o operation: Represents the actual function of the chaincode

  o metadata: Represents attributes about the operation

- **Deploy transaction**: These transactions are required for deployment of chaincode; however, they are not often used as administrators do most of the deployments through CLI.

  `txPayload = <source, metadata, policies>`
  The parameters are described as follows:

  o `source`: Denotes the chaincode source code

  o `metadata`: Represents attributes related to the chaincode and application

  o **policies**: It contains policies applicable to the chaincode such as the endorsement policy

A simplified pictorial description of transaction proposal is shown below:

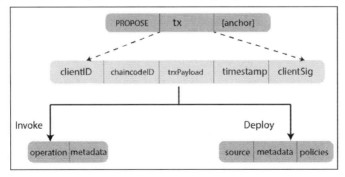

Figure 7.3: Transaction proposal structure

In this example, the client is submitting a transaction proposal for chaincode A. Because of endorsement policy; it needs to send the request to all endorser peers, which are Endorser 0, Endorser 1, and Endorser 2 in this case. So, simply, the client has created a transaction proposal using SDK provided for its programming language and sending the proposal request to all endorsing peers who are required to endorse the transaction to be able to change the state of the ledger. Targeted chaincode, in this case, is Smart contract A:

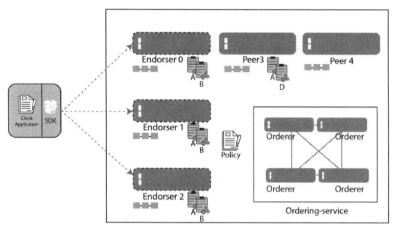

Figure 7.4: Propose transaction

Execute propose transaction

Once endorsing peer Endorser 0, Endorser 1, and Endorser 2 receive the transaction proposal as a next step, they need to execute the transaction. The endorsing peer would:

- Ensure and verify that the transaction proposal is correctly formed and as the specified format
- It makes sure the transaction submitted already in the past to protect against replay-attack
- It verifies that the client signature is valid
- It also checks that the submitter is authorized correctly to perform the proposed operation on that channel

More technically, once endorsing peer receives, <PROPOSE, tx, [anchor]> from a client, the endorsing peer would verify the client signature (clientSig), recall clientSig is part of tx (transaction) and then simulates a transaction. Simulating a transaction means endorsing peer executing a transaction (txPayload) by invoking the chaincode that has been referenced in the transaction itself (chaincodeID). As a result of chaincode execution, the endorsing peer shall compute and come up with a read version (readset) and state updates (writeset).

After the readset and writeset have been formed, the peer than internally forwards the `tx` to part of peer logic for transaction endorsement. Endorsing logic at the peer accepts the transaction proposal (`tran-proposal`) and simply signs it. Once a transaction has been endorsed, it shall be sent back to the submitting client in the form:

`<TRANSACTION-ENDORSED, tid, tran-proposal,epSig>`

The parameters are as follows:

- `tran-proposal` =
  `epID,tid,chaincodeID,txContentBlob,readset,writeset`
- `epSig` is the endorsing peer's signature on `tran-proposal`

In case, endorsing client does not endorse the transaction, then it would send the following message to submitting client:

`(TRANSACTION-INVALID, tid, REJECTED)`

In summary, the transaction proposal inputs work as an argument to invoke the chaincode function to execute business functionality. Endorsing peers would then execute the chaincode against the current state database and shall produce transaction results. The result includes response value, read set and write set which essentially is the updated key-value pair set of an attribute of the asset that has changed as a result of execution transaction business logic as part of chaincode execution. At this stage, the ledger state remains unchanged, and no updates are made in the ledger. The set of changed values, along with the endorser peer signature, are sent back to the client as a proposal response for its consumption:

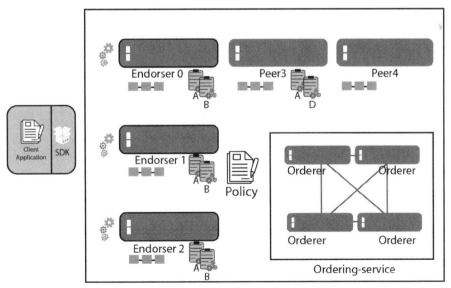

Figure 7.5: *Execute Propose transaction*

Proposal response

In this step, the application client receives a back transaction proposal response from endorser peers. These are returned asynchronously from endorsers to the client. At this stage, the client application shall verify the endorsing peer signatures and compares the proposal responses to determine if the proposal responses are the same. In the case, if the transaction were sent only to query ledger, then the application would simply inspect the query response and would not go ahead with the submission of the transaction to ordering service as there is nothing to update the ledger and rather information is meant to be used by N application client.

If the query were meant to update the state of ledger through chaincode invocation, then the client would collate all the responses and make sure that the endorsement policy has been fulfilled before submitting it further to ordering service. In case the client chooses not to inspect resources and forwards this to ordering service even then, the endorsement policy shall be enforced at the commit validation phase and shall be disregarded by the peers.

More technically, submitting the client would wait for (TRANSACTION-ENDORSED, tid, *, *) from the required number of peers to establish the fact that the endorsement policy criteria is met. The act of collection of signed TRANSACTION-ENDORSED messages from required endorsing peers is called an endorsement and establishes the fact that the transaction is endorsed. If the submitting client does not manage to collect required endorsements for the submitted transaction proposal, then it would abandon this transaction and retry later.

In a nutshell, in this step, the client application collates all the transaction proposal responses, verifies the endorsing peer signatures, makes sure the endorsement policy is followed, and then prepares for the next step. The below image shows the collation of the transaction proposal response:

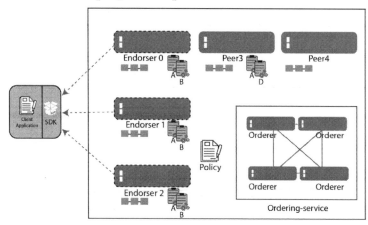

Figure 7.6: Proposal Response

Order transaction

Once all the transaction proposal responses are received, verified, and endorsement policy validated as required, then the client application broadcasts a transaction message to ordering service. This transaction message contains the transaction proposal and response in it. The transaction shall contain the read/write sets that were received as part of the proposal response, signatures of endorsing peers, and the Channel ID. The ordering service is not involved in the inspection of the content of the transaction. In contrast, its job is to simply receive transactions from all the channels in the network, then order them chronologically by channel, and then get into the process of creating blocks of transactions per channel.

More technically, submitting the client invokes the ordering service using the broadcast(blob) where the blob is the collection of endorsement that we have seen in the last step.

Though we have been illustrating the flow with the request coming from client SDK, at the same time, we could see that other requests are coming from other clients to the ordering service, which may pertain to the same channel or could be for another channel. The ultimate objective of this step of transaction flow is to ordering service receives transactions from the client, and then order them.

The below image shows how the client is sending the transaction message to the ordering service, and now the orderer would order the transactions before it could be sent to all participating peers:

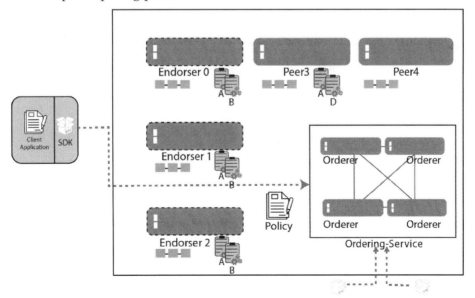

Figure 7.7: Order transaction

Deliver transaction

After collecting transactions and collating them in blocks, it's time to broadcast these blocks to peers; ordering service now would send the blocks to all peers. So, all peers would now get all the transactions in a block in an ordered fashion. Ordering service is a modular and pluggable component in Hyperledger Fabric, and you may choose to have your implementation. As of now, Hyperledger Fabric provides three implementations of ordering service:

- Solo
- Raft
- Kafka

More technically, ordering service emits an event with `deliver(seqno, prevhash, blob)`. In the following image, we can see that ordering service is delivering the ordered blocks to different peers in the network:

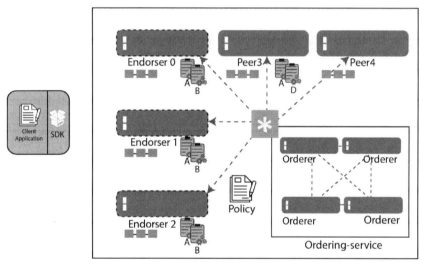

Figure 7.8: Deliver transactions

Validate transaction

More technically, when a peer is notified of `deliver(seqno, prevhash, blob)` and it realizes that it has applied all state updates for blobs with a sequence number lower than provided `seqno`, it would then perform the following step:

- It will check if the endorsement (`blob.endorsement`) is valid as per the defined policy of the chaincode (`blob.tran-proposal.chaincodeID`).
- It then verifies that the dependencies (`blob.endorsement.tran-proposal. readset`) are in order, and there is no violation.

- It also verifies the version associated with every key in the `readset` to be equal to that key's version in the state.

- If all these verification checks are through, then the transaction is considered valid and is committed. In this case, the peer marks the transaction with '1' in the bitmask of the PeerLedger and applies proposal writeset (`blob.endorsement.tran-proposal.writeset`) to ledger state.

- If the endorsement policy verification of `blob.endorsement` fails, the transaction is considered invalid, and the peer marks the transaction with '0' in the bitmask of the PeerLedger. An important note is that invalid transactions do not change the state.

In a nutshell, blocks are received by the peers, the transactions within the block are validated for endorsement policy, and it also checks that all read-write sets still valid for the current state of the world state to ensure that there is no change to ledger state for read set variables from the time the read set was generated during the initial steps of transaction execution. Transactions in the block shall be marked as valid and invalid; invalid transactions would be retained on the ledger for later compliance and audit purposes. Still, they shall not be updated on the world state database:

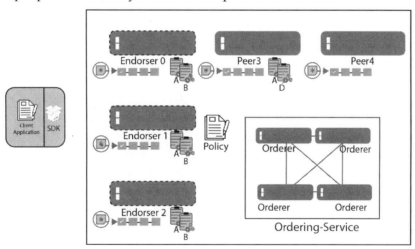

Figure 7.9: *Transaction validation*

Notify transaction

It is not exactly a step in the transaction flow, but for the sake of completion, this has been added. In this step, client applications can be notified if the transactions were succeeded or failed to make it to the ledger:

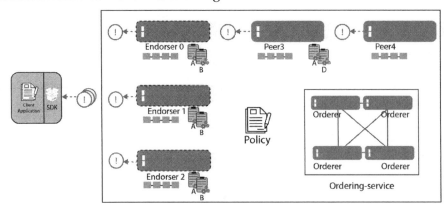

Figure 7.10: Notify transaction

Endorsement policies

Endorsement policies are again an essential concept in Hyperledger Fabric, and it plays a vital role in the transaction workflow. An endorsement policy is a set of rule or condition that determines the transaction endorsement success criteria. Every chaincode deployed on a fabric blockchain network has an endorsement policy associated with it that specifies the set of peers in a prescribed combination that must execute chaincode function logic and endorse the transaction execution results for the transaction to be deemed valid. Endorsement policy, in one way, guarantees security in blockchain as it enables the transaction evaluation process with enough peer participants taking part in it. It defines which organization should take part in endorsing a specific transaction that would make it valid.

A transaction would only be declared valid if it has been endorsed according to the policy, and then only it can be committed to the ledger. Invoking a transaction for a chaincode needs to get an endorsement that satisfies the defined chaincode policy; otherwise, it will not be seen as following endorsement policy and shall not be committed. It takes place through the interaction between the client and endorsing peers, as we have seen in the last section of the transaction workflow.

Endorsement policies are chaincode specific, which means that any transaction invocation happening in a chaincode follows the same policy. In contrast, there are business use cases where state-based endorsement policy might be required, state-based endorsement overrides the default chaincode-level endorsement policies by a different policy for the specified keys.

Chaincode-level endorsement policies

Chaincode level endorsement policies are the default and most commonly used endorsement policies in the fabric network. These policies are specified at the time of chaincode instantiation. Chaincode life cycle has installed, instantiate, and invoke stages, and this shall be discussed thoroughly in later chapters. The specification can be done either through Peer CLI (Command Line Interface), which is again a common way of specifying policies or through SDK as well from the client.

There is a syntax that gets followed for specifying endorsement policy; complete CLI looks like:

```
peer chaincode instantiate -C <channelid> -n mychaincode -P "AND('Orgz1.peer', 'Orgz2.peer')"
```

Figure 7.11: Chaincode endorsement

Whereas this command would be made clear during further chapters when we delve into setting up a network; however, the part of interest is specifying endorsement policy on a specific channel which is represented by channel ID is an AND condition with arguments as two peers, one respectively from Orgz1 and another one from Orgz2. Applying such an endorsement policy means that any transaction invoked on mychaincode needs to be endorsed by peers of two organizations to be considered to be valid.

Principals are used to expressing the notation of Endorsement policies; principals are specified in a format such as 'MSP.ROLE' where MSP is the MSP ID, and ROLE represents the predefined roles. As in fabric, these roles are peer, admin, member, and client.

Few of examples are:

- Company1.admin: Any administrator of Company1 MSP
- Company1.member: Any member of Company1 MSP
- Company2.client: Any client of Company2 MSP
- Company3.peer: Any peer of Company3 MSP

Whereas the parameters inside represent the principal responsible for carrying out endorsement, there is an expression (EXPR) bounding all principals, which could be of following types:

- AND
- OR
- OutOf

So, the syntax looks like:

```
EXPR( E [, E.. ] )
```

More examples covering this syntax which can be used for defining endorsement policies are:

- `OR('Company1.member', 'Company2.member', 'Company3.member')` requests one signature from any of the three principals.
- `AND('Company1.member', 'Company2.member')` requests one signature from both the principals.
- `OR('Company1.member', AND('Company2.member', 'Company3.member'))` requests either one signature from a member of the Company1 MSP or one signature from a member of the Company2 MSP and one signature from a member of the Company3 MSP.
- `OutOf(1, 'Company1.member', 'Company2.member')`, which evaluates to the same thing as `OR('Company1.member', 'Company2.member')`.
- `OutOf(2, 'Company1.member', ' Company2.member', ' Company3.member')` is equivalent to `OR(AND(' Company1.member', ' Company2.member'), AND(' Company1.member', ' Company3.member'), AND(' Company2.member', ' Company3.member'))`.

That is the level of flexibility that fabric provides to participant organizations to define by themselves a more granular level of policy to validate the transaction. It has been a significant shift in terms of how consensus is defined in public/permissionless blockchain where consensus rules are written in the software itself and needs to be agreed by every participant or joining node. In enterprises, this may vary and gives the flexibility to approach the part of the consensus in the mutually agreed way by way of configurations that have provided by Hyperledger Fabric.

Key-level endorsement policies

Whereas chaincode level endorsement policies are most commonly used, there are certain business use cases where key level endorsement policies suit more to address the business need. Another notable difference that arises is, chaincode-level endorsement policies are closely tied to the lifecycle of the chaincode and are restricted to be updated only when instantiation or up-gradation of chaincode is happening on the channel. In the case of key-level endorsement policies, it can be very controlled from within the chaincode in a more granular fashion.

SHIM API is the way by which smart contract interact with the ledger, the same way there have been additional functions provided by the SHIM API that can be used to set the endorsement policy at the key level. The provided methods are:

```
•   SetStateValidationParameter(key string, ep []byte) error
•   GetStateValidationParameter(key string) ([]byte, error)
```

Figure 7.12

Where ep stands for endorsement policy, which could simply be expressed either by using the same syntax as we have just seen or by using a function as described below:

```
type KeyEndorsementPolicy interface {
    // Policy returns the endorsement policy as bytes
    Policy() ([]byte, error)

    // AddOrgs adds the specified orgs to the list of orgs that are required
    // to endorse
    AddOrgs(roleType RoleType, organizations ...string) error

    // DelOrgs delete the specified channel orgs from the existing key-level endorsement
    // policy for this KVS key. If any org is not present, an error will be returned.
    DelOrgs(organizations ...string) error

    // ListOrgs returns an array of channel orgs that are required to endorse changes
    ListOrgs() ([]string)
}
```

Figure 7.13

For instance, to set an endorsement policy for a key where two specific organizations are required to endorse the transaction involving a specific key, we need to pass both organizations MSPIDs first to AddOrgs() function. We then need to call Policy() function to construct the endorsement policy byte array that can be passed to SetStateValidationParameter().

An important fact to note here is that, when a key-level endorsement level policy is set up for the very first time, the new key-level endorsement policy needs to be endorsed first before that transaction is committed, and this happens through pre-existing chaincode-level endorsement policy. If a key is modified and key-level endorsement policy is in place, then it overrides the default chaincode level endorsement policy. The key-level endorsement policies could be more or less restrictive than chaincode level endorsement policy. And since, while setting up key-level endorsement policy chaincode level endorsement has already been executed, there is no policy breach at any level. Also, when the key level endorsement policy is removed, then the default chaincode enforcement policy would become useful again and become the default one.

Customized transaction endorsement and validation

One of the most significant benefits that we can leverage from the Hyperledger Fabric blockchain network is its ability to provide options for custom and pluggable module replacement. In the public blockchain, almost everything is embedded in the software that runs the node, and it's hard to change any implementation logic, and that needs to go through a set process through the established community before any change could be taken up. In the real-world, every organization would rather have different choices to be implemented as part of their ways of working; for instance, a group of organizations operating a blockchain network might want to have customized transaction endorsement and validation process, Hyperledger Fabric provides that flexibility.

In general, when a transaction in fabric gets validated before it is committed in the ledger, there are various checks that peer performs such as:

- Validating the peer identities that have signed the transaction
- To cross-check the signatures of the endorsers who are part of endorsement policy
- Ensuring endorsement policy

However, there could be a need for custom transaction validation, which might be a bit different from what has been specified by default transaction endorsement and validation logic as defined in fabric.

To address this need, fabric provides the flexibility of implementation and deployment of custom endorsement and validation logic that can be associated with the chaincode. This logic can be separately built and deployed alongside with the peer as a GoLang plugin. A peer administrator may alter the endorsement/validation logic that is selected by extending the peer's local configuration with the customization of the endorsement/validation logic, which is loaded and applied at peer start-up.

Default configurations

A peer or node that represents an organization in the form of leader, anchor, or regular peer is a binary implementation of peer usually provided as a docker image. This peer also has a local configuration in the form of a YAML file (`core.yaml`), it declares the endorsement and validation logic name and the implementation that it runs. These configurations are found under the handlers section as follows:

```
handlers:
    endorsers:
      escc:
        name: DefaultEndorsement
    validators:
      vscc:
        name: DefaultValidation
```

Figure 7.14

The `escc` stands for **Endorsement System Chaincode**, and `vscc` means `Validation System Chaincode`. To build custom endorsement and validation as a go-lang plugin, this handlers section can be extended by adding attributes that identify custom logic implementation name and location.

The entries in the local configuration file of a peer can be extended as:

```
handlers:
    endorsers:
      escc:
        name: DefaultEndorsement
      custom:
        name: customOrgEndorsement
        library: /etc/hyperledger/fabric/plugins/customOrgEndorsement.so
    validators:
      vscc:
        name: DefaultValidation
      custom:
        name: customOrgValidation
        library: /etc/hyperledger/fabric/plugins/customOrgValidation.so
```

Figure 7.15

The .so plugin files need to be placed in the peer's local file system. Implementing custom endorsement and validation logic needs implementation done in a fashion which follows the extension of prescribed interfaces such that peer can use the functionalities as required. Other than implementing custom logic, Hyperledger Fabric emphasizes on maintaining validation plugin consistency across the peers such that all peers follow the same validation rules and should be able to do error handling as desired.

Conclusion

This chapter has been an important one in understanding the architecture considerations of Hyperledger fabric. We started by discussing the architecture and consensus approach taken in public/permissionless blockchain, which exhibits order-execute architecture. We did discuss the limitation that this architecture throws and how that is not viable for private/permissioned blockchain network. We also saw the approach taken by Hyperledger Fabric as execute-order-validate architecture and how this architectural approach has been able to solve most of the issues for the fabric blockchain network. We also looked into details of this approach and various steps that it performs at every step.

Moving on, we took a deep dive into the transaction flow that constitutes multiple steps. In every detail, we discussed every step, responsibilities taken up in that step. Wherever possible, we complemented it with the message structure with an elaborate description of all the parameters used in the message and a detailed diagrammatic description to supplement the understanding.

We finally moved to understand the endorsement policy syntax, structure it applicability, and its importance in the transaction workflow of Hyperledger Fabric. It was an important concept to understand and would help us define the right set of policies in the real-world and also when we move to set up our network example in the later chapter. Whereas the chapter before has given us a good understanding of the individual components, this chapter has set the ground for working them jointly and how the message flows among themselves. In the next chapter, leveraging the understanding of this and the last chapter, we would get into setting up of network and see how the theory described in the last two chapters gets into practical use.

CHAPTER 8

Setting up Hyperledger Fabric Network

This chapter intends to be quite technical in terms of experimenting and understanding as to what it takes to set up a Hyperledger Fabric blockchain network. Learnings of the concepts from the previous chapter, specifically around Hyperledger Fabric, shall be put to use in this chapter. The outcome of going through this chapter should result in you be able to set up a blockchain network, understanding how core components are deployed and put to work, and then finally installing smart contracts and seeing them in action where you can update and retrieve transactions in the ledger. This chapter intends to come up to the level where you can visualize how a blockchain network looks like and what all steps do we need to do to set that up and to run.

Structure

- Introduction
- Defining a business network
- Designing network topology
- Deploying smart contracts
- Making client work
- Examples
    - o   Adding a new organization

      o   Adding a new peer
- Some Important concepts
    - o   Network configuration and policies
    - o   Access Control List
    - o   RAFT
    - o   Transport Layer Security
        - i.   Peer Configuration
        - ii. Orderer Configuration
    - o   Fabric Client (SDK)
    - o   Monitoring (Prometheus & Grafana)

Objective

This chapter covers total hands-on for the setting up of the actual blockchain network and what it takes on the ground to set that up. We shall touch upon the system requirements, configuration files, and chaincode that do the actual magic.

Introduction

While this chapter intends to be a technical one with the steps laid down to prepare the Hyperledger fabric blockchain network, this also touches upon the groundwork that needs to be done to be able to complete the solution technically. As in any other software development, we go for requirement understanding and designing of the system before we finally delve into implementation, we would look for establishing the context around the business need, participants, and so on, for whom we are going to set up the network for.

And then, we would also be spending some time around technical definitions and other requirements of the business participants. We would then move to smart contract installation, instantiation, and invocation part of the setup to complete the process. Smart contracts, as discussed previously, do encapsulate the agreed business transaction rules that get executed based on different workflows in business processes.

Below is the high-level visualization of the entire setup assuming prerequisites have been set up and necessary binaries have been installed. In the subsequent section, we shall be discussing every step in detail:

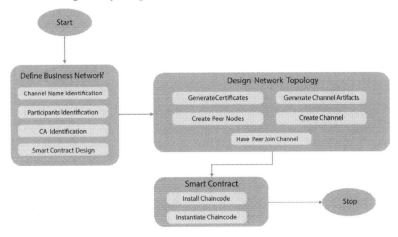

Figure 8.1

Defining a business network

First thing first, before getting into actual designing of the blockchain network, it makes sense to understand who we are creating this blockchain network for, mostly what problem are we trying to solve and what capabilities we are leveraging that we have been studying all through this book.

Identifying participants

Blockchain is a peer to peer network where peer plays the role of the member node in the network. Like in public, permissionless blockchain any member node can join and leave the network at its own will, in permissioned network such as Hyperledger it is different, the entities are well known to each other as they plan to come together to achieve a common business objective. So, while before setting up a network, all member nodes are known. For instance, in the example network that we would be setting up, we would assume that **Org1, Org2**, and **Org3** are the participant members for whom we are going to create a network.

To understand Hyperledger blockchain network setup, we would not be addressing any specific business problem as a use case rather we would merely set up a network and then see how they can carry out a simple transaction and leave it on readers to enhance this network to give it more meaningful and business-specific network.

Hyperledger gives us the flexibility of adding any member node post the network is up and running with several transactions done which could be a real-life scenario such as an airline consortium which started with a limited number of airlines being its member, and then more and more airlines coming and joining the network at a later point of time. We shall explore the scenario of adding new member node/peer in the network.

Channel Name Identification

It is essential to identify the number of channels that are required to carry out secure transactions between groups of participants. Though in a blockchain network there could be multiple channels depending on the need of participants trying to carry out the transaction among themselves, however in an attempt to keep the network simple for understanding the purpose and to suit the business need as defined in setting up the context, we would create a single channel with all participants being a member of that.

We do also need to have the name of the channel for identification purpose, so would have a name of the channel as well.

In a real-life scenario, we may end up having multiple channels and a peer taking part in different channels.

Rule definition (foundation for Smart Contracts)

The sole purpose of entities coming together and creating a business network is to achieve a common business objective by way of agreed transaction rules. Smart contracts help achieve that. Smart contracts are mostly programs written in different languages (available ones are Go, Java, and NodeJS) that help encapsulate business rules in them. Practically, any transaction rule that is possible otherwise can be coded in smart contracts. Depending on the member participants and business goals, these rules could be different; think of business rules of financial institutions would be different from the airline industry.

However, in the example network setup, we would limit ourselves to simple operations of creating, retrieving, and updating records in the ledger, which could be transformed into complex real-time business transactions by the readers themselves.

The idea here would be to understand the structure of smart contracts, various interfaces they use, and other necessary APIs that are used to fulfill the transaction completeness.

Certificate Authority

Every actor (peer\client) that connects and takes part in the Hyperledger blockchain network needs to have an identity by which it can be recognized in the system. Each of these actors would have a digital identity encapsulated in X.509 digital certificate, which helps make them valid. These identities ensure the access level control of information and resources that are part of the blockchain network. Digital identities are issued by a **Certificate Authority (CA)** in the form of cryptographically validated digital certificates that complies with the X.509 standard. On top of that, there is a notion of **Membership Service Provider (MSP)** in Hyperledger fabric; MSP abstracts away all cryptographic mechanisms and protocols behind issuing and validating certificates, and user authentication. An MSP defines its notion of identity and the rules by which governs these identities as in identity validation and authentication. MSP configuration plays a vital role in setting up of network and how it utilizes the digital identities.

Coming back to the identities issued by the CA, to help set up network faster mostly for development and testing of the blockchain network and related client application, Hyperledger Fabric provides a command-line utility by the name of 'cryptogen' which would help generate certificates and other cryptographic material that is required by a member to participate and access the resources in the blockchain network.

Please keep in mind that *cryptogen* is not meant for production, and there we must be using certificates and other material issued by the trusted certificate authority. Whereas, 'cryptogen' would help us generate the cryptographic material for now, but the steps would help us understand the setup in such a way that we can use cryptographic material issues by trusted CA as well.

For the setup, we shall be using the following:

- **Participant Identification:**
    - Org1, Org2, and Org3
    - Org4 (peer joining the already running network)
- **Channel Name:**
    - `samplechannel` (should be a meaningful name which describes the purpose of the channel)
- **Rule definition**:
    - We would keep this simple and have simple operations.
- **Certificate Authority:**
    - We shall use cryptogen tools for creating cryptographic material to provide identities to Org1, Org2, Org3, and their respective admin and users
    - MSP structure is defined in the config files, which uses the cryptographic material

With the original thinking and design completed, we shall now proceed to set up the machine and the blockchain network; we shall keep on exploring all bit and pieces en route our journey towards creating the network and making it work.

Designing network topology

This section is dedicated to setup environment for Hyperledger based blockchain network right from starting with having a machine/VM made available then moving on with the installation of Prerequisite then installing Hyperledger Fabric binaries. Once we reach till this step, we shall have everything setup required for creating a business network that may be catered for the specific use case.

We shall then move on to generate certificate and channel artifacts specific to the identified participants. After that, we shall start proceeding towards setting up the network, that is, peer nodes and orderer nodes, and attaching the cryptogen materials generated for them. In the process, we shall create a channel and have peers join the channel. Once we have reached this step that ensures the network is up and running, and we shall process to next section for deploying smart contracts, and then we would have a client ready to access the blockchain network and invocation of smart contracts by these clients.

In this section, we shall take the help of script files and Docker to ease out the setup process, though there are ways of directly installing the binaries and going command by command in setting up the network. In contrast, we would take up the mix of script files and commands to make steady progress, along with getting an understanding of what we are doing. I leave it up to the readers to fine-tune script files, and so on, to speed up the process of setting up/starting/stopping the network, but it's prudent for now to understand it at the core level to gain an in-depth understanding.

- Have a machine\environment ready
  - o A VM on cloud
  - o Setup on the local machine

First thing first, we need to have a machine to setup the blockchain network. In the real world, this would be scattered among a cluster of machines with every organization bringing up their set of machines as peers and then joining the network through channels. For this setup, and to keep it simple, we shall be using a single machine.

Hyperledger Fabric network installation can be done on any operating system such as MACOSX, *nix, or on Windows-based system. Setup steps are nearly the same for all the different OS, other than the older version of Windows, such as Windows 7.

Other than installing Hyperledger fabric on windows directly, you could opt for Linux based VM that can be brought up using Vagrant or Oracle Virtual Box. In a nutshell, whereas a lot of installation options available, the best way to get started is to have a *nix based VM either on a cloud or your local machine.

To set up the network, I shall be using a VM on Amazon web services just to focus on Hyperledger for now and save myself from spending time on infrastructural aspects. I would assume once you are comfortable with Hyperledger, than probably you can get started in exploring it on different deployment options.

To set up a network, I am using AWS free tier single instance, which is t2.micro (Variable ECUs, one vCPUs, 2.5 GHz, Intel Xeon Family, 1 GiB memory, EBS only). It should suffice purpose for now from understanding and setup perspective; however, a well thought through deployment architecture and adequate infrastructure setup shall be required while you move to address a real-world business problem involving multiple organizations and taking into considerations your traffic requirement, throughput and latency needs and storage that you envisioned based on the number of transactions that shall be required.

Setting up an instance on AWS is relatively straight forward and is usually a web wizard-based console that guides you through setting up the instance. You need to sign up on AWS to be able to proceed with setting up an instance. AWS has provided proper enough documentation that could help you through setting up your VM. One of the links that could be helpful is **https://docs.aws.amazon.com/efs/latest/ug/ gs-step-one-create-ec2-resources.html.**

Make sure, when you are setting up the instance, you take good care of setting up the security group, which is nothing but a set of firewall rules around inbound and outbound traffic for the VM.

You may need to connect to VM through the local machine, for which you could follow the link to use Putty to connect to VM instance remotely **https://docs.aws. amazon.com/AWSEC2/latest/UserGuide/putty.html.**

Please note, though, we have been talking about AWS specifically, but you are free to choose your environment either on the cloud or getting your local machine ready. However, further steps shall assume AWS instance as a base environment for simplicity.

Once VM is ready, and you can log into using an SSH client such as putty, you should be able to see the following screen:

Figure 8.2: VM Console

Once we have the VM instance setup, now we would progress with the prerequisite installations for HLF:

- Prerequisite
  - o Docker
  - o Docker Compose
  - o Go Lang

Docker installation

First, we shall install Docker CE (Community Edition); all required steps are provided here on the official website link **https://docs.docker.com/install/linux/docker-ce/ubuntu/.**

However, for the sake of simplicity and to understand what we are doing, all steps are shown below as well:

```
1   sudo apt-get update
2   sudo apt-get install \
    apt-transport-https \
    ca-certificates \
    curl \
    gnupg-agent \
    software-properties-common
3   curl -fsSL https://download.docker.com/linux/ubuntu/gpg | sudo apt-key add -
4   sudo apt-key fingerprint 0EBFCD88
5   sudo add-apt-repository "deb [arch=amd64] https://download.docker.com/linux/ubuntu $(lsb_release -cs) stable"
6   sudo apt-get update
7   sudo apt-get install -y "docker-ce"
```

Figure 8.3: Docker CE installation steps

At this point your Docker installation should be completed, you can run docker –v command to verify the installation

The following screenshot should confirm that Docker installation is complete:

```
ubuntu@ip-172-31-33-127: ~
ubuntu@ip-172-31-33-127:~$ docker -v
Docker version 19.03.1, build 74b1e89
ubuntu@ip-172-31-33-127:~$
```

Figure 8.4: Docker version check

> Though the steps mentioned above are valid at the time of writing this book, I strongly encourage you to follow the latest documentation at the same time while trying to follow the steps.

Docker Compose installation

Docker Compose is required to be installed as we end up having a lot of Docker containers to set up the network, and Docker Compose helps us orchestrate the creation and managing of Docker containers.

Docker Compose installation is relatively more straightforward and once can follow the steps as mentioned in the link **https://docs.docker.com/compose/install/.**

Again for simplicity:

```
1.  sudo curl -L "https://github.com/docker/compose/releases/download/1.24.0/docker-compose-$(uname -s)-$(uname -m)"
    -o /usr/bin/docker-compose
2.  sudo chmod +x /usr/bin/docker-compose
```

Figure 8.5: Docker Compose installation

At this step, Docker compose installation is complete and you can verify that by running `docker-compose -version`:

```
ubuntu@ip-172-31-33-127:~$ docker-compose -version
docker-compose version 1.24.0, build 0aa59064
ubuntu@ip-172-31-33-127:~$
```

Figure 8.6: Docker Compose version check

Go Lang installation

After Docker and Docker Compose is installed, we shall now install Go Lang, below are the steps that can be used for Go Lang installation. It is recommended that you figure out the latest compatible version of Go Lang is available and can be installed. Below steps are generic steps and can be found online specific to the version:

```
1. sudo apt-get update
2. sudo apt-get -y upgrade
3. wget https://dl.google.com/go/go1.13.3.linux-amd64.tar.gz
4. sudo tar -xvf go1.13.3.linux-amd64.tar.gz
5. sudo mv go /usr/local
```

Figure 8.7: Go Lang installation steps

Once Go Lang is installed, three environment variables need to be set, and they are :

- `GOROOT:` `GOROOT` is the path where the GO package is installed
- `GOPATH:` `GOPATH` is the work directory location, will set it later
- `PATH:` `PATH` variable like in other languages gives access to GO binary across the system

Below are the commands that are required to run into order to set GOROOT and PATH. Note that this setting of values is limited to the current session only and so it's recommended to set them in profile:

```
export GOROOT=/usr/local/go
export PATH=$PATH:/usr/local/go/bin
```

Figure 8.8: GO variable setup

By running above two commands we have set GO in our instance, we would set GOPATH later on, you can verify GO installation go version:

```
ubuntu@ip-172-31-33-127: ~
ubuntu@ip-172-31-33-127:~$ go version
go version go1.13.3 linux/amd64
ubuntu@ip-172-31-33-127:~$
```

Figure 8.9: Go version verification

Once this is done, we are done with prerequisites, and now we would move to the installation of Hyperledger Fabric Binaries.

HLF binary installation

There are no installable that come from Hyperledger Fabric; instead, they provide a script file that can be executed to get all the binaries that shall be required to set up the network.

The link for the script file is provided at **https://hyperledger-fabric.readthedocs.io/ en/release-1.4/install.html.**

Please note that you are encouraged to check the latest release link and get the script file URL from there. For now, we would go with release 1.4.

We shall create a project folder by the name of `sample` in the user's home directory so that we can confine our work there. After that, we would run `curl` command in the sample directory to download Hyperledger binaries:

```
mkdir sample
cd sample
sudo curl -sSL http://bit.ly/2ysbOFE | bash -s
```

Figure 8.10: HLF Binary download script

Make sure you recheck this command on the link given above; however, this gets changes only with a release. You might see permission denied while running this and see something like `permission denied while trying to connect to the Docker daemon socket at unix:///var/run/docker.sock`. Refer to the troubleshooting section in the chapter below.

Once you have successfully run this command, you would see the following output at the end that shows all the docker images have been downloaded. We can see a lot of images: for most of them, we have not discussed, though we would as we progress. However, you could see the Docker container of a peer (hyperledger/ fabric-peer) and orderer (hyperledger/fabric-orderer) as well.

```
===> List out hyperledger docker images
hyperledger/fabric-javaenv      1.4.2       1cd707531ce7    4 weeks ago     1.76GB
hyperledger/fabric-javaenv      latest      1cd707531ce7    4 weeks ago     1.76GB
hyperledger/fabric-ca           1.4.2       f289675c9674    4 weeks ago     253MB
hyperledger/fabric-ca           latest      f289675c9674    4 weeks ago     253MB
hyperledger/fabric-tools        1.4.2       0abc124a9400    4 weeks ago     1.55GB
hyperledger/fabric-tools        latest      0abc124a9400    4 weeks ago     1.55GB
hyperledger/fabric-ccenv        1.4.2       fc0f502399a6    4 weeks ago     1.43GB
hyperledger/fabric-ccenv        latest      fc0f502399a6    4 weeks ago     1.43GB
hyperledger/fabric-orderer      1.4.2       362021998003    4 weeks ago     173MB
hyperledger/fabric-orderer      latest      362021998003    4 weeks ago     173MB
hyperledger/fabric-peer         1.4.2       d79f2f4f3257    4 weeks ago     178MB
hyperledger/fabric-peer         latest      d79f2f4f3257    4 weeks ago     178MB
hyperledger/fabric-zookeeper    0.4.15      20c6045930c8    5 months ago    1.43GB
hyperledger/fabric-zookeeper    latest      20c6045930c8    5 months ago    1.43GB
hyperledger/fabric-kafka        0.4.15      b4ab82bbaf2f    5 months ago    1.44GB
hyperledger/fabric-kafka        latest      b4ab82bbaf2f    5 months ago    1.44GB
hyperledger/fabric-couchdb      0.4.15      8de128a55539    5 months ago    1.5GB
hyperledger/fabric-couchdb      latest      8de128a55539    5 months ago    1.5GB
```

Figure 8.11: Hyperledger Docker images

Along with Docker images, this script also downloads a folder by the name of fabric-samples, you can see the listing of your project folder and then finally see the listing of fabric-samples:

```
ubuntu@ip-172-31-33-127:~/sample/fabric-samples$ ls -ll
total 92
-rw-rw-r-- 1 ubuntu ubuntu   597 Aug 20 08:13 CODE_OF_CONDUCT.md
-rw-rw-r-- 1 ubuntu ubuntu   935 Aug 20 08:13 CONTRIBUTING.md
-rw-rw-r-- 1 ubuntu ubuntu  6386 Aug 20 08:13 Jenkinsfile
-rw-rw-r-- 1 ubuntu ubuntu 11358 Aug 20 08:13 LICENSE
-rw-rw-r-- 1 ubuntu ubuntu   470 Aug 20 08:13 MAINTAINERS.md
-rw-rw-r-- 1 ubuntu ubuntu  1805 Aug 20 08:13 README.md
drwxrwxr-x 5 ubuntu ubuntu  4096 Aug 20 08:13 balance-transfer
drwxrwxr-x 4 ubuntu ubuntu  4096 Aug 20 08:13 basic-network
drwxrwxr-x 2 ubuntu ubuntu  4096 Jul 17 21:01 bin
drwxrwxr-x 8 ubuntu ubuntu  4096 Aug 20 08:13 chaincode
drwxrwxr-x 3 ubuntu ubuntu  4096 Aug 20 08:13 chaincode-docker-devmode
-rw-rw-r-- 1 ubuntu ubuntu   968 Aug 20 08:13 ci.properties
drwxrwxr-x 3 ubuntu ubuntu  4096 Aug 20 08:13 commercial-paper
drwxrwxr-x 2 ubuntu ubuntu  4096 Jul 17 21:01 config
drwxrwxr-x 2 ubuntu ubuntu  4096 Aug 30 08:13 docs
drwxrwxr-x 5 ubuntu ubuntu  4096 Aug 20 08:13 fabcar
drwxrwxr-x 6 ubuntu ubuntu  4096 Aug 20 08:13 first-network
drwxrwxr-x 4 ubuntu ubuntu  4096 Aug 20 08:13 high-throughput
drwxrwxr-x 4 ubuntu ubuntu  4096 Aug 20 08:13 interest_rate_swaps
drwxrwxr-x 4 ubuntu ubuntu  4096 Aug 20 08:13 scripts
```

Figure 8.12: fabric-samples listing

There are a lot of folders that are of interest and use to us, basic-network, for instance, is a project with all required scripts files that can start/stop/run a network. You would gain more insight into these once you have created a network from scratch by going through the steps in the book, and then you can go back into various projects and explore other things, for now, we would choose to ignore these folders.

However, if you go inside the bin folder, you would see:

```
ubuntu@ip-172-31-33-127:~/sample/fabric-samples/bin$ ll
total 175464
drwxrwxr-x  2 ubuntu ubuntu     4096 Jul 17 21:01 ./
drwxrwxr-x 17 ubuntu ubuntu     4096 Aug 20 08:13 ../
-rwxrwxr-x  1 ubuntu ubuntu 20477536 Jul 17 21:00 configtxgen*
-rwxrwxr-x  1 ubuntu ubuntu 22613744 Jul 17 21:01 configtxlator*
-rwxrwxr-x  1 ubuntu ubuntu 13554544 Jul 17 21:00 cryptogen*
-rwxrwxr-x  1 ubuntu ubuntu 21542928 Jul 17 21:01 discover*
-rwxrwxr-x  1 ubuntu ubuntu 18187680 Jul 17 21:01 fabric-ca-client*
-rwxrwxr-x  1 ubuntu ubuntu 12188272 Jul 17 21:00 idemixgen*
-rwxrwxr-x  1 ubuntu ubuntu 32263568 Jul 17 21:01 orderer*
-rwxrwxr-x  1 ubuntu ubuntu 39823440 Jul 17 21:01 peer*
ubuntu@ip-172-31-33-127:~/sample/fabric-samples/bin$ 
```

Figure 8.13: bin folder content

And this is important because we would use a couple of binaries given in this folder, especially `cryptogen` and `configtxgen`, for creating crypto material and other channel artifacts for the rest of binaries we would talk about at the appropriate time.

We shall move binaries from the `fabric-samples/bin` folder into the local bin so that we can run these binaries without giving absolute path, and they are available at any console.

Just to verify that binaries can be run from anywhere you can try using `cryptogen` command:

```
cp fabric-samples/bin/*   /usr/local/bin
cryptogen
```

Figure 8.14: Cryptogen

The below figure shows two things, one we can run cryptogen from anywhere once we have moved that to the bin and also `cryptogen` syntax for using it, we shall go through in detail:

```
ubuntu@ip-172-31-33-127:~$ cryptogen
usage: cryptogen [<flags>] <command> [<args> ...]

Utility for generating Hyperledger Fabric key material

Flags:
  --help  Show context-sensitive help (also try --help-long and --help-man).

Commands:
  help [<command>...]
    Show help.

  generate [<flags>]
    Generate key material

  showtemplate
    Show the default configuration template

  version
    Show version information

  extend [<flags>]
    Extend existing network
```

Figure 8.15

With this step completed, we are done with an initial requirement of making prerequisites available and installation of HLF, a quick snapshot of what we have done so far:

- Provision a VM
- Install Prerequisite
    - o Docker
    - o Docker Compose
    - o Go Lang (along with setting up of environment variables)
- HLF Binaries Installation
    - o Verify docker images
    - o Verify Hyperledger Binaries (`fabric-samples/bin`)
    - o Copy binaries to bin

With this, we have the base infrastructure ready, and we can go ahead and create any Hyperledger based business network to fulfill our use case.

Now, we would move on to the specific setup of the network, which is, defining Network Topology of the business network that we have thought through.

The output of the network topology section shall be the actual Hyperledger blockchain network up and running as defined in the business network; this is going to be a more detailed section as we would run through actual configuration files, Hyperledger binaries and scripts used. On a high level, the following are the work items that we would do:

- Network Setup
    - o Certificate Generation
    - o Channel Artifacts Generation
        - ▪ Genesis Block
        - ▪ Channel Transaction
        - ▪ Anchor Peer Transaction
    - o Setting up Ordering Node
    - o Create Peer Nodes
    - o Create Channel
    - o Peer Nodes Joining Channel

Let's get started with the understanding of the most crucial section of the setting up of the Hyperledger blockchain network. We shall go through a working example. The objective is that you should understand every command and file that is the bare minimum required to set up the network.

> **To follow along, you can download the code bundle or clone the repository and go through README.md from https://github.com/ashwanihlf/ sample_3PeerNetwork.git. Read till the section end and try to understand the commands, and then, in the end, there shall be a set of commands that can be executed together to set up the network. There are many files in that folder; we will go one by one through each file.**

Following is the listing of the working folder; it contains a lot of script and YAML files. YAML files are:

- configtx.yaml:
  - o It contains details about Genesis block, which is required by Orderer to initialized
  - o Contains details about application channel
  - o Contains details about anchor peers

- crypto-config.yaml:
  - o It contains details about the crypto material that needs to be generated for orderers, peers, admins, and users.

- docker-compose.yaml:
  - o It contains details about the entities (docker containers) that are to be brought up as part of the network; for this setup, we would have:
    - ▪ Orderer
    - ▪ Three peers, one from each Org
    - ▪ CLI (command-line interface utility to interact with peers)

Similarly, scripts files are as follows:

- generate.sh: A utility script to run cryptogen and configtxgen in one go to generate crypto material and channel-artifacts

- start.sh: To start the network

- stop.sh: To stop the network

- teardown.sh: To tear down the network

```
ubuntu@ip-172-31-33-127: ~/sample_3PeerNetwork
ubuntu@ip-172-31-33-127:~/sample_3PeerNetwork$ ll
total 68
drwxrwxr-x  5 ubuntu ubuntu 4096 Mar 25 08:29 ./
drwxr-xr-x 13 ubuntu ubuntu 4096 Mar 25 07:22 ../
-rwxr-xr-x  1 root   root     25 Feb  3 05:20 .env*
drwxr-xr-x  3 root   root   4096 Feb  3 04:21 chaincode/
-rw-r--r--  1 root   root   5682 Feb 25 07:17 configtx.yaml
-rwxr-xr-x  1 root   root   3753 Feb 25 07:17 crypto-config.yaml*
-rwxr-xr-x  1 root   root   8668 Mar  9 12:57 docker-compose.yml*
drwxrwxr-x 18 ubuntu ubuntu 4096 Feb  2 12:28 fabric-samples/
-rwxr-xr-x  1 root   root   1213 Feb  1 12:47 generate.sh*
-rwxr-xr-x  1 root   root    277 Feb  1 12:47 init.sh*
drwxrwxr-x  2 ubuntu ubuntu 4096 Mar 16 09:37 scripts/
-rwxr-xr-x  1 root   root   1562 Feb 25 19:33 start.sh*
-rwxr-xr-x  1 root   root    258 Feb  1 12:47 stop.sh*
-rwxr-xr-x  1 root   root    468 Feb  1 12:47 teardown.sh*
ubuntu@ip-172-31-33-127:~/sample_3PeerNetwork$
```

Figure 8.16: Listing of sample_3PeerNetwork

Generate certificates

Since we have identified that we shall be setting up a network of three organizations by the name of Org1, Org2, and Org3, we would first generate the crypto material for them. For generating the crypto materials, we shall be using one of the binaries that have been provided by Hyperledger, and that got downloaded when we executed the script. The name of the binary is `cryptogen`

Cryptogen takes a YAML file which contains the detail of all the organizations for which we want to generate crypto materials. In the setup, following `crypto-config.yaml` has been used.

The entire process looks like:

Figure 8.17: Generating Crypto

We provide crypto-config.yaml file to cryptogen tool and that results in the generation of the required crypto material for the identities, that is, orderer and peer. In the real-world, this might not be the case, and you would instead get this material from Certificate Authorities.

The YAML file that we are using in the setup is given below; it generates the material for network components such as orderer and respective peers of the organization.

It's a straightforward file that governs how many identities we want to generate. The below image is the trim down version of the file:

```
# "OrdererOrgs" - Definition of organizations managing orderer nodes
# --------------------------------------------------------------------
OrdererOrgs:
  - Name: Orderer
    Domain: example.com
    Specs:
      - Hostname: orderer
# "PeerOrgs" - Definition of organizations managing peer nodes
# --------------------------------------------------------------------
PeerOrgs:
  - Name: Org1
    Domain: org1.example.com
    Template:
      Count: 1
    Users:
      Count: 1
  - Name: Org2
    Domain: org2.example.com
    Template:
      Count: 1
    Users:
      Count: 1
  - Name: Org3
    Domain: org3.example.com
    Template:
      Count: 1
    Users:
      Count: 1
```

Figure 8.18: crypto-config.yaml

This file contains two sections OrdererOrgs and PeerOrgs. OrdererOrgs defines the name and domain of the organization that shall host the orderer node for the network. In this case, we have kept it simple, and the orderer node shall be orderer. example.com.

The next section is PeerOrgs that defines the participating organization in the network. In the setup, we have defined three organizations Org1, Org2, and Org3, which are represented by their domain name as org1.example.com, org2. example.com, and org3.example.com.

There is another configuration of the Template count that defines the number of peers that we would want to generate crypto material for that specific organization. Now, in this case, since we have given Template count as 1, then it would automatically generate crypto material for peer0.org1.example.com. In the case of 2, it would have generated peer0.org1.example.com and peer1.org1.example.com.

Another configuration is User count; it is the number of crypto material that we need to generate for users belonging to that organization. It starts from Users<n> where n starts from 1 and goes up to user count. Additionally, it also generates crypto material for Admin as well by the name of `Admin@<domain name>,` so in our case, it would be `Admin@org1.example.com` and so on.

For full reference, you can always refer to the `crypto-config` file in `fabric-samples` and run over the documentation. However, I have kept it simple here as that was barely required to meet our objective.

The command that needs to run to generate crypto material is:

```
cryptogen generate --config=./crypto-config.yaml
```

`crypto-config.yaml` is present in the base directory of the project, that is, `sample_3PeerNetwork` in our case. The output of running this command would be the generation of a `crypto-config` folder, and the exciting part is, it creates two folders inside, one for peer and another one for the orderer:

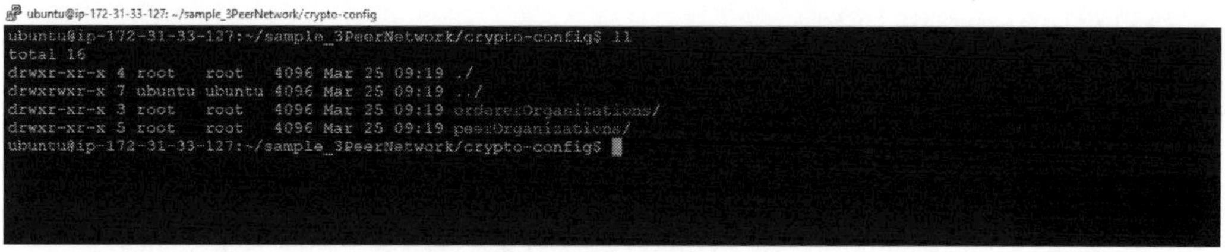

Figure 8.19: crypto-config listing

We would now move inside `peerOrganizations` folder, and we would see the following screenshot:

Figure 8.20: peerOrganizations listing

In the `crypto-config` file, we wanted to create crypto material for three organizations, and we gave domain name as well, now we could see that it has created three separate folders, each belonging to an organization.

We would now explore one organization folder, and rest two would be the same as that only; we go inside `org1.example.com`:

Figure 8.21: Org1 listing

It is the standard set of folders that get created inside any organization; we would now look into the peers and users folder; first, we would into peer folder and would see, remember we gave Template count as 1, and we could see 1 peer folder has been generated:

```
ubuntu@ip-172-31-33-127:~/sample_3PeerNetwork/crypto-config/peerOrganizations/org1.example.com/peers$ ll
total 12
drwxr-xr-x 3 root root 4096 Mar 25 09:19 ./
drwxr-xr-x 7 root root 4096 Mar 25 09:19 ../
drwxr-xr-x 4 root root 4096 Mar 25 09:19 peer0.org1.example.com/
ubuntu@ip-172-31-33-127:~/sample_3PeerNetwork/crypto-config/peerOrganizations/org1.example.com/peers$
```

Figure 8.22: Peers listing

Inside peers folder, since we have only peer, that is, peer0.org1.example.com, and inside that, we have two folders `msp` and `'tls`. `msp` is an essential folder as it carries all the cryptographic material that is required by the peer to carry out any activity on the blockchain network:

```
ubuntu@ip-172-31-33-127:~/sample_3PeerNetwork/crypto-config/peerOrganizations/org1.example.com/peers$ tree
└── peer0.org1.example.com
    ├── msp
    │   ├── admincerts
    │   │   └── Admin@org1.example.com-cert.pem
    │   ├── cacerts
    │   │   └── ca.org1.example.com-cert.pem
    │   ├── keystore
    │   │   └── 1962c98e6ea042f45f9aad9ef9a60fea5b93412837afbc84742cf3c2ec1d7b8c_sk
    │   ├── signcerts
    │   │   └── peer0.org1.example.com-cert.pem
    │   └── tlscacerts
    │       └── tlsca.org1.example.com-cert.pem
    └── tls
        ├── ca.crt
        ├── server.crt
        └── server.key
```

Figure 8.23: Peer msp

We would now come out of this folder and look into the user's folder, and we see the following screenshot:

```
ubuntu@ip-172-31-33-127:~/sample_3PeerNetwork/crypto-config/peerOrganizations/org1.example.com/users$ tree
├── Admin@org1.example.com
│   ├── msp
│   │   ├── admincerts
│   │   │   └── Admin@org1.example.com-cert.pem
│   │   ├── cacerts
│   │   │   └── ca.org1.example.com-cert.pem
│   │   ├── keystore
│   │   │   └── 93d5c137c3189699e08b51bff45c8d2a96212cb9071942db474d528f6fdb175f_sk
│   │   ├── signcerts
│   │   │   └── Admin@org1.example.com-cert.pem
│   │   └── tlscacerts
│   │       └── tlsca.org1.example.com-cert.pem
│   └── tls
│       ├── ca.crt
│       ├── client.crt
│       └── client.key
└── User1@org1.example.com
    ├── msp
    │   ├── admincerts
    │   │   └── User1@org1.example.com-cert.pem
    │   ├── cacerts
    │   │   └── ca.org1.example.com-cert.pem
    │   ├── keystore
    │   │   └── 764b0183a23012d809829866c573b17f2b3c4f29caf50da800f6bc674458a4ae_sk
    │   ├── signcerts
    │   │   └── User1@org1.example.com-cert.pem
    │   └── tlscacerts
    │       └── tlsca.org1.example.com-cert.pem
    └── tls
        ├── ca.crt
        ├── client.crt
        └── client.key
```

Figure 8.24: Users listing

Admin is something that gets generated by default, and User gets generated based on the count that we gave since we provided 1, we have one user created by User1, and in case we want to have more, we would simply increase the count and rerun the cryptogen tool.

Now, we could go back and look into orderer, we gave the domain as `example.com,` and that is what we see here:

```
ubuntu@ip-172-31-33-127: ~/sample_3PeerNetwork/crypto-config/ordererOrganizations
ubuntu@ip-172-31-33-127:~/sample_3PeerNetwork/crypto-config/ordererOrganizations$ ll
total 12
drwxr-xr-x 3 root root 4096 Mar 25 09:19 ./
drwxr-xr-x 4 root root 4096 Mar 25 09:19 ../
drwxr-xr-x 7 root root 4096 Mar 25 09:19 example.com/
ubuntu@ip-172-31-33-127:~/sample_3PeerNetwork/crypto-config/ordererOrganizations$
```

Figure 8.25: Orderer domain listing

Peeking inside example.com:

```
ubuntu@ip-172-31-33-127:~/sample_3PeerNetwork/crypto-config/ordererOrganizations/example.com$ ll
total 28
drwxr-xr-x 7 root root 4096 Mar 25 09:19 ./
drwxr-xr-x 3 root root 4096 Mar 25 09:19 ../
drwxr-xr-x 2 root root 4096 Mar 25 09:19 ca/
drwxr-xr-x 5 root root 4096 Mar 25 09:19 msp/
drwxr-xr-x 3 root root 4096 Mar 25 09:19 orderers/
drwxr-xr-x 2 root root 4096 Mar 25 09:19 tlsca/
drwxr-xr-x 3 root root 4096 Mar 25 09:19 users/
```

Figure 8.26: example.com listing

For now, folders that are of interest to use are orderers and users, looking inside the orderer, we have `orderer.example.com and its msp` folder, which provides identity to orderer in the network:

```
ubuntu@ip-172-31-33-127:~/sample_3PeerNetwork/crypto-config/ordererOrganizations/example.com/orderers$ tree
.
└── orderer.example.com
    ├── msp
    │   ├── admincerts
    │   │   └── Admin@example.com-cert.pem
    │   ├── cacerts
    │   │   └── ca.example.com-cert.pem
    │   ├── keystore
    │   │   └── bee7b271637b98edc20b484f14b425ef6c1f94481bd762b0916804c03dc617c3_sk
    │   ├── signcerts
    │   │   └── orderer.example.com-cert.pem
    │   └── tlscacerts
    │       └── tlsca.example.com-cert.pem
    └── tls
        ├── ca.crt
        ├── server.crt
        └── server.key
```

Figure 8.27: Orderer msp listing

We created orderer.example.com; under that, there are two folders: `msp` and `tls`. Under the `msp` folder, there is a folder by the name of the Keystore, which holds the private key of the orderer and signcerts folder, which contains the public key/ certificate of the orderer. This private/public key pair is used by the orderer for carrying out various actions in a blockchain network.

While we would setup orderer in the network, we need to pass the path of `msp` and `tls` (in case we want to have transport layer security) for orderer set up so that once orderer is up and running, it knows which certificates it needs to use to prove its identity and carry out the transaction. We shall show you how we use that when we would be doing the setup.

Similarly, there is an admin msp for the orderer:

```
ubuntu@ip-172-31-33-127:~/sample_3PeerNetwork/crypto-config/ordererOrganizations/example.com/users$ tree
└── Admin@example.com
    ├── msp
    │   ├── admincerts
    │   │   └── Admin@example.com-cert.pem
    │   ├── cacerts
    │   │   └── ca.example.com-cert.pem
    │   ├── keystore
    │   │   └── a047378198823b1cd01c2d09a2ea90c62bd8058a2febefa9a42438f5e2646ec1_sk
    │   ├── signcerts
    │   │   └── Admin@example.com-cert.pem
    │   └── tlscacerts
    │       └── tlsca.example.com-cert.pem
    └── tls
        ├── ca.crt
        ├── client.crt
        └── client.key
```

Figure 8.28: orderer admin listing

With the above step, we have used cryptogen successfully to create crypto materials that shall be provided to the orderer and peer installation as part of the network setup. Also, at the same time, we have created crypto material for Admin and User for orderer and peer, which we shall be used at an appropriate time.

Generate Channel Artifacts

After generating the crypto material, we shall now move on to generate other artifacts that are required for network setup. There are three artifacts that we generate through the use of a utility by the name of configtxgen, and those artifacts are necessary to set up the network. As in the case of cryptogen, configtxgen also takes a YAML file as an input. configtxgen is a command-line utility to generate and manage configuration artifacts. It also gets downloaded along with the cryptogen and other binaries when we run script files to download Hyperledger binaries and is present in the bin folder.

The artifacts that get produced are:

- Genesis Block
- Create Channel Tx
- Anchor Peer Update Transaction

The process of generation of artifacts looks like as:

Figure 8.29: configtxgen

While we would soon be creating channel artifacts by providing configtx.yaml to configtx binary, it is worthwhile to get the understanding of the content of the configtx.yaml file. Configtx file contains six sections:

- **Organizations**: This includes a list of member organizations
- **Orderer**: It contains configurations for the orderer
- **Application**: Application configuration parameters
- **Channel**: Parameters for Channel configuration
- **Profiles**: Configuration for setting up multiple profiles
- **Capabilities**: Version Management for binary files

A combination of the above-given six sections ultimately helps us generate genesis block, channel transaction, and anchor peer update.

Creating Genesis Block

To create a genesis block for the network, we need configuration for the orderer, orderer organizations, and consortium; consortium is nothing but a group of peer organizations that would make part of the network. Additionally, since the organization needs to provide their identities, which can be done through MSP so we would need MSP of orderer and organizations as well.

We shall place configtx.yaml in the root project folder, the file looks like, and it does have sections for:

- Organizations
- Orderer
- Profile
- Channel
- Application

Please note that this file has been kept simple for understanding purpose and we shall delve into more details of and add relevant sections later on.

Below is the *Organizations* section of configtx.yaml file; organizations that shall be taking part in the network are defined here. In our setup example, we could see that there are an OrdererOrg and three different orgs. & sign is used as an anchor in this file, which means that Org definitions are being provided in this section and can be referenced elsewhere in the document. The attributes are Name, ID, and MSPDir and AnchorPeer (for peer organization). Note that MSPDir is the path of the folder where we have created the crypto material:

```
Organizations:

    # SampleOrg defines an MSP using the samplecontig.  It should never be used
    # in production but may be used as a template for other definitions
    - &OrdererOrg
        Name: OrdererOrg
        ID: OrdererMSP
        # MSPDir is the filesystem path which contains the MSP configuration
        MSPDir: crypto-config/ordererOrganizations/example.com/msp

    - &Org1
        Name: Org1MSP
        ID: Org1MSP
        MSPDir: crypto-config/peerOrganizations/org1.example.com/msp
        AnchorPeers:
            # AnchorPeers defines the location of peers which can be used
            # for cross org gossip communication.  Note, this value is only
            # encoded in the genesis block in the Application section context
            - Host: peer0.org1.example.com
              Port: 7051
    - &Org2
        Name: Org2MSP
        ID: Org2MSP
        MSPDir: crypto-config/peerOrganizations/org2.example.com/msp

    - &Org3
        Name: Org3MSP
        ID: Org3MSP
        MSPDir: crypto-config/peerOrganizations/org3.example.com/msp
```

Figure 8.30: Organization Section (configtx.yaml)

It is the second section of the Orderer, which defines its configuration and properties. These values become part of the genesis block that is required for the initialization of the orderer. There are three ways by which orderer can be started:

- Solo
- Kafka
- RAFT

For now, we are using solo in our example to keep the setup simple; however, I would share the setup for RAFT as well. OrdererType is what defines the type of orderer. Orderer is responsible for creating the batch of transactions before finally relaying that to peers for updating the ledger. So, various batch and time out properties can be configured here, which are self-explanatory:

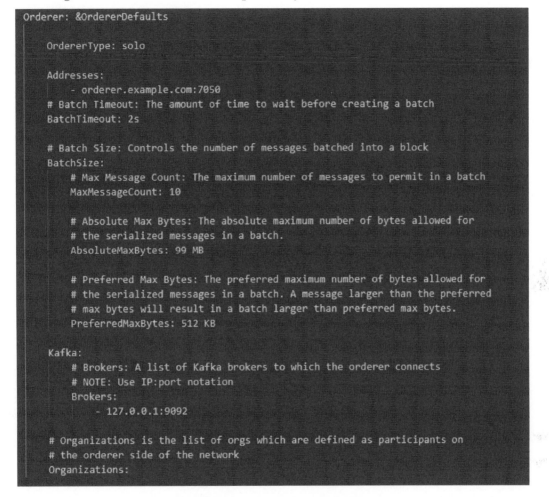

```
Orderer: &OrdererDefaults

    OrdererType: solo

    Addresses:
        - orderer.example.com:7050
    # Batch Timeout: The amount of time to wait before creating a batch
    BatchTimeout: 2s

    # Batch Size: Controls the number of messages batched into a block
    BatchSize:
        # Max Message Count: The maximum number of messages to permit in a batch
        MaxMessageCount: 10

        # Absolute Max Bytes: The absolute maximum number of bytes allowed for
        # the serialized messages in a batch.
        AbsoluteMaxBytes: 99 MB

        # Preferred Max Bytes: The preferred maximum number of bytes allowed for
        # the serialized messages in a batch. A message larger than the preferred
        # max bytes will result in a batch larger than preferred max bytes.
        PreferredMaxBytes: 512 KB

    Kafka:
        # Brokers: A list of Kafka brokers to which the orderer connects
        # NOTE: Use IP:port notation
        Brokers:
            - 127.0.0.1:9092

    # Organizations is the list of orgs which are defined as participants on
    # the orderer side of the network
    Organizations:
```

Figure 8.31: Orderer Section (configtx.yaml)

Profiles are the third relevant section of the configtx.yaml file, genesis block, and application channel are defined as a profile in this section. Genesis block needs information on Orderer organization, orderer configuration, and peer organization, which all can be referenced from here. The second profile is for Channel, which shows that which all organization shall be part of the channel:

```
###############################################################################
Profiles:

    MultiOrgOrdererGenesis:
        Orderer:
            <<: *OrdererDefaults
            Organizations:
                - *OrdererOrg
        Consortiums:
            SampleConsortium:
                Organizations:
                    - *Org1
                    - *Org2
                    - *Org3
    MultiOrgChannel:
        Consortium: SampleConsortium
        Application:
            <<: *ApplicationDefaults
            Organizations:
                - *Org1
                - *Org2
                - *Org3
```

Figure 8.32: Profiles Section (configtx.yaml)

Given now, we have our `configtx.yaml` ready for our three peer setup, we would now create channel artifacts, and individual commands that are used are as below. First of all, we shall create a folder by the name of config; there is where we would create a genesis block, and so on.

Please note that these commands are for reference and understanding purposes, though we would be using the same set of commands but hold on for now and try grasping the concepts. We shall use one of the script files, as mentioned earlier, to carry out these steps, and you can very go and view the contents of these scripts. You would be in a better position to relate as to what we are doing once we know the individual commands and their motives:

```
mkdir config

# generate genesis block for orderer
configtxgen -profile MultiOrgOrdererGenesis -outputBlock ./config/genesis.block
```

Figure 8.33: Channel Artefacts (Genesis Block) Generation

It is simply, we ran configtxgen with the profile as `MultiOrgOrdererGenesis`, and we want the output to be redirected to the **config** folder. This command shall generate a genesis block that we shall use in bring up the network.

Let's have a look at the content of the `configtx.yaml` file again. If you look into the file, under the Profiles section, we have a section by the name of

`MultiOrgOrdererGenesis`, and that is something that we have passed on to `configtxgen` to generate genesis file. The information that is passed in this section is about Orderer and Consortium, that is, member organizations:

```
Profiles:

    MultiOrgOrdererGenesis:
        Orderer:
            <<: *OrdererDefaults
            Organizations:
                - *OrdererOrg
        Consortiums:
            SampleConsortium:
                Organizations:
                    - *Org1
                    - *Org2
                    - *Org3
```

Figure 8.34: *MultiOrgOrdererGenesis Profile*

* means it is referring to Orderer and Org1, Org2 and Org3 and these entities are defined in `Organizations` section:

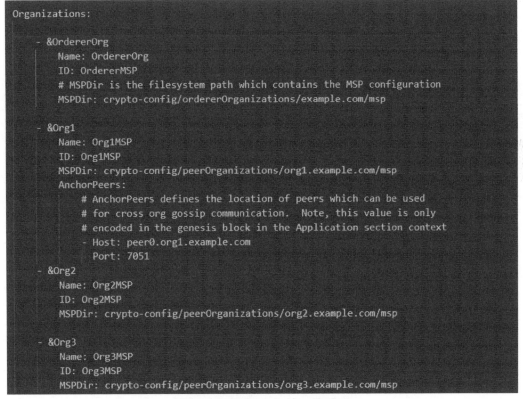

```
Organizations:

    - &OrdererOrg
        Name: OrdererOrg
        ID: OrdererMSP
        # MSPDir is the filesystem path which contains the MSP configuration
        MSPDir: crypto-config/ordererOrganizations/example.com/msp

    - &Org1
        Name: Org1MSP
        ID: Org1MSP
        MSPDir: crypto-config/peerOrganizations/org1.example.com/msp
        AnchorPeers:
            # AnchorPeers defines the location of peers which can be used
            # for cross org gossip communication.  Note, this value is only
            # encoded in the genesis block in the Application section context
            - Host: peer0.org1.example.com
              Port: 7051
    - &Org2
        Name: Org2MSP
        ID: Org2MSP
        MSPDir: crypto-config/peerOrganizations/org2.example.com/msp

    - &Org3
        Name: Org3MSP
        ID: Org3MSP
        MSPDir: crypto-config/peerOrganizations/org3.example.com/msp
```

Figure 8.35: *Organizations Section*

& means that they are defined here and can be used anywhere in the file like they have been used in the Genesis profile section. Organizations are defined with a couple of properties such as Name, MSP ID, and the location where crypto material is located by the attribute name MSPDir. Anchor peer is defined for organizations, and they are ones that are exposed over the network. Only these peers are accessible over the network and not the rest of the peer of the organization, whereas anchor peers can talk to external networks as well as other member peers of the network.

The content generated for the genesis block is in binary format, which is not readable, and `configtxgen` gives us a way to find out what is written inside the genesis block. Following command is not required for setting up the network but still, you can run this command to see the content of genesis block:

```
configtxgen –inspectBlock ./config/genesis.block
```

Figure 8.36: Inspect Block command

Create Channel Transaction (Channel Tx)

Moving on with creating the artifacts for channel set up, now we would create Channel Transaction the same way as we did for creating genesis block. While creating a channel, we would also pass the name of the profile, in this case, `MultiOrgChannel`:

```
Profiles:

    MultiOrgOrdererGenesis:
        Orderer:
            <<: *OrdererDefaults
            Organizations:
                - *OrdererOrg
        Consortiums:
            SampleConsortium:
                Organizations:
                    - *Org1
                    - *Org2
                    - *Org3
    MultiOrgChannel:
        Consortium: SampleConsortium
        Application:
            <<: *ApplicationDefaults
            Organizations:
                - *Org1
                - *Org2
                - *Org3
```

Figure 8.37: Channel Profile

In the `MultiOrgChannel` profile, we have channel consortium and Application configuration; MSP is attached with the organizations which help `configtxgen` generate channel, which knows about which organization would be part of the channel and as well the identities by way of MSP. We also need to provide the `channelID`, which identifies a channel uniquely:

```
# generate channel configuration transaction
configtxgen -profile MultiOrgChannel -outputCreateChannelTx ./config/channel.tx -channelID mychannel
```

Figure 8.38: *Channel Tx Generation*

Once we run this command, a file by the name of `channel.tx` would be created in the config folder. Please note that `MultiOrgChannel` is the name of the profile, and `mychannel` is the name of the channel that we have created, and we shall be using later on for peers to use this channel.

When we run these commands, we might get some warnings, ignore them for now, as with new release, it is expected to provide policies that we shall cover later on.

Creating Anchor Peers Update Tx

We shall now move into the last step of configuration and generate Anchor Peer Update Transactions, like for earlier configuration artifacts, this information also comes from profile definition in `configtx.yaml,` and separate transaction update for anchor peers for respective org is created.

The commands that are required to be run to generate anchor peers are as follow:

```
# generate anchor peer transaction
configtxgen -profile MultiOrgChannel -outputAnchorPeersUpdate ./config/Org1MSPanchors.tx -channelID mychannel -asOrg Org1MSP

# generate anchor peer transaction
configtxgen -profile MultiOrgChannel -outputAnchorPeersUpdate ./config/Org2MSPanchors.tx -channelID mychannel -asOrg Org2MSP

# generate anchor peer transaction
configtxgen -profile MultiOrgChannel -outputAnchorPeersUpdate ./config/Org3MSPanchors.tx -channelID mychannel -asOrg Org3MSP
```

Figure 8.39: *Anchor Peer Update Tx*

Once we have run this for all three peers as part of network setup and if we go and have a look at the config folder, it would look like:

```
ubuntu@ip-172-31-33-127:~/sample_3PeerNetwork/config$ ll
total 36
drwxrwxr-x 2 ubuntu ubuntu  4096 Mar 26 05:22 ./
drwxrwxr-x 7 ubuntu ubuntu  4096 Mar 26 05:22 ../
-rw-r--r-- 1 root   root     284 Mar 26 05:22 Org1MSPanchors.tx
-rw-r--r-- 1 root   root     284 Mar 26 05:22 Org2MSPanchors.tx
-rw-r--r-- 1 root   root     284 Mar 26 05:22 Org3MSPanchors.tx
-rw-r--r-- 1 root   root     334 Mar 26 05:22 channel.tx
-rw-r--r-- 1 root   root   11970 Mar 26 05:22 genesis.block
ubuntu@ip-172-31-33-127:~/sample_3PeerNetwork/config$
```

Figure 8.40: *Config listing (all config artifacts)*

Setting up ordering node

After all the crypto material created and channel artifacts available, now we shall setup orderer service. Orderer service needs genesis block for setup, and then it also needs some runtime properties that are again managed in the YAML file. Also, the orderer needs MSP information; of course, we can provide that as we had generated in earlier steps.

Orderer configuration is provided in a YAML file, and likewise, different peer configurations can be provided in the YAML file. To merely the deployment of the network, that is, bringing up the orderer and peer network, creating a channel, and making peer join the channel can be done through a one consolidated yaml file and with the help of script files.

From now on, we shall be discussing some snippets of the YAML file, which describe orderer, peer, and CLI and a couple of scripts file. Once we have gone through them, in the end, we shall discuss them in entirety and see how they work together.

Docker Compose helps orchestrate Docker containers and rather than running docker containers one by one, compose files gives us the option of defining docker containers and then can be brought up together at once.

In the sample folder, now we shall have docker-compose.yaml file, which has the definition of the orderer as given below:

```yaml
orderer.example.com:
    container_name: orderer.example.com
    image: hyperledger/fabric-orderer
    environment:
      - FABRIC_LOGGING_SPEC=info
      - ORDERER_GENERAL_LISTENADDRESS=0.0.0.0
      - ORDERER_GENERAL_GENESISMETHOD=file
      - ORDERER_GENERAL_GENESISFILE=/etc/hyperledger/configtx/genesis.block
      - ORDERER_GENERAL_LOCALMSPID=OrdererMSP
      - ORDERER_GENERAL_LOCALMSPDIR=/etc/hyperledger/msp/orderer/msp
    working_dir: /opt/gopath/src/github.com/hyperledger/fabric/orderer
    command: orderer
    ports:
      - 7050:7050
    volumes:
        - ./config/:/etc/hyperledger/configtx
        - ./crypto-config/ordererOrganizations/example.com/orderers/orderer.example.com/:/etc/hyperledger/msp/orderer
        - ./crypto-config/peerOrganizations/org1.example.com/peers/peer0.org1.example.com/:/etc/hyperledger/msp/peerOrg1
    networks:
      - basic
```

Figure 8.41: Orderer configuration

This section defines the orderer docker container that we would want to bring up, with properties as follows:

- **container_name:** This is the name of the docker container that would come up with an orderer image in it.

- **image:** This is the image name that we want Docker Compose to use while bringing up the container since we are going to have an orderer node, fabric-orderer image name has been given.

- **environment**: Orderer relies on a lot of environmental variables that help customize and initialize orderer during runtime, there are a lot of environment properties that orderer can use, for now, we are referring to a bare minimum, which is essential to bring up the orderer. We shall be listing down and talk out about other properties in the *Appendix*.

    o   A valuable property to note here is `ORDERER_GENESIS_METHOD`. There are two methods by which genesis block information can be provided to the orderer; one is the `file`, which we have used here. And to provide a file path, we have used and `ORDERER_GENERAL_GENESISFILE` to provide the path of the genesis block that we created in the earlier steps. The other method for providing genesis is `provisional`, where orderer creates genesis block at run time during initialization. This information is provided to the orderer through a profile in the genesis block.

    o   Also, we have provided the orderer with the MSP information that it is supposed to carry, that is name and location of the crypto material, which in this case is something that we created during crypto material generation.

- **working_dir**: It is the path of the location on the docker container having orderer where if you get a chance to log in, it will take you there.

- Ports are the mapping between VM ports and the docker container ports. Any traffic coming on to port 7050 on the VM shall be routed to 7050 port of orderer container.

- Volumes: This is used for volume mounting from the perspective of providing the orderer with the relevant materials that the orderer is supposed to use based on the environment variables. We had created all crypto material and configuration on the VM, where we ran all the cryptogen and configtxgen command. However, these need to be provided to the orderer container. The first part of the volume is the source where everything is present on the VM, and the second part is the location on the docker container.

    For instance:

```
- ./crypto-config/ordererOrganizations/example.com/orderers/orderer.example.com/:/etc/hyperledger/msp/orderer
```

Figure 8.42: Crypto config volume mapping

All crypto material was generated under the `orderer.example.com/msp` folder on the VM, and then while creating the orderer container; we mounted these to `/etc/hyperledger/msp/orderer/msp` location of the container so that these are available to orderer which would use its environment variables to locate that.

While we are done with the orderer setup, we would now go on and create peer nodes.

Create peer nodes

Similarly, like we have defined orderer node in the Docker Compose file, we shall now define peer nodes, we started with taking into consideration that we would set up the network between three organizations and so we would set three peer nodes, one each from the organization:

Following is the snippet of the Docker Compose file for defining the peer:

```
peer0.org1.example.com:
    container_name: peer0.org1.example.com
    image: hyperledger/fabric-peer
    environment:
        - CORE_VM_ENDPOINT=unix:///host/var/run/docker.sock
        - CORE_PEER_ID=peer0.org1.example.com
        - FABRIC_LOGGING_SPEC=info
        - CORE_CHAINCODE_LOGGING_LEVEL=info
        - CORE_PEER_LOCALMSPID=Org1MSP
        - CORE_PEER_MSPCONFIGPATH=/etc/hyperledger/msp/peer/
        - CORE_PEER_ADDRESS=peer0.org1.example.com:7051
        - CORE_VM_DOCKER_HOSTCONFIG_NETWORKMODE=${COMPOSE_PROJECT_NAME}_basic
        - CORE_LEDGER_STATE_STATEDATABASE=CouchDB
        - CORE_LEDGER_STATE_COUCHDBCONFIG_COUCHDBADDRESS=couchdb:5984
        - CORE_LEDGER_STATE_COUCHDBCONFIG_USERNAME=
        - CORE_LEDGER_STATE_COUCHDBCONFIG_PASSWORD=
    working_dir: /opt/gopath/src/github.com/hyperledger/fabric
    command: peer node start
    ports:
        - 7051:7051
        - 7053:7053
    volumes:
        - /var/run/:/host/var/run/
        - ./crypto-config/peerOrganizations/org1.example.com/peers/peer0.org1.example.com/msp:/etc/hyperledger/msp/peer
        - ./crypto-config/peerOrganizations/org1.example.com/users:/etc/hyperledger/msp/users
        - ./config:/etc/hyperledger/configtx
    depends_on:
        - orderer.example.com
```

Figure 8.43: Peer configuration

The above section defines a peer node in the compose file, which shall result in the creation of a peer node in the form of a docker container with the properties as specified in this section.

On a high level, if you see it is no different than we saw in orderer configuration, just that peer image has been used in this container. As well, the environment variables are different. This snapshot is for `peer0.org1.example.com`, the same way in compose file, we would define peer configuration for Org2 and Org3 peer, which would then result in peer nodes coming up in the network.

Create a channel

The next step after we have brought up orderer and peer nodes up is to create a channel and making sure that all peers are joining the channel which effectively would make a network where any transaction happening on the channel would be available and visible to all the peers and orderer playing the role of ordering the transaction blocks.

Creating a channel and making peers join the network is essentially a set of individual commands that we can run. To further simplify the developer's work we intend to use a command-line utility provided by the Hyperledger Fabric itself by the name of cli, so first, we would bring up a CLI container and then run commands from this `cli` container that too in a script file that would then knit the orderer and peer together with the channel.

To move further, we shall have a quick look at the cli that shall help us run the script file that would be knitting the network together:

```
cli:
  container_name: cli
  image: hyperledger/fabric-tools
  tty: true
  environment:
    - GOPATH=/opt/gopath
    - CORE_VM_ENDPOINT=unix:///host/var/run/docker.sock
    - FABRIC_LOGGING_SPEC=info
    - CORE_PEER_ID=cli
    - CORE_PEER_ADDRESS=peer0.org1.example.com:7051
    - CORE_PEER_LOCALMSPID=Org1MSP
    - CORE_PEER_MSPCONFIGPATH=/opt/gopath/src/github.com/hyperledger/fabric/peer/crypto/peerOrganizations/org1.example.com/users/Admin@org1.example.com/msp
    - CORE_CHAINCODE_KEEPALIVE=10
    - CORE_PEER_TLS_ENABLED=false
  working_dir: /opt/gopath/src/github.com/hyperledger/fabric/peer
  command: /bin/bash -c './scripts/script.sh ${CHANNEL_NAME} ${TIMEOUT}; bash'
  volumes:
    - /var/run/:/host/var/run/
    - ./chaincode/:/opt/gopath/src/github.com/
    - ./crypto-config:/opt/gopath/src/github.com/hyperledger/fabric/peer/crypto/
    - ./scripts:/opt/gopath/src/github.com/hyperledger/fabric/peer/scripts/
    - ./config:/opt/gopath/src/github.com/hyperledger/fabric/peer/channel-artifacts
  networks:
    - basic
  depends_on:
    - orderer.example.com
    - peer0.org1.example.com
    - peer0.org2.example.com
    - peer0.org3.example.com
    - couchdb
```

Figure 8.44: cli configuration

Similarly, as we have created the orderer and peer, we shall now be creating a `cli` container. It is provided by Hyperledger Fabric and helps us connect to the orderer and peer, which is required to set up the network by way of creating channels and making peers joining the channel. Once the `cli` container is created, it is expected to run a script file provided in the `scripts` folder that does a lot of things in one shot. You can create a cli container and then run commands one by one, but that might be too time-consuming; hence we have seen the practice of providing a script file to cli container.

One thing that you could notice in the volume section is that we have provided the mapping of the chaincode folder as well, which contains smart contract code which we shall be deploying and then run some commands from cli to see how smart contract is invoked.

Additionally, you could also see that environment variables that are set are about Org1; this is done on the assumption that when a peer is joining channel or chaincode is being installed on that peer, then environment variables related to the peer are available.

We shall now go through the code snippets of the script file to better understand it what is happening, mostly in the script file we are:

- Creating a channel
- Peers joining the channel
- Installation of Chaincode
- Instantiation of Chaincode

To accomplish all this, there are also certain utility and helper functions in the script file. Every step that we have mentioned above is encapsulated in a function that runs a command to achieve said functionality. We shall go through individual functions one by one to see what is happening here:

```
echo "Creating channel."
createChannel

echo "Peers joining the channel."
joinChannel
echo "_____Installing chaincode on Org1/peer0."
installChaincode 0
echo "_____Installing chaincode on Org2/peer0."
installChaincode 1
echo "_____Install chaincode on Org3/peer0."
installChaincode 2


#Instantiate chaincode in one of the peers
echo "_____Instantiating chaincode on _____"
instantiateChaincode 0
```

Figure 8.45: Channel operations

Just to recap that, what we have done so far is:

- Created Crypto
- Created Channel Artifacts
- Started Orderer
- Started Peers
- Started cli container

The central command from `createChannel()` method looks like below, (please note that there are particular boilerplate code and channel create command if TLS is enabled, you can ignore that for now):

```
peer channel create -o orderer.example.com:7050 -c $CHANNEL_NAME -f ./channel-artifacts/channel.tx >&channellog.txt
```

Figure 8.46: create channel command

`$CHANNEL_NAME` is a variable and value that has been defined at the start of the script file. This command generates a channel with the orderer details and creates channel transaction configurations that we created initially with configtxgen utility.

After that, there shall be the execution of the `joinChannel()` method; the line of interest is, the block that is used to join the channel gets created as part of the `channel create` command. Since we ran peer channel create in `cli` container, then block is created there and is available further to be used for joining the channel:

```
peer channel join -b $CHANNEL_NAME.block  >&retrylog.txt
```

Figure 8.47

However, since we have three peers that need to join channel so this is being done in loop and `setGlobals()` is the method that provides cli with different parameters of peers at different times, `cli` emulates itself as a peer for Org1, Org2, and Org3 based on different environment variables.

After the channel has been created and peers have joined the channel. The next step is to install and instantiate the chaincode.

Deploying Smart Contracts

Having a network of orderer and peers joined together through a channel is still a network but without any business objective and purpose. To organizations do meaningful business, they need to agree on the rules of business or transactions that can be written in smart contracts. Smart contracts are deployed on endorser peers, that is, peer whom we want to endorse the transaction.

We have read in detail about the committing and endorser peer and how endorsement policy plays an essential role in getting a transaction through. While setting up a network, identification of channel and endorsement policy is an important consideration. The sample chaincode that we are deploying on the network is straightforward logic, not the likes of business rules.

The script does the job of installing and instantiating chaincode.

```
#installChaincode()

peer chaincode install -n samplecc -v 1.0 -p github.com/ >&installlog.txt


#instantiateChaincode()

peer chaincode instantiate -o orderer.example.com:7050 -C $CHANNEL_NAME -n samplecc -v 1.0 -c '{"Args":[""]}'
                                                              -P "OR('Org1MSP.member','Org2MSP.member')"
```

Figure 8.48: Install and instantiate

Peer chaincode install command takes a couple of flags:

- -n: Name of the chaincode (samplecc is the name of chaincode)
- -v: Version of chaincode, we can have multiple versions of chaincode installed
- -p: Path of chaincode (in cli container, as we mounted our chaincode directory of our VM to the /github.com directory of cli container)

What this command does is, it directly installs the chaincode on the specified peer, however at this point if you do the 'docker ps' you would not see any container, installation simply means availability of the chaincode to the specific peer, we shall delve into more into this in next chapter that is on smart contracts.

Once the installation is done, we would need to do the instantiation of the chaincode on the specified peer. This command would instantiate the chaincode for a specific peer as a separate docker container; this command also takes a couple of flags:

- -o: Specifies the orderer
- -C: Specifies the channel name
- -n: Specifies the name of chaincode
- -c: It is a constructor argument that is required to pass the argument, which we are passing null for now
- -P: Endorsement Policy

Once we have done this and if we do docker ps then we would get, and yes, we are successful in bringing up the network:

Figure 8.49: Hyperledger 3 Peer Network

Check the first container in the list; it is the Docker container for chaincode that is deployed on a peer for Org1:

With this, our network setup is complete with chaincode deployed, and now we can run the client or queries from cli to invoke the chaincode to make changes in the ledger. In this chapter, we shall go through a couple of simple commands, and in later chapters, we shall develop a decent client to interact with the Hyperledger network.

Before we go any further, we shall have a quick look at the smart contract that we have deployed.

The chaincode is written in the Go Lang, whereas we have the option of deploying chaincode in NodeJS and Java as well.

In the sample chaincode, we shall be working on a straightforward smart contract with 'Car' as an asset that has three attributes, namely owner, model, and color. The idea is to get an understanding of the basic structure of the smart contract and to play around a little bit with simple operations on the asset that is a car for now. In the real world, there shall be involved and business savvy rules that need to be put in this.

Within this chapter, we shall only be trying to invoke the chaincode and see how we can interact with the chaincode that eventually updates the ledger.

Making client work

Now is the time to interact with the blockchain network by way of invoking the chaincode. As mentioned earlier, usually, there shall be a client application that would interact with the blockchain network. Hyperledger Fabric provides SDK for specific languages such as Java, NodeJS, Python that can be leveraged to interact with the Hyperledger Fabric blockchain network, which is, eventually, can invoke smart contracts. For this chapter, we shall invoke the smart contract using `cli`.

We have `cli` container up and running, and we would log into the container by running the following command:

```
docker exec -it cli /bin/bash
```

Once we are logged into the container, now we need to invoke the chaincode which we could do:

```
peer chaincode invoke -C mychannel -n samplecc -c '{"function": "initCar", "Args" : ["Ashwani","Blue","BMW"]}'
```

What we are doing here is, we are invoking chaincode bypassing the channel name and chaincode name. And then, we are passing constructor arguments, function names, and argument value. Though the code is self-explanatory by looking at it; however, we shall have an in-depth discussion around that in the next chapter. Let's keep our focus on setting up the network and understanding its nuances.

Once we run this command, we would get a response back as:

```
[chaincodeCmd] InitCmdFactory -> INFO 001 Retrieved channel (mychannel)
orderer endpoint: orderer.example.com:7050
```

```
[chaincodeCmd] chaincodeInvokeOrQuery -> INFO 002 Chaincode invoke
successful. result: status:200
```

Next command that we are going to run is following, in this, we are merely querying the data that we persisted in last command (invoke):

```
peer chaincode query -C mychannel -n samplecc -c
'{"function":"readCar","Args":["Ashwani"]}'
```

Once we run this command, we shall get back, data that we stored in the ledger:

```
{"docType":"Car","owner":"Ashwani","color":"blue","model":"bmw"}
```

So far, what we have done is we saved the data on Org1 peer and then queried it from there; however, given there are three Orgs, and they all share the same channel so the same data should be there in Org2 peer ledger in case we try to fetch it from there.

We shall run the following command:

```
docker exec -e "CORE_PEER_ADDRESS=peer0.org2.example.com:7051"

 -e "CORE_PEER_LOCALMSPID=Org2MSP" -e "CORE_PEER_MSPCONFIGPATH=/
opt/gopath/src/github.com/hyperledger/fabric/peer/crypto/
peerOrganizations/org2.example.com/users/Admin@org2.example.
com/msp" cli peer chaincode query -C mychannel -n samplecc -c
'{"function":"readCar","Args":["Ashwani"]}'
```

This command is interesting to note and essential to understanding; in this, we are invoking cli with peer chaincode query by giving the channel name, chaincode name, and constructor arguments. Along with that, we are setting the Identity Context of the cli container to Org2; we are setting the core peer address, MSP ID, and so on, to Org2. If you go back again and check the docker-compose.yml file, you would realize that when we initialized the network, then the cli container was set with an identity context of Org1. It gives us a convenient way to interact with any Org through cli container by way of setting up the identity context.

The result that we would get running above command is:

```
{"docType":"Car","owner":"Ashwani","color":"blue","model":"bmw"}
```

Please recall that we have installed the chaincode on the Org2 peer but didn't instantiate it. After a chaincode is installed on the peers, a single network member instantiates the chaincode on the channel.

Another interesting thing to note here is that, now, if you do 'docker ps' on your VM, you shall get the following listing, which shows that there has been a new spin-up of the docker chaincode container for Org2 Peer:

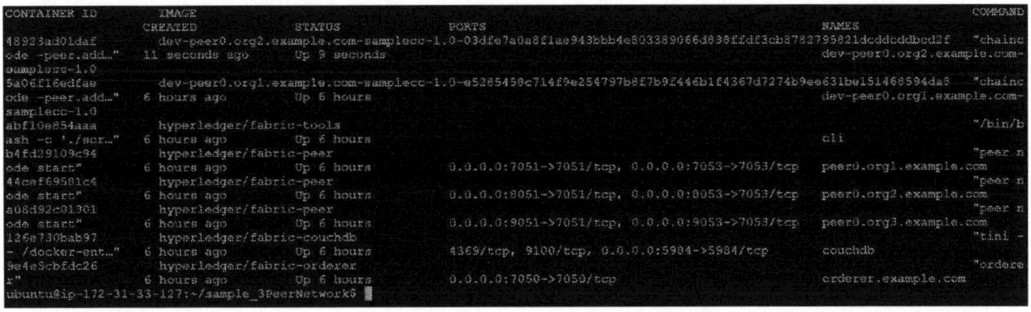

```
CONTAINER ID        IMAGE                                                                                                             COMMAND
                    CREATED             STATUS              PORTS                                            NAMES
48923ad01daf        dev-peer0.org2.example.com-samplecc-1.0-03dfe7a0a8f1ae943bbb4e803389066d838ffdf3cb8782795821dcddcddbcd2f   "chainc
ode -peer.add…"   11 seconds ago      Up 9 seconds                                                         dev-peer0.org2.example.com-
samplecc-1.0
5a06f16edfae        dev-peer0.org1.example.com-samplecc-1.0-e5285458c714f9e254797b8f7b9f446b1f4367d7274b9ee631be151468594da8   "chainc
ode -peer.add…"   6 hours ago         Up 6 hours                                                           dev-peer0.org1.example.com-
samplecc-1.0
abf10e854aaa        hyperledger/fabric-tools                                                                                          "/bin/b
ash -c './scr…"   6 hours ago         Up 6 hours                                                           cli
b4fd29109c94        hyperledger/fabric-peer                                                                                           "peer n
ode start"        6 hours ago         Up 6 hours          0.0.0.0:7051->7051/tcp, 0.0.0.0:7053->7053/tcp   peer0.org1.example.com
44caf69581c4        hyperledger/fabric-peer                                                                                           "peer n
ode start"        6 hours ago         Up 6 hours          0.0.0.0:8051->7051/tcp, 0.0.0.0:8053->7053/tcp   peer0.org2.example.com
a08d92c01301        hyperledger/fabric-peer                                                                                           "peer n
ode start"        6 hours ago         Up 6 hours          0.0.0.0:9051->7051/tcp, 0.0.0.0:9053->7053/tcp   peer0.org3.example.com
136e730bab97        hyperledger/fabric-couchdb                                                                                        "tini -
- /docker-ent…"   6 hours ago         Up 6 hours          4369/tcp, 9100/tcp, 0.0.0.0:5984->5984/tcp       couchdb
9e4e5cbfdc26        hyperledger/fabric-orderer                                                                                        "ordere
r"                6 hours ago         Up 6 hours          0.0.0.0:7050->7050/tcp                           orderer.example.com
ubuntu@ip-172-31-33-127:~/sample_3PeerNetwork$
```

Figure 8.50: new chaincode container

Following is the crisp set of command that you can run through to set up the 3 Peer and 1 Orderer set up along with the chaincode setup on Org1 and Org2. Going through the understanding of every file, step, and purpose should relate you with the steps that you should be performing now.

These are the contents of `README.md` from **https://github.com/ashwanihlf/sample_3PeerNetwork/:**

1. create a working folder, change directory to working folder
2. git clone https://github.com/ashwanihlf/sample_3PeerNetwork.git
3. sudo chmod -R 755 sample_3PeerNetwork/
4. cd sample_3PeerNetwork
5. mkdir config
   <remove config and crypto-config if they are existing before creation of config folder (Optional)> 5a. sudo rm -rf config 5b sudo rm -rf crypto-config
6. export COMPOSE_PROJECT_NAME=net
7. sudo ./generate.sh
8. sudo ./start.sh
9. docker exec -it cli /bin/bash
10. peer chaincode invoke -C mychannel -n samplecc -c '{"function":"initCar","Args":["Ashwani","Blue","BMW"]}'
11. peer chaincode query -C mychannel -n samplecc -c '{"function":"readCar","Args":["Ashwani"]}'

> returns {"color":"bmw","docType":"Car","model":"blue","owner":"Ashwani"}

12. docker exec -e "CORE_PEER_ADDRESS=peer0.org2.example.com:7051" -e "CORE_PEER_LOCALMSPID=Org2MSP" -e "CORE_PEER_MSPCONFIGPATH=/opt/gopath/src/github.com/hyperledger/fabric/peer/crypto/peerOrganizations/org2.example.com/users/Admin@org2.example.com/msp" cli peer chaincode query -C mychannel -n samplecc -c '{"function":"readCar","Args":["Ashwani"]}'

> returns {"color":"bmw","docType":"Car","model":"blue","owner":"Ashwani"}

13. docker ps

you should see 2 chaincode container one for Org1 and Org2 each

Figure 8.51: README

Hoping you have been able to run through these steps and can see all the containers up and running, and along with you can run chaincode.

Examples

To further strengthen the understanding of some more concepts, we shall now be going through some more examples, code samples, and README files that are also available on GitHub or in different projects in downloaded code sample.

Adding a new organization

In this example, we would try to add a new organization is already running setup; the reason for choosing this case is:

- It is close to the real-world case, where new organizations would keep coming in the network as and when they would see value in getting onto the network

- Use of configtxlator utility and its commands, we have gone through cryptogen and configtxgen; likewise, this is a vital utility

- Use of jq utility, this is not directly related to hyperledger rather its lightweight command-line JSON processor

- Protocol Buffers (.pb extension) files, which are something that is the platform-neutral mechanism for serializing structured data

- Some more commands from peer binary

To execute and do the setup, you can follow the project from downloaded code sample or at **https://github.com/ashwanihlf/sample_AddNewOrg.** README files have all the steps that you can go through step by step for a successful setup.

In this section, we would try to explain what we are doing most in the entire process:

1. *Step 1–Step 12* is the same as what we did in the last example, the result of running these steps is there shall be a network with 1 Orderer node, 3 Peer Nodes each from an organization. Chaincode also gets involved with all peers. Along with two chaincode containers of Org1 and Org 2 peers.

2. Now, since we need to add a new Organization, that is, Org 4, so before that, we need to have corresponding crypto material information (`org4-crypto.yaml`) and Organization MSP detail (in `configtx.yaml`) file.

3. *Steps 13–Step 20* are around running cryptogen and configtxgen for Org4 configuration files. PeerOrganization folder with Org4 Peer crypto gets generated in the `crypto-config` folder, and `org4.json` contains `channel-artefcats` for Org 4.

4. For an org to be part of the network, its configuration needs to go into the configuration block of the network.

5. Steps 21–Step 23 is where we fetch the config block from the orderer by providing the specific channel name where we want this new org to join. We run the following command:

```
> peer channel fetch config config_block.pb -o orderer.example.
com:7050 -c $CHANNEL_NAME
```

6. Now an important point, whereas so far, we have been seeing peer binary as specific Peer instance running for an organization by way of definition in the docker-compose file. Same time, the peer also work as a utility which provides certain command, subcommand, and flags that can be used to interact with a specific peer:

```
ubuntu@ip-172-31-33-127:~$ peer
Usage:
  peer [command]

Available Commands:
  chaincode   Operate a chaincode: install|instantiate|invoke|package|query|signpackage|upgrade|list.
  channel     Operate a channel: create|fetch|join|list|update|signconfigtx|getinfo.
  help        Help about any command
  logging     Logging configuration: getlevel|setlevel|getlogspec|setlogspec|revertlevels.
  node        Operate a peer node: start|status|reset|rollback.
  version     Print fabric peer version.

Flags:
  -h, --help   help for peer

Use "peer [command] --help" for more information about a command.
ubuntu@ip-172-31-33-127:~$
```

Figure 8.52: Peer commands

7. Now, you can relate to how we were using peer command for installing and instantiating chaincode. It shows us clearly how many operations we can do with the peer. In *Step 23*, we are using peer channel fetch. The whole idea of doing fetch was to get the channel configuration and then append the configurations that we have created.

8. Before we finally move further talking about the rest of the steps, we shall have a look at the **configtxlator** utility, which is also a vital utility such as cryptogen and configtxgen:

```
ubuntu@ip-172-31-33-127:~$ configtxlator
usage: configtxlator [<flags>] <command> [<args> ...]

Utility for generating Hyperledger Fabric channel configurations

Flags:
  --help  Show context-sensitive help (also try --help-long and --help-man).

Commands:
  help [<command>...]
    Show help.

  start [<flags>]
    Start the configtxlator REST server

  proto_encode --type=TYPE [<flags>]
    Converts a JSON document to protobuf.

  proto_decode --type=TYPE [<flags>]
    Converts a proto message to JSON.

  compute_update --channel_id=CHANNEL_ID [<flags>]
    Takes two marshaled common.Config messages and computes the config update which transitions between the two.

  version
    Show version information
```

Figure 8.53: configtxlator

9. While we are adding a new org in the existing setup, fundamentally, we are changing the configuration, and configtxltor is the utility that helps us change the configuration. Configuration comes in a form that is protocol buffer (.pb extension), which is a binary form and is not human readable. So, this needs to be converted into JSON for modifying, and that is where `configtxlator` helps. Similarly, .pb is the format that is updated back, and the modified JSON file is converted back .pb file using `configtxlator`.

10. Additionally, another utility is `jq`, which is not directly related to Hyperledger Fabric but is a command-line JSON processor that helps modify the JSON file.

11. So, in the entire process, we are using configtxlator to change the .pb to a JSON file that uses `jq` to do some operation on the JSON file, use configtxlator again to convert the modified JSON into .pb file.

12. `proto_encode` and `proto_decode` are two commands that are used by configtxlator foe conversion between .pb and JSON format.

13. *Step 24*, Converting `config_block.pb` into `common.Block` json and then using jq utility to fetch only config part of the JSON.

14. *Step 25*, Using `jq` utility and by using `config.json` (channel configuration in JSON format) and `org4.json` (we created using `configtxgen`) and creating a modified JSON file.

15. *Step 26–Step 27* creating .pb file for original config JSON and the modified JSON file.

16. `config_update` is another command in the `configtxlator` that takes the two config messages and computes the config update.

17. *Step 28*, Running `compute_update` on original config and modified config and result is updated Org4 config in pb.

18. *Step 29*, Generate JSON out of org4 update .pb file

19. *Step 30*, Need to add an envelope to generated JSON file

20. *Step 31*, Get complete .pb file with updated config and envelope, and .pb is something that goes back to the channel for updation of configuration.

21. In an attempt to simplify steps from *Step 21–Step 31*, below is an image that just helps you understand what all this process goes through, especially from fetching the original config block from the channel and then coming back into a position where the block is ready with necessary modified configuration to be supplied back to the network. It's a raw representation of

all the commands that we need to execute and the file transformations that take place during this course:

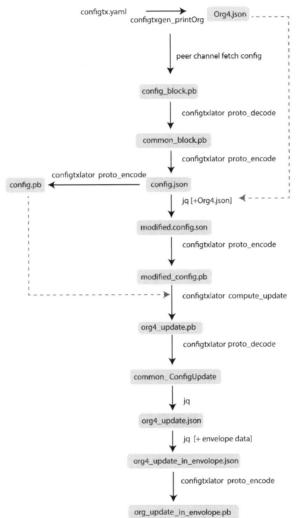

Figure 8.54: The config update process

22. *Step 32,* Since we are running all these commands in a cli docker container that has the Identity context of Org1 and now before we could update this modified channel configuration this needs to be signed by the peer of all Orgs, so in this case Org1 peer is signing using the command:

```
> peer channel signconfigtx -f org4_update_in_envelope.pb
```

23. *Step 33–Step 36,* Change Identity context to Org2 and sign the file.

24. *Step 37–Step 39,* Change Identity context to Org3 and sign the file.

25. *Step 40*, actual step, updating the channel with this new configuration so that now the network is aware that now we have another Org, that is, Org4 as a member.

26. *Step 41–Step 45*, bringing the Org 4 peer container and cli container up and joining the network.

27. *Step 46*, install the same chaincode as we did for other orgs.

28. *Step 47*, run the chaincode query, and we would get back the result, please not we didn't do any invoke from this peer, but still, we got the updated result.

It brings us to the end of this section; it been a length and bit complex scenario; however, it allowed us to play around with channel configurations, docker files for the addition of new Org, and then use of configtxlator and jq utility.

Adding a new peer

It is relatively simple; we would try to add a new peer for an organization in an already running setup.

To execute and do the setup, you can follow the project downloaded code or at **https://github.com/ashwanihlf/sample_AddNewPeer**. README files have all the steps that you can go through step by step for a successful setup.

In this section, we would try to explain what we are doing most in the entire process:

1. *Step 1–Step 12* is the same as what we did in the last example; the result of running these steps is there shall be a network with 1 Orderer node, 3 Peer Nodes each from an organization. Chaincode also gets involved with all peers. Along with two chaincode containers of Org1 and Org 2 peers.

2. *Step 13,* since we need to add a new `Peer in Org3, that is, peer1.org3.example.com`, we only need to generate crypto material for this specific peer. We shall make Template count from 1 to 2 in `crypto-config.yaml` and run `cryptogen extend` command. Please recall we ran cryptogen generate in our earlier projects.

3. *Steps 14* for adding a new peer, we need to define everything for new peer and run the `docker-compose` file.

4. *Step 15–Step 18* open up cli container and set the Identity Context for Org3.

5. *Step 19* set `CORE_PEER_ADDRESS` to new peer address.

6. *Step 20* Install Chaincode.

7. *Step 21* run query on chaincode and you would get the result back.

With these examples and trying to make use of most of the utility binaries provided now, we should have gained a good understanding of setting up the network, which is an essential learning path for Hyperledger Fabric.

Network configuration and policies

So far, we have been able to set up the network from scratch, going step by step, going through required configuration and script files to understand how it all works. With that, we also went through the steps of adding a new org and a new peer, which mainly was configuration updates. If you would have realized, during the course, we made the peers signed the updates, and then we finally ran the peer channel update command. So, what we did during this was satisfying a policy for channel updates. However, we never gave any policy anywhere, though we must have seen the following warning running every time we generated the genesis block or generated channel config transactions:

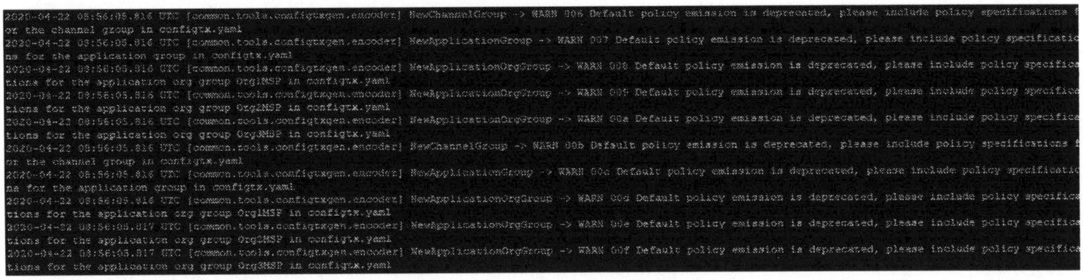

```
2020-04-22 08:56:05.816 UTC [common.tools.configtxgen.encoder] NewChannelGroup -> WARN 006 Default policy emission is deprecated, please include policy specifications f
or the channel group in configtx.yaml
2020-04-22 08:56:05.816 UTC [common.tools.configtxgen.encoder] NewApplicationGroup -> WARN 007 Default policy emission is deprecated, please include policy specificatio
ns for the application group in configtx.yaml
2020-04-22 08:56:05.816 UTC [common.tools.configtxgen.encoder] NewApplicationOrgGroup -> WARN 008 Default policy emission is deprecated, please include policy specifica
tions for the application org group Org1MSP in configtx.yaml
2020-04-22 08:56:05.816 UTC [common.tools.configtxgen.encoder] NewApplicationOrgGroup -> WARN 009 Default policy emission is deprecated, please include policy specifica
tions for the application org group Org2MSP in configtx.yaml
2020-04-22 08:56:05.816 UTC [common.tools.configtxgen.encoder] NewApplicationOrgGroup -> WARN 00a Default policy emission is deprecated, please include policy specifica
tions for the application org group Org3MSP in configtx.yaml
2020-04-22 08:56:05.816 UTC [common.tools.configtxgen.encoder] NewChannelGroup -> WARN 00b Default policy emission is deprecated, please include policy specifications f
or the channel group in configtx.yaml
2020-04-22 08:56:05.816 UTC [common.tools.configtxgen.encoder] NewApplicationGroup -> WARN 00c Default policy emission is deprecated, please include policy specificatio
ns for the application group in configtx.yaml
2020-04-22 08:56:05.816 UTC [common.tools.configtxgen.encoder] NewApplicationOrgGroup -> WARN 00d Default policy emission is deprecated, please include policy specifica
tions for the application org group Org1MSP in configtx.yaml
2020-04-22 08:56:05.817 UTC [common.tools.configtxgen.encoder] NewApplicationOrgGroup -> WARN 00e Default policy emission is deprecated, please include policy specifica
tions for the application org group Org2MSP in configtx.yaml
2020-04-22 08:56:05.817 UTC [common.tools.configtxgen.encoder] NewApplicationOrgGroup -> WARN 00f Default policy emission is deprecated, please include policy specifica
tions for the application org group Org3MSP in configtx.yaml
```

Figure 8.55: *Policy emission warning*

These are the warnings where we have been asked to include policy specifications, in case of no policy provided, the fabric gives default policy parameters. For dev environment, it's still okay to not provide them for now, but when we shall be deploying the network on production-like environments, we need to make sure that we have given proper policies.

A policy, in general, is a set of rules that governs how decisions shall be made, and outcomes are achieved. In Hyperledger Fabric, policies encompass the rules for accessing and updating the network and channel configuration. Hyperledger Fabric is a permissioned blockchain with known participants joining the network, and hence users are well known and recognized by the underlying infrastructure. On one side, where these users have the responsibility to provide the governance to the network, they can decide the parameters required for the governance of the network before the start of the network and also once the network is up and running, and there is where Policies help.

Hyperledger Fabric supports policies implementation at a different level of the network:

- **System Channel Configuration:** In Hyperledger Fabric, a network starts with a bootstrap channel or also known as ordering system channel. This channel contains all the information about Orderer Organizations, Consortium Organizations, and as well knows about the consensus mechanism used by Ordering Service and how the new blocks are created. Just to connect the dots, all these things are we specify under various section heads in `configtx.yaml` file, and then we create genesis block out of it, which we provide during orderer initialization in compose file and orderer gets initialized. However, so far we have done without policies, that is why we were getting warnings all over again.

- **Application Channel Configuration:** We have read about the application channel; this provides a private communication mechanism between an agreed set of organizations in a specific channel. The policies defined in a channel (application) govern the rules to add or remove members from the channel. Whenever an application channel is created for the first time, it inherits all the ordering service parameters from the orderer system channel by default.

System Channel and Application Channel Configuration are the vital aspects of hyperledger blockchain infrastructure with policies defined in both set controls a range of aspects. An important point to note here is that its mostly orderer organizations that govern System Channel, and a part of it is controlled by consortiums. For an application channel, it's mostly consortium organizations that govern that including channel modification part of System Channel.

Other than channel configuration, there is another aspect, which is the **Access Control List (ACL)**, which again works as a policy for Smart contracts, Ledger data, and Events. We shall talk about that in the next section.

Before we finally move to understand the different policy types and how do we write and interpret them, I just wanted to let you know about Modification Policies Think of this as Policies policies; that is, it defines how a policy by itself can be updated. So, we would see that every configuration element points a reference to a policy that governs its modification.

We have talked about the network configuration in terms of system and application channel, and now first, we would talk about how do we write policy, what are types of policies available with Fabric. Then we would look at a couple of examples to understand it better.

To be able to change anything in the network, we need to figure out the policy attached to the resource that describes the role who can do that, and with the signature from allowed parties, the desired change can be achieved.

The policy defines a specific rule, and rules are expressed as a Boolean expression in terms of Principals. A principal is just a signer's role in the organization. When an organization issues identities to its members, that time, they are associated with a role. Four roles are off now, and they are admin, member, peer, and client. So, if an organization MSP looks like Org1MSP, then the identity issued to the peer could have a principal like `Org1MSP.peer`. These principals play an essential role in the definition of policies.

There are two kinds of policies that can be attached to the resources:

- **Signature policies**: These policies define a specific type of identities having specific principals that can sign to satisfy a policy. For example, `Org1MSP.Admin` or `Org1MSP.peer`. Signature policies syntax supports the use of AND, OR, and NOutOf. We have seen the use of AND and OR in case of endorsement policies; they work the same way. NOutOf can be used with a set of principals, and the first argument with the number that tells out of total principals given the specific number must sign. For example, `NOutOf(1, Org1MSP.admin,Org2MSP.Admin)` is satisfied if 1 out of two principals sign.

- **ImplicitMeta policies**: This is different than signature policies and is only valid mostly in the case of channel configurations. It follows a hierarchial level of policies in a configuration tree. Policy invoked at any level goes down till the end, where it eventually gets signature policy. Interestingly they are called Implicit because these are created automatically based on the organizations in the channel configuration. They are called Meta because the evaluation of these policies is against the sub-policies down the tree than actual specific MSP principals. ImplicitPolicies rule in the form of `<ANY | ALL \ MAJORITY > <READERS | WRITERS | ADMINS > | <SubPolicyName>>`.

All of these policies, along with the network configuration, becomes part of the genesis block and then eventually config block, which works as the orderer system channel. The policy follows a number that shows if a policy is a `Signature (Type = 1)` or `ImplicitMeta (Type =3)`.

Now, we would run into some examples that show the mapping of policies defined in `configtx.yaml` for various network elements configurations and how that is represented as system channel configuration in Hyperledger Fabric.

First of all, you need to set up a network; you can do it in any of running network, I have used one of the earlier samples just that am using two organizations and have added policy changes in the `configtx.yaml` file, which I will walk you through. You can always refer to Hyperledger GitHub for the sample `configtx.yaml` file, for your reference, so that you can take one and modify **https://github.com/hyperledger/fabric/blob/master/sampleconfig/configtx.yaml.**

Once the network is up, the following commands can be run to fetch the config block, and then we would run configtxlator to convert it into JSON file so that this could be readable:

```
docker exec -it cli bash

peer channel fetch config config_block.pb -o orderer.example.com:7050 -c mychannel

configtxlator proto_decode --input config_block.pb --type common.Block > config.json
```

Figure 8.56: *Command to get config*

If you recall, we define organizations in the configtx.yaml that represent organizations that take part in Orderer and as well in the consortium. Now in the below section, we would see how we define policies. They are of Readers, Writers, and Admins type and is type=1 policy that is signature policy:

```
Organizations:
    - &OrdererOrg
        Name: OrdererOrg
        ID: OrdererMSP
        MSPDir: crypto-config/ordererOrganizations/example.com/msp
        #    /Channel/<Application|Orderer>/<OrgName>/<PolicyName>
        Policies:
            Readers:
                Type: Signature
                Rule: "OR('OrdererMSP.member')"
            Writers:
                Type: Signature
                Rule: "OR('OrdererMSP.member')"
            Admins:
                Type: Signature
                Rule: "OR('OrdererMSP.admin')"
    - &Org1
        Name: Org1MSP
        ID: Org1MSP
        MSPDir: crypto-config/peerOrganizations/org1.example.com/msp
        #    /Channel/<Application|Orderer>/<OrgName>/<PolicyName>
        Policies:
            Readers:
                Type: Signature
                Rule: "OR('Org1MSP.admin', 'Org1MSP.peer', 'Org1MSP.client')"
            Writers:
                Type: Signature
                Rule: "OR('Org1MSP.admin', 'Org1MSP.client')"
            Admins:
                Type: Signature
                Rule: "OR('Org1MSP.admin')"
```

Figure 8.57: *Organization policies*

Now, if you open up the content of the generated JSON file in a JSON viewer, you would notice a bit complicated structure. It is the entire configuration that we define in configtx.yaml and goes inside as genesis file, and then an update of configuration goes inside this config only.

If you see under `channel_group` which represents `/Channel` we have:

- `groups`
- `mod_policy`
- `policies`
- `values`

`mod_policy` is Admins that is any change of anything undervalues can only be done by "Admins". Policies define the policy rule attached to various roles that can read, write, and make changes to the values undervalues. Groups follow the hierarchy further to /Channel:

Figure 8.58: *Channel policies*

Now, if we further expand policies under `channel_group`, we would see that Admins policy is `type : 3`, that is, it is ImplictMeta policy and value is `MAJORITY Admins,` so to change the policy itself of this `channel_group` policies majority of admins should sign. Likewise, if we see Writers policy, to change any values related to this level can be changed by writers provided they have the Writers policy:

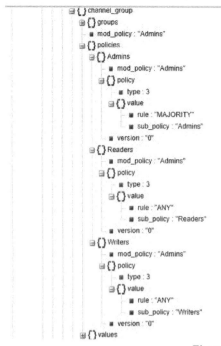

Figure 8.59: Channel policies

Now, if we expand the values section under channel_group, we could see that the values we could change and the related policy attached to it. For changing the HashingAlgorithm, the mod_policy is "Admins", and we just saw that the rule for the "Admins" policy is MAJORITY Admins. Similarly, if we could see that OrdererAddresses can be modified by /Channel/Orderer/Admins policy. So far, we have been going through /`Channel` policies, and further down, we would go to /`Channel/Orderer` and /`Channel/Application policies`:

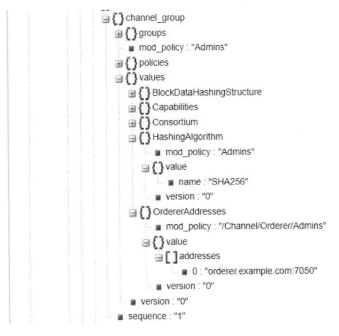

Figure 8.60: Channel values

If you go further down the /`Channel`, you would see, which essentially represents /`Channel/Application` and /`Channel/Orderer`:

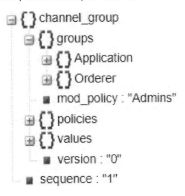

Figure 8.61: Further channels

We would now look at the exciting aspect where we would look at how ImplicitMeta eventually traverses to Signature policy. We have expanded /`Channel/Orderer,` and `max_message_count` value under batch size has `mod_policy` of "Admins".

Now if you look at "**Admins**" under policies, you would see that its `type : 3,` that is, ImplicitMeta and `rule` is `MAJORITY Admins:`

Figure 8.62: Channel/Orderer policies

As we know that ImplicitMeta policy goes deep in the hierarchy to evaluate the expression. Now the next level is `/Channel/Orderer/<Org>`. If we expand OrdererOrg and look into Admin's policy under policies, then we would realize this is a type 1 policy with signature required as `OrdererMSP.admin,` which we provided in `configtx.yaml` file:

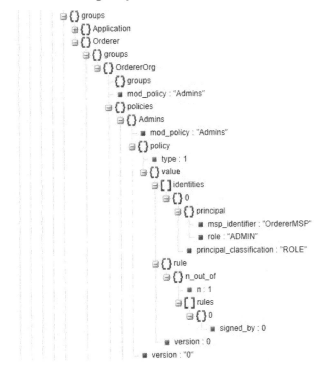

Figure 8.63*: OrdererOrg policies*

Likewise, I would encourage you to go through the policy defined in the `configtx.yaml` and corresponding representation in the config.

Access Control List

While we have to talk about policies and how we can control access at various levels. We have talked about managing the configurations which control system and application channel configurations. This topic would not be complete if we do not talk about another way of controlling access through policies, and that is the **Access Control List (ACL).**

Users through the use of application SDK and peer binaries can interact with Hyperledger Fabric; in that, they eventually interact with the resources. In general, these resources are system chaincode, user-developed custom chaincode, and events that fabric emits. ACLs are the way by which access to these resources could be controlled. ACLs make use of policy to allow and manage access to these resources. All of the available resources that for now are internal resources and are currently given by Fabric. The way to name resources follows the convention of

`<component>/<resource>`. Again, you can have a look at the sample `configtx.yaml` file for the complete list.

A sample definition of ACL's look like this is for reference and not complete, but would help you understand the concept. If you remember, we ran `peer chaincode list –instantiated –c mychannel` for getting the list of instantiated chaincode:

```
Application: &ApplicationDefaults
  ACLs: &ACLsDefault

    # ACL policy for lscc's "getid" function
    lscc/ChaincodeExists: /Channel/Application/Readers

    # ACL policy for lscc's "getdepspec" function
    lscc/GetDeploymentSpec: /Channel/Application/Readers

    # ACL policy for lscc's "getccdata" function
    lscc/GetChaincodeData: /Channel/Application/Readers

    # ACL Policy for lscc's "getchaincodes" function
    lscc/GetInstantiatedChaincodes: /Channel/Application/Readers

    #---Query System Chaincode (qscc) function to policy mapping for access control---#

    # ACL policy for qscc's "GetChainInfo" function
    qscc/GetChainInfo: /Channel/Application/Readers

    # ACL policy for qscc's "GetBlockByNumber" function
    qscc/GetBlockByNumber: /Channel/Application/Readers

    # ACL policy for qscc's  "GetBlockByHash" function
    qscc/GetBlockByHash: /Channel/Application/Readers

    # ACL policy for qscc's "GetTransactionByID" function
    qscc/GetTransactionByID: /Channel/Application/Readers
```

Figure 8.64: ACL list

The first section is a resource, and the second part is the policy applied to that resource. it is the default policy settings for these resources:

```
# Default policies
Policies: &ApplicationDefaultPolicies
  Readers:
      Type: ImplicitMeta
      Rule: "ANY Readers"
  Writers:
      Type: ImplicitMeta
      Rule: "ANY Writers"
  Admins:
      Type: ImplicitMeta
      Rule: "MAJORITY Admins"
```

Figure 8.65: ACL policies

You can carry out the simple exercise of defining a custom policy and then overriding that policy and go and try out the earlier steps which were giving you out the desired result.

In the following image, the first line is that you can change in default ACL to override the default policy with custom policy and then add `OnlyAdmins` in Policies and then when you run the peer command to get the list of instantiated chaincode, only Admin would be able to fetch that not anyone else. Try this out would help you get a better understanding of the ACLs:

```
lscc/GetInstantiatedChaincodes: /Channel/Application/OnlyAdmins

OnlyAdmins:
        Type: ImplicitMeta
        Rule: "ANY Admins"
```

Figure 8.66: *ACL custom policy*

RAFT

We did talk about ordering service and various type of types of ordering service that Hyperledger Fabric supports in *Chapter 6*. Throughout all the examples, we have used ordering service as solo, which comes as part of orderer binaries, and we don't need to install anything else for that. Apart from solo, the other supported types are Kafka and raft. Both are **crash fault-tolerant (CFT); that is,** they can tolerate nodes going down and still helping in the ordering of the blocks and helping reach consensus.

In this section, we shall be talking about RAFT and have a look at one of the setup examples from downloaded code samples or **https://github.com/ashwanihlf/ sample_raft.git.** We shall not be talking about RAFT as a protocol as we have already discussed that in *Chapter 4* and shall more talk about how to setup RAFT in Hyperledger Fabric setup. Again, this is a very trimmed down version of the setup provided by hyperledger Fabric in `fabric-samples` to help you understand it quickly and staying relevant with what is needed to set up for RAFT as the consensus protocol.

RAFT has become a preferred choice for the Hyperledger Fabric because of the issues associated with Kafka and solo being only limited to use in development mode. Solo and Kafka's support has been depreciated with fabric version 2.0. RAFT uses the leader and follower model and with the leader chosen dynamically. The group of ordering nodes that makes up the RAFT nodes are called the consenter set in the fabric. RAFT ordering service still keeps working till the quorum is maintained; that is, the majority of nodes are running. RAFT supports a fault tolerance of *2f+1* nodes, that is, in a set of 2f+1 nodes; it can sustain f faulty nodes.

In the setup, we would see that in a RAFT ordering setup with five nodes, the system would be working if two nodes go down even if there is any leader among the faulty nodes. We would look through the various configurations that are required to bring the raft nodes and well see what happens if we bring down the ordering service node in between and if that impacts the transaction flow in the fabric.

The configuration for RAFT is required at two places, first is, channel configuration where we provide consenters as part of `configtx.yaml` as given below. It is from the profile section, which is used for generating a genesis block. The same can be defined in the Orderer section as well. Notice that we need to provide client and server TLS certificates. TLS is mandatory for now for RAFT:

```
OrdererType: etcdraft
EtcdRaft:
    Consenters:
    - Host: orderer.example.com
      Port: 7050
      ClientTLSCert: crypto-config/ordererOrganizations/example.com/orderers/orderer.example.com/tls/server.crt
      ServerTLSCert: crypto-config/ordererOrganizations/example.com/orderers/orderer.example.com/tls/server.crt
    - Host: orderer2.example.com
      Port: 7050
      ClientTLSCert: crypto-config/ordererOrganizations/example.com/orderers/orderer2.example.com/tls/server.crt
      ServerTLSCert: crypto-config/ordererOrganizations/example.com/orderers/orderer2.example.com/tls/server.crt
    - Host: orderer3.example.com
      Port: 7050
      ClientTLSCert: crypto-config/ordererOrganizations/example.com/orderers/orderer3.example.com/tls/server.crt
      ServerTLSCert: crypto-config/ordererOrganizations/example.com/orderers/orderer3.example.com/tls/server.crt
    - Host: orderer4.example.com
      Port: 7050
      ClientTLSCert: crypto-config/ordererOrganizations/example.com/orderers/orderer4.example.com/tls/server.crt
      ServerTLSCert: crypto-config/ordererOrganizations/example.com/orderers/orderer4.example.com/tls/server.crt
    - Host: orderer5.example.com
      Port: 7050
      ClientTLSCert: crypto-config/ordererOrganizations/example.com/orderers/orderer5.example.com/tls/server.crt
      ServerTLSCert: crypto-config/ordererOrganizations/example.com/orderers/orderer5.example.com/tls/server.crt
Addresses:
    - orderer.example.com:7050
    - orderer2.example.com:7050
    - orderer3.example.com:7050
    - orderer4.example.com:7050
    - orderer5.example.com:7050
```

Figure 8.67: RAFT changes in configtx.yaml

In channel configuration itself, there are a couple of other configuration values as part of Options in `Orderer\Etcdraft` section; however, there are advisable to be not changed unless you are too sure about it. These attributes are:

- TickInterval
- ElectionTick
- HeartbeatTick
- MaxInflightblocks
- SnapshotIntervalSize

For the complete description and usage of these attributes, please refer to sample `configtx.yaml` provided by fabric.

The second configuration is the local configuration, which is given in the `orderer.yaml` file. These local configurations again have two groups:

- Cluster parameters
- Consensus parameters

In the setup, that we are running, we have used bare minimum configurations that are required for raft cluster to run and assuming other defaults should be okay for now:

```
orderer.example.com:
  container_name: orderer.example.com
  image: hyperledger/fabric-orderer
  environment:
    - FABRIC_LOGGING_SPEC=info
    - ORDERER_GENERAL_LISTENADDRESS=0.0.0.0
    - ORDERER_GENERAL_GENESISMETHOD=file
    - ORDERER_GENERAL_GENESISFILE=/etc/hyperledger/configtx/genesis.block
    - ORDERER_GENERAL_LOCALMSPID=OrdererMSP
    - ORDERER_GENERAL_LOCALMSPDIR=/etc/hyperledger/msp/orderer/msp
    # enabled TLS
    - ORDERER_GENERAL_TLS_ENABLED=true
    - ORDERER_GENERAL_TLS_PRIVATEKEY=/etc/hyperledger/msp/orderer/tls/server.key
    - ORDERER_GENERAL_TLS_CERTIFICATE=/etc/hyperledger/msp/orderer/tls/server.crt
    - ORDERER_GENERAL_TLS_ROOTCAS=[/etc/hyperledger/msp/orderer/tls/ca.crt]
    - ORDERER_GENERAL_CLUSTER_CLIENTCERTIFICATE=/etc/hyperledger/msp/orderer/tls/server.crt
    - ORDERER_GENERAL_CLUSTER_CLIENTPRIVATEKEY=/etc/hyperledger/msp/orderer/tls/server.key
    - ORDERER_GENERAL_CLUSTER_ROOTCAS=[/etc/hyperledger/msp/orderer/tls/ca.crt]
  working_dir: /opt/gopath/src/github.com/hyperledger/fabric/orderer
  command: orderer
  ports:
    - 7050:7050
  volumes:
    - ./config/:/etc/hyperledger/configtx
    - ./crypto-config/ordererOrganizations/example.com/orderers/orderer.example.com/:/etc/hyperledger/msp/orderer
    - ./crypto-config/ordererOrganizations/example.com/orderers/orderer.example.com/tls/:/etc/hyperledger/msp/orderer/tls
  networks:
    - basic
```

Figure 8.68: RAFT changes in orderer.yaml

All files are present in downloaded code samples or GitHub, so you can go through these files to understand it fully and follow through the README file to see how it runs.

Once you have a complete setup running and chaincode instantiated, you can go and check logs of any orderer, and you could see relevant logs related to raft

One additional change you would notice is as part of peer configuration is that we have enabled TLS, so creating a channel and instantiating chaincode needs TLS configurations to be passed. You could see relevant changes in script.sh. And then while you are invoking chaincode, you can also see the difference:

```
root@ee03c59e5a92:/opt/gopath/src/github.com/hyperledger/fabric/peer# peer chaincode invoke -o orderer.example.com:7050 --
yperledger/fabric/peer/crypto/ordererOrganizations/example.com/orderers/orderer.example.com/msp/tlscacerts/tlsca.example.c
resses peer0.org1.example.com:7051 --tlsRootCertFiles /opt/gopath/src/github.com/hyperledger/fabric/peer/crypto/peerOrgani
ple.com/tls/ca.crt -c '{"function":"initCar","Args":["Ashwani","Blue","BMW"]}'
                                                              Chaincode invoke successful. result: status:
root@ee03c59e5a92:/opt/gopath/src/github.com/hyperledger/fabric/peer# peer chaincode query -C mychannel -n samplecc -c '{"
["docType":"Car","owner":"Ashwani","color":"blue","model":"bmw"]
root@ee03c59e5a92:/opt/gopath/src/github.com/hyperledger/fabric/peer#
root@ee03c59e5a92:/opt/gopath/src/github.com/hyperledger/fabric/peer#
```

Figure 8.69: Chaincode Invoke

Till this it looks, however now you can test the quorum feature of the RAFT protocol by stopping any three containers out of five using the following command:

```
>> docker container stop orderer<x>.example.com  [x could be any number
of your orderers]
```

Now, if you would try to run the invoke command with initCar function with new arguments, you would get an error as follows:

```
root@ee03c59e5a92:/opt/gopath/src/github.com/hyperledger/fabric/peer# peer chaincode invoke -o orderer.example.com:7050 --
tls true --cafile /opt/gopath/src/github.com/hyperledger/fabric/peer/crypto/ordererOrganizations/example.com/orderers/orde
rer.example.com/msp/tlscacerts/tlsca.example.com-cert.pem -C mychannel -n samplecc --peerAddresses peer0.org1.example.com:
7051 --tlsRootCertFiles /opt/gopath/src/github.com/hyperledger/fabric/peer/crypto/peerOrganizations/org1.example.com/peers
/peer0.org1.example.com/tls/ca.crt -c '{"function":"initCar","Args":["Naman","Red","Merc"]}'
Error: error sending transaction for invoke: got unexpected status: SERVICE_UNAVAILABLE -- no Raft leader - proposal respo
nse: version:1 response:<status:200 > payload:"\n 3\300\004RS\366:\372\032\331\313\273\322Og\324\306\226N\230X\265\3365M\2
27\025\350$\272\316\315\022\222\001\nz\022\030\n\0041scc\022\020\n\016\n\010samplecc\022\002\010\001\022^\n\010samplecc\02
2R\n\007\n\005Naman\032G\n\005Naman\032>[\"docType\":\"Car\",\"owner\":\"Naman\",\"color\":\"red\",\"model\":\"merc\"}\032
\003\010\310\001\"\017\022\010samplecc\032\0031.0" endorsement:<endorser:"\n\007org1MSP\022\252\006-----BEGIN CERTIFICATE-
----\nMIICKDCCAc6gAwIBAgIQMtAn2mibkIdZfpYBOK7xpzAKBggqhkjOPQQDAjBzMQsw\nCQYDVQQGEwJVUzETMBEGA1UECBMKQ2FsaWZvcm5pYTEWMBQGA1
UEBxMNU2FuIEZy\nYW5jaXNjbzEZMBcGA1UEChMQb3JnMS5leGFtcGxlLmNvbTEMBoGA1UEAxMTY2Eu\nb3JnMS5leGFtcGxlLmNvbTAeFw0yMDA0MjcwNDM0
MDBaFw0zMDA0MjUwNDM0MDBa\nMGoxCzAJBgNVBAYTAlVTMRMwEQYDVQQIEwpDYWxpZm9ybmlhMRYwFAYDVQQHEw1T\nYW4gRnJhbmNpc2NvMRMwMQYwCwYDVQQLEw
RwZWVyMR8wHQYDVQQDExZwZWVyMC5vcmcxLmV4YW1wbGUuY29tMFkwEwYHKoZIzj0CAQYIKoZIzj0DAQcDQgAEO7gZLX1p3d6I\nCWsjk4VxfErGvFNReRYm
apyNwz0Pz3yHCsF1R8/I/hZ1onYVPEn6mhJdrxByEtyX\n8CA5ywCuJ6NNMEswDgYDVR0PAQH/BAQDAgeAMAwGA1UdEwEB/wQCMAAwKwYDVR0j\nBCQwIoAghO
RJuSCkAEuh2qnuqlsqcsej4xirXDJVXyvVHsNAQ6owCqYIKoZIzj0E\nnAwIDSAAwRQIhAJz1QqA1Ja7oF3nUb7h62XS7HBu2/sRXf8yGygoQTsSlAiAg44eX\n
XwY+mefmcef0eT5B7zZzEcxTzeIUR/L4qnD7fQ=="\n-----END CERTIFICATE-----\n" signature:"0D\002 *\341\374\037\i\220z\272\303:\36
5\272\006na\211\341\303\302\2759\251\311\237\241\235_\302\231+\354\002 =\253\375yHo\304ED^\233yzy\034\266-\306\340\333\234
o\332\275\331W\034Ep\036\343|" >
```

Figure 8.70: *RAFT error*

And if you go and check orderer logs, you can simply make out that since quorum is not reached, the transaction was not successful. Now you can bring any of the orderers up that you stopped by giving the command:

```
>> docker container start orderer<x>.example.com
```

And then run the same command of initCar invoke again, and it would be through.

I would suggest to go through configtx.yaml, docker-compose, and script. sh files and see the differences from the earlier projects. You would be in a better position to understand RAFT from the configuration point of view, and if you play around with docker containers, start and stop while observing the logs that would give you a much better understanding of RAFT protocol. I hope going through this section would have helped you understand one of the niche parts of the fabric that is playing around with consensus.

Transport Layer Security (TLS)

Transport Layer Security or TLS is an industry-wide, widely adopted security protocol that is designed to provide privacy and data security for communications over a computer network. TLS has become a de facto standard for secure communications over the internet with the most common use case is secure communication between web applications and clients, that is, browser in most of the cases. HTTPS is the most common implementation of TLS that provides such security between web applications and clients.

Likewise, in Hyperledger Fabric, we do establish a network where different systems interact with each other, could be peer, orderer, application client, or cli. A peer serving application client requests, cli request can act as a server. And peer communicating with the orderer or other peer acts as a client. TLS communication can happen one way (server only) and also work as two way (client-server) authentication.

Peer configuration

TLS configuration for a peer in Hyperledger Fabric is managed through properties. The following are the properties that we can define as part of the service definition of peer in the docker compose file. We need to enable the TLS flag to true, which is false by default, and at the same time, we need to provide values for other variables:

```
- CORE_PEER_TLS_ENABLED=true
- CORE_PEER_TLS_CERT_FILE=/etc/hyperledger/msp/peer/tls/server.crt
- CORE_PEER_TLS_KEY_FILE=/etc/hyperledger/msp/peer/tls/server.key
- CORE_PEER_TLS_ROOTCERT_FILE=/etc/hyperledger/msp/peer/tls/ca.crt
```

Figure 8.71: *Peer TLS properties*

TLS certificates are also generated as part of the crypto material generation that we do use cryptogen utility. And if you get a chance to look under the crypto-config folder and further down till tls folder, you would see the certificates and key generated that needs to be provided here:

```
ubuntu@ip-172-31-33-127:~/sample_raft/crypto-config/peerOrganizations/org1.example.com/peers/peer0.org1.example.com/tls$ tree
├── ca.crt
├── server.crt
└── server.key
```

Figure 8.72: *Peer TLS certificates*

This configuration enables the TLS on peers.

Even in the case of TLS enabled on the peer, it would still not validate the certificates of the client connecting to it. To enable TLS client authentication on the peer node, then there are additional properties that are required to set. It enables two-way TLS on the peer. To set these, we need to set the following properties:

- CORE_PEER_TLS_CLIENTAUTHREQUIRED
- CORE_PEER_TLS_CLIENTROOTCAS_FILES

The first property needs to be set true, and the second property contains the location of trusted CA certificates.

So far, we have seen two cases where the peer is acting as a server for one way TLS, so it has its required certificates, and then to the provider to provide two-way TLS and authenticating client, it needs to enable that property and provide the trusted CAs certificates.

However, there is a case when per acts as a client, let's say to the orderer, and the peer is required to present its certificates as client auth is required at the orderer side so for that following flags needs to be populated with right values:

- `CORE_PEER_TLS_CLIENTCERT_FILE`
- `CORE_PEER_TLS_CLIENTKEY_FILE`

Orderer configuration

Same way as we have done TLS configuration for peer, there are configurations available for the orderer. We can set them using the following properties:

```
- ORDERER_GENERAL_TLS_ENABLED=true
- ORDERER_GENERAL_TLS_PRIVATEKEY=/etc/hyperledger/msp/orderer/tls/server.key
- ORDERER_GENERAL_TLS_CERTIFICATE=/etc/hyperledger/msp/orderer/tls/server.crt
- ORDERER_GENERAL_TLS_ROOTCAS=[/etc/hyperledger/msp/orderer/tls/ca.crt]
```

Figure 8.73: Orderer TLS properties

If you recall, in our RAFT example, we saw that RAFT uses TLS protocol, and so if you look at the orderer service definition in the docker compose file, you would see these configurations.

For enabling client authentication on Orderer, we can use the following properties:

- `ORDERER_GENERAL_TLS_CLIENTAUTHREQUIRED`
- `ORDERER_GENERAL_TLS_CLIENTROOTCAS`

Fabric Client (SDK)

In all the examples that we have seen so far, we have been interacting with the Hyperledger Fabric network mostly through the cli. It comes as a handy option as we are quite quickly able to interact with the network and get the desired results. However, this may not work in the real world. In the actual scenario, we may provide users with a graphical user interface that they can use to interact with the network.

To develop such applications that can interact with the network to manage and process data on the network, Hyperledger Fabric provides client SDK. These SDK comes for different languages, and they are:

- Hyperledger Fabric SDK for NodeJS
- Hyperledger Fabric SDK for Java
- Hyperledger Fabric SDK for Go
- Hyperledger Fabric SDK for Python

So, you have the option of developing your application in any of these languages, and by using respective client SDK, we can interact with the fabric network. Developing client applications shall again follow the desired enterprise pattern for integration.

For instance, you can have an integration layer developed that can interact with fabric using any of the SDK. Then this integration layer can expose a set of API that user interface application or any other application that wishes to interact with fabric network can use.

Hyperledger Fabric has provided a good amount of documentation and examples that can help you with the development of applications that can interact with the network and as well be an interface to other applications that want to connect with the network. These APIs provide us with the facility of sending the transactions by way of invoking the chaincode, querying the ledger, and in fact, we can install and instantiate chaincode as well. Fabric network also emits events in certain instances that can be captured by these applications and further used by other applications such as reporting and monitoring applications.

The objective of this section is to give you an idea of how we can leverage one of the SDK to connect with the network. We shall be going through an example of fabric NodeJS client SDK for reference. Please note that the effort is to provide you with enough ground to get started then exploring each and everything. Readers who wish to go with client SDK in any other language, can refer to the documentation and provided examples.

We shall be looking into fabric SDK for NodeJS, and it provides the following modules and available high-level functionality to interact with the network.

- `fabric-network` (mainly for chaincode interactions)
  - Transaction submission to smart contracts
  - To query the smart contract
- `fabric-client` (to access fabric run time)
  - Channel creation
  - Installation and instantiation of chaincode
  - Event monitoring
  - Configuration related queries
- `fabric-ca-client` (to interact with fabric-ca-server)
  - Registering and enrolling of a new user
  - Revoking an existing user

In the following NodeJS client example, we shall be invoking and querying the sample chaincode, where we have used the car as an asset. Since we would be limiting ourselves to chaincode interaction, we shall be mainly focusing on the fabric-network module.

Following are the classes in the fabric-network module; there are a lot of other classes in other modules as well; we might not be able to go through each one of them, would try to cover a couple of classes. However, highly recommended to go and explore modules, classes, and functions available in case you wish to create NodeJS client for your network:

fabric-network.AbstractEventHubSelectionStrategy

fabric-network.AbstractEventListener

fabric-network.BaseCheckpointer

fabric-network.BaseWallet

fabric-network.CommitEventListener

fabric-network.Contract

fabric-network.ContractEventListener

fabric-network.CouchDBWallet

fabric-network.EventHubDisconnectError

fabric-network.EventHubManager

fabric-network.FabricError

fabric-network.FileSystemCheckpointer

fabric-network.FileSystemWallet

fabric-network.Gateway

fabric-network.HSMWalletMixin

fabric-network.InMemoryWallet

fabric-network.Network

fabric-network.Query

fabric-network.RoundRobinEventHubSelectionStrategy

fabric-network.TimeoutError

fabric-network.Transaction

fabric-network.X509WalletMixin

Figure 8.74: fabric-network classes

Since in our example, we would be doing chaincode interactions, so we would be using `Contract` and `Transaction` class. Meanwhile, we would also be required to use the `Gateway` class, which acts as a handle to connect to the `network` and as well Network class. In due course, we would also use `FileSystemWallet`, which helps us manage and interact with the required crypto material for providing the identity on the network to interact with the fabric network.

Starting with the `Gateway` class, it provides the connection point for an application to access the Fabric network. It can simply be instantiated with the default constructor. It then uses the connect method for connecting by using connection profile definition and configuration options:

`<async> connect(config,options)`

`config` is a connection profile definition that can be passed as a YAML file, and `options` is an instance of `GatewayOptions` that contains information about the wallet, identity, and so on.

Once we have the instance of `Gateway` class, then by merely passing the network (channel) name, we get the instance of the network, and bypassing the contract name to this network instance we get the Contract object which can further be used for submitting a transaction and querying a chaincode.

We shall now look at the connection profile in detail, which is an argument to the Gateway connect method. Profile contains the details of the network, such as Orderer and Peer addresses, channel, and organization details. You can refer to the complete connection profile file in the sample, here is the trim down version of the section for better understanding.

Following is the organization's section; it merely shows the list of organizations, its MSPID, and peers in it:

```
organizations:
  Org1:
    mspid: Org1MSP
    peers:
      - peer0.org1.example.com

  Org2:
    mspid: Org2MSP
    peers:
      - peer0.org2.example.com

  Org3:
    mspid: Org3MSP
    peers:
      - peer0.org3.example.com
```

Figure 8.75: Profile - Organizations details

The below screenshot shows the `orderers` and peers section; we have omitted the `tls` section just for simplicity:

```
orderers:
  orderer.example.com:
    url: grpc://localhost:7050

    grpcOptions:
      ssl-target-name-override: orderer.example.com
peers:
  peer0.org1.example.com:

    url: grpc://127.0.0.1:7051

  peer0.org2.example.com:

    url: grpc://localhost:8051
```

Figure 8.76: Profile - Orderer and Peers Detail

The last section is channels that include the name of the channel and listed orders and peers in the channel. There are specific attributes under peer that help client SDK identify peers:

```
channels:
  # name of the channel
  mychannel:
    # List of orderers designated by the application to use for transactions on this channel.
    orderers:
      - orderer.example.com

    # Required. list of peers from participating orgs
    peers:
      # Org1 peer - with roles played by the peer
      peer0.org1.example.com:
        # Roles for which this peer may be used
        endorsingPeer: true
        chaincodeQuery: true
        ledgerQuery: true
        eventSource: true

      # Org2 peer - with roles played by the peer
      peer0.org2.example.com:
        # Roles for which this peer may be used
        endorsingPeer: true
        chaincodeQuery: true
        ledgerQuery: true
        eventSource: false    # SDK will NOT allow event subscribers for this peer
```

Figure 8.77: Profiles – channels

We have spoken about connection profile; now we would talk about another essential aspect that is Wallet, it goes in the GatewayOptions. The Wallet maintains the identity context of the user that is connecting to the network. It holds the private key, public key, and certificate. Please note that users may connect to different networks under different contexts. Wallet maintains the identity in the form of a label mapped to an identity object that uses X509 credentials. We can create an identity context by passing a label and an instance of an identity object that can be created using the createIdentity method of X509WalletMixin and bypassing mspID, certificate, and key.

Just to simplify:

- Create an identity label, a string that represents a user and the organization
- Create identity by passing mspID, cert and key to X509WalletMixin class
- Import the label and identity in the wallet
- Pass this wallet in options
- Along with the configuration and options created above, connect to the network

Now, we would go through the small application that we have created using NodeJS SDK that performs initCar and readCar chaincode operation on samplecc. The sample program can be found at downloaded code samples or **https://github.com/ashwanihlf/sample_sdk_client.git.**

Please keep in mind that it is a scarce example and doesn't use any modularization of code, parametrization, error handling, and so on. The main motive is to make you aware and provide a foundation step stone to move upwards.

As a pre-requisite you need to install node and npm, I have installed below mentioned versions, would suggest you refer to the documentation for applicable versions. Make sure that installation goes without errors. Also, note that the client that we shall be going as an example is deployed on the same machine where we have carried out all other samples. This client application shall be using our 3 Peer Network deployed chaincodes:

```
ubuntu@ip-172-31-33-127:/$ node -v
v10.20.1
ubuntu@ip-172-31-33-127:/$ npm -v
6.14.4
ubuntu@ip-172-31-33-127:/$
```

Figure 8.78: Node version

Follow along with the steps as given in the README file to see the example working:

We need to start the 3PeerNetwork application so that a network could be established, and chaincode is deployed so that we can make client working. Another thing to note here is that we need to have a valid identification at the client-side to interact with the network, so you would see that we have referred the Admin certificates and keys generated for the peer of Org1.

Once we have the network up and running and we have set up the client application, we would be invoking two client programs `initCar.js` and `readCar.js`. The `initCar.js` is a client version of the `cli` command of peer chaincode invoke that we were using to create the `car` asset, and `readCar.js` is analogous to peer chaincode query that we were doing to read the car asset based on the owner name. While executing both client files, we need to pass specific arguments to invoke the chaincode functions.

We would now go through the content of `initCar.js` and `readCar.js` to see what we are doing. Following image shows the initial statements of the program:

```
const fs = require('fs');
const yaml = require('js-yaml');
// Import fabric-network classes
const { Gateway, FileSystemWallet,X509WalletMixin, DefaultEventHandlerStrategies, Transaction  } = require('fabric-network');

const CONNECTION_PROFILE_PATH = '../profiles/connection.yaml'
// Identity context used
const USER_ID = 'Admin@org1.example.com'
// Channel name
const NETWORK_NAME = 'mychannel'
// Chaincode
const CONTRACT_ID = "samplecc"

// Create an instance of the file system wallet
const wallet = new FileSystemWallet('./wallet');
const gateway = new Gateway();

var myArgs = process.argv.slice(2)

if (myArgs.length !=3) {
        console.log("Enter three Arguments 'Name' 'Colour' 'Model'")
        process.exit(1)
}
main()
```

Figure 8.79: initCar.js

In the above image, we are merely creating instances of the required modules; we need to use the file system ('fs') module as we would be reading certificate and key files for wallet and, most importantly, is the fabric-network package. Please pay closer attention to the README file that guides us through the installation of required node modules; the error-free installation is very much required for the successful execution of this program. Then we are providing a path of the connection profile and initializing a couple of other variables required for the program. We are also using FileSystemWallet as this points to the location where we would be keeping our identity that is required for interacting with the network. We are expecting arguments from the command line, and then we are calling the main() method.

Following are the contents of the **main** method, it's self-explanatory:

```
async function main() {

        await addIdentityToWallet()
        await setupGateway()
        let network = await gateway.getNetwork(NETWORK_NAME)
        const contract = await network.getContract(CONTRACT_ID);
        await submitTxnContract(contract)
}
```

Figure 8.80: initCar.js main method

Below image shows the execution statements in `addIdentityToWallet()`:

```
async function addIdentityToWallet() {

    try {
        // hard coded path to read cert and key of Admin from sample_3PeerNetwork
            // check for private key file name, your generate command might have generated with a different name
                var certPath = "../../../sample_3PeerNetwork/crypto-config/peerOrganizations/org1.example.com/users
                /Admin@org1.example.com/msp/signcerts/Admin@org1.example.com-cert.pem"
        var cert = fs.readFileSync(certPath).toString();
        var keyPath = "../../../sample_3PeerNetwork/crypto-config/peerOrganizations/org1.example.com/users
        /Admin@org1.example.com/msp/keystore/ea5ef499a069aaa04cba3aa54e00917f3985687a1cc8384f280714d3b83b2176_sk"
                var key = fs.readFileSync(keyPath).toString();

    } catch (e) {
        console.log("Error reading certificate or key!!! ")
        process.exit(1)
    }
    let mspId = "Org1MSP"
    const identity = X509WalletMixin.createIdentity(mspId, cert, key);
    await wallet.import("Admin@org1.example.com", identity);
}
```

Figure 8.81: initCar.js addIdentityToWallet method

In this, we are reading key and certificate for Org1 Admin as that would help us create an identity to interact with the network. You can see that I have used the certificates generated from our `sample_3PeerNetwork setup`. While executing this program, you need to make sure that `keyPath` is matching; this most likely would be different. In this, we are simply creating an identity using key and cert and then importing that identity in the wallet with a label.

You may not notice this instantly, but when the `import` statement is run on wallet instance, and identity is imported, then a folder gets created since we used `FileSystemWallet`. And this folder contains a certificate, public and private key:

Figure 8.82: wallet folder

Following are the contents of `setupGateway()` function:

```
async function setupGateway() {

    let connectionProfile = yaml.safeLoad(fs.readFileSync(CONNECTION_PROFILE_PATH, 'utf8'));
    const wallet = new FileSystemWallet('./wallet')
    let connectionOptions = {
        identity: USER_ID,
        wallet: wallet,
        discovery: { enabled: false, asLocalhost: true }
        , eventHandlerOptions: {
            strategy: null
        }
    }
    await gateway.connect(connectionProfile, connectionOptions)
}
```

Figure 8.83: initCar setupGateway() function

The first thing that we are doing is loading the connection profile so that client gets to know where it needs to connect. We provide the path of the `wallet` where `identity` can be looked for. Then we create config instance; in this, we provide wallets and the label that we need to look for in the wallet. Recall, when we talked about `Gateway.connect()` method, we talked about two arguments that we pass, connection profile, and config, so we would just pass those arguments, and the gateway is ready to connect.

Follow the code to submit the transaction:

```
async function submitTxnContract(contract){
    try{
        // Submit the transaction
        let response = await contract.submitTransaction('initCar', myArgs[0],myArgs[1],myArgs[2])
        console.log("Response= ",response.toString())
    } catch(e){
        console.log(e)
    }
}
```

Figure 8.84: initCar submitTransaction

We submit the transaction after getting the network and contract instance; please refer to the `main` method. We are invoking the `initCar` method on the chaincode with passing the required arguments. It looks similar to peer chaincode invoke for `initCar`.

Now, we need to run the following command to see that in action:

```
ubuntu@ip-172-31-33-127:~/sample_3PeerNetwork_Client/app/gateway$ sudo node ./initCar.js Ashwani Blue BMW
Response=
ubuntu@ip-172-31-33-127:~/sample_3PeerNetwork_Client/app/gateway$ sudo node ./readCar.js Ashwani
Query Response={"docType":"Car","owner":"Ashwani","color":"blue","model":"bmw"}
```

Figure 8.85: Node client run

Monitoring (Prometheus and Grafana)

Monitoring is an important aspect of enterprise applications. Whereas it is important for organizations to embrace new technologies, incorporate new methodologies of build and deployment for greater success, at the same time, monitoring the systems proactively is equally important to sustain that success. Healthy systems are key for businesses to keep operating. Any inadvertent fault in the system could disrupt the functioning of the system, resulting in negative user experience and jeopardize the organization's reputation.

Hyperledger Fabric, being an enterprise solution, also provides the options for network operators to monitor the deployed solution. Peer and Orderer are the key components of the fabric blockchain network. In addition to the core services offering, peer and orderer have an inbuilt HTTP server that exposes operations API that is RESTful. The objective is to provide as much information of the operators that could help monitor the health check and operational metric. On a high level, the following are the capabilities that are exposed:

- **Log level management:**
  - o Peer and Orderer expose a REST resource `/logspec` that can help manage the active logging specification
  - o It supports GET and PUT requests, where GET gets you the current logging specification, PUT would let you set the new logging specification

- **Health check:**
  - o A REST resource `/healthz` is exposed that gives out the details of the liveness and health of peers and orderer
  - o It supports GET and gives out the details of the health checkers of that process

- **Metrics:**
  - o To provide greater insight into the working and behavior of the system, peer and orderer expose metrics, that is, a lot of vital parameters that can help determine how the system is working.
  - o For instance, in peer, it gives out the value of `chaincode_execute_timeouts` that tells the number of times Init or Invoke chaincode execution has timed out. One another example is `chaincode_shim_requests_received` that tells how many requests have been received.
  - o Similarly, for the orderer, one of the properties is broadcast_processed_count, which tells the number of transactions that have been processed.
  - o The complete list can be found at https://hyperledger-fabric.readthedocs.io/en/release-1.4/metrics_reference.html.
  - o Peer and Orderer provide all this metric information on a specific port, and then we would need tools that pick up this metrics information and display it in a meaningful way. Prometheus is supported to pick this information, and the same way StatsD can also be used.

- **Version:**
  - o It is just an information endpoint with a resource `/version` which gives out a JSON document that tells about the version of the orderer or peer and also contains information about the hashcode of the commit on which the release was made.

Now, we would talk about the configuration to enable operational metrics for peer and orderer, and same time we would see how Prometheus and Grafana can help us enabling this monitoring in a more useful and meaningful way.

Whereas we would use Prometheus and Grafana to monitor the operational metrics, we shall focus on integrating both of them into one of our networks. This integration is done on a very minimal basis, and the objective is to show the basics of integration and no way we would delve into Prometheus and Grafana. They both are established products on their own with a wide range of functionalities that they offer. Readers are suggested to look at them separately to gain more insights into them. In this example, we shall focus only on the integration part and limited visualization.

The monitoring project is present at downloaded code sample or **https://github.com/ ashwanihlf/sample_monitoring.git**; again, this is the same 3 Peer sample network where we have added operational support and as well added service definition for Prometheus and Grafana.

If you look at the orderer environment variables, we have added ORDERER_ OPERATIONS_LISTENADDRESS and OPERATIONS_METRICS_PROVIDER:

```
services:
  orderer.example.com:
    container_name: orderer.example.com
    image: hyperledger/fabric-orderer
    environment:
      - FABRIC_LOGGING_SPEC=info
      - ORDERER_GENERAL_LISTENADDRESS=0.0.0.0
      - ORDERER_GENERAL_GENESISMETHOD=file
      - ORDERER_GENERAL_GENESISFILE=/etc/hyperledger/configtx/genesis.block
      - ORDERER_GENERAL_LOCALMSPID=OrdererMSP
      - ORDERER_GENERAL_LOCALMSPDIR=/etc/hyperledger/msp/orderer/msp
      - ORDERER_OPERATIONS_LISTENADDRESS=0.0.0.0:9446
      - ORDERER_METRICS_PROVIDER=prometheus
    working_dir: /opt/gopath/src/github.com/hyperledger/fabric/orderer
    command: orderer
    ports:
      - 7050:7050
      - 9446:9446
    volumes:
      - ./config/:/etc/hyperledger/configtx
      - ./crypto-config/ordererOrganizations/example.com/orderers/orderer.example.com/:/etc/hyperledger/msp/orderer
      - ./crypto-config/peerOrganizations/org1.example.com/peers/peer0.org1.example.com/:/etc/hyperledger/msp/peerOrg1
    networks:
      - basic
```

Figure 8.86: Operation configuration for Orderer

Similarly, if you have a look at the below figure, we have added support for operation metric in one of the peers:

```
peer0.org1.example.com:
  container_name: peer0.org1.example.com
  image: hyperledger/fabric-peer
  environment:
    - CORE_VM_ENDPOINT=unix:///host/var/run/docker.sock
    - CORE_PEER_ID=peer0.org1.example.com
    - FABRIC_LOGGING_SPEC=info
    - CORE_CHAINCODE_LOGGING_LEVEL=info
    - CORE_PEER_LOCALMSPID=Org1MSP
    - CORE_PEER_MSPCONFIGPATH=/etc/hyperledger/msp/peer/
    - CORE_PEER_ADDRESS=peer0.org1.example.com:7051
    - CORE_OPERATIONS_LISTENADDRESS=peer0.org1.example.com:9444
    - CORE_METRICS_PROVIDER=prometheus
```

Figure 8.87: Operation configuration for peer

With these configurations, operation service starts listening to these addresses to be able to respond to any request that comes asking for any information.

You can see that we have enabled port **9446** for orderer and **9444** for Org1 peer and now if we hit log level and health resource endpoints, we shall get information as given in below screenshot:

```
ubuntu@ip-172-31-33-127:~/sample_monitoring$ curl localhost:9446/healthz
{"status":"OK","time":"2020-05-22T06:11:03.495131162"}ubuntu@ip-172-31-33-127:~/sample_monitoring$
ubuntu@ip-172-31-33-127:~/sample_monitoring$
ubuntu@ip-172-31-33-127:~/sample_monitoring$ curl localhost:9444/healthz
{"status":"OK","time":"2020-05-22T06:11:14.720105096Z"}ubuntu@ip-172-31-33-127:~/sample_monitoring$
ubuntu@ip-172-31-33-127:~/sample_monitoring$
ubuntu@ip-172-31-33-127:~/sample_monitoring$ curl localhost:9444/logspec
{"spec":"info"}
ubuntu@ip-172-31-33-127:~/sample_monitoring$
```

Figure 8.88: Operation endpoints

Same way we can call `/version` endpoint as well. So far, so good, we have been able to explore three out of four operation capabilities, and now we would talk about the Metrics part for which we shall be using Prometheus and Grafana.

In the same `docker-compose` file where we have given service definition for all of our containers, we shall now provide service details for Prometheus and Grafana. The configuration given here is the bare minimum, which enables us to download and run the container for both. To make full use of both of these, I would suggest to read more about their configuration properties and enable them:

```
prometheus:
  container_name: prometheus
  image: prom/prometheus
  ports:
    - 9090:9090
  command:
    - --config.file=/etc/prometheus/prometheus.yml
  volumes:
    - ./prometheus.yml:/etc/prometheus/prometheus.yml
  networks:
    - basic
  depends_on:
    - orderer.example.com
    - peer0.org1.example.com

grafana:
  container_name: grafana
  image: grafana/grafana
  ports:
    - 3000:3000
  networks:
    - basic
  depends_on:
    - prometheus
```

Figure 8.89: Prometheus and Grafana definition

Whereas we have our operational metrics enabled on orderer and peer, Prometheus and Grafana are available. Still, we need to define certain configurations for Prometheus so that it can start fetching the operational metrics, and that is done via the YAML file. If you closely look at the Prometheus definition in the command section, we are passing a config file flag along with the path of the `prometheus.yaml` file. This file defines the configurations that Prometheus is supposed to use:

```
global:
  scrape_interval: 15s
  evaluation_interval: 15s
scrape_configs:
- job_name: 'prometheus'
  scrape_interval: 10s
  static_configs:
    - targets: ['localhost:9090']
- job_name: 'hyperledger_metrics'
  scrape_interval: 10s
  static_configs:
    - targets: ['peer0.org1.example.com:9444', 'orderer.example.com:9446']
```

Figure 8.90: prometheus.yaml

If you look at the file, you will notice that we have provided two jobs of scrape configurations. One is for Prometheus itself, and the second one is for the fabric network. We enabled **9446** for orderer, and **9444** for Org1 peer both are given as targets, and scrape interval is given as 10 seconds. Again, this is a very simplistic view, and readers are encouraged to explore more of this.

Now, we have Prometheus scraping the orderer and peer operational metrics, and we would look at how this can be viewed in the Prometheus dashboard. Prometheus server runs at **9090** port and if we hit `http://<host>:9090` then we shall get the following dashboard:

Figure 8.91: Prometheus dashboard

If we expand the dropdown right next to the Execute button, you would realize that it is showing all the operational metrics parameters that we looked earlier:

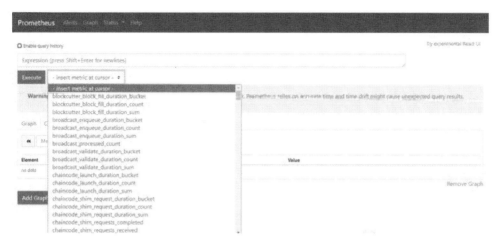

Figure 8.92: Operation metric parameters

It proved to be a great resource of information to determine the status of orderer and peer as to how they are behaving, in the below picture just to explore it bit further, we selected one of the parameters of `ledger_blockchain_height` and clicked on **Execute** button, and we were displayed following results. It shows the real power that the enabling of operational metrics and Prometheus bring for us:

Figure 8.93: ledger_blockchain_height

We have now been able to monitor the operational metrics using Prometheus, then why would we need Grafana. It is quite a popular analytical and visualization tool that helps bring data together in such a fashion that it is efficient and organized. Grafana works on the concept of data source, and they could be Prometheus, AWS CloudWatch, MySQL, and many others. So, from an enterprise perspective, it provides a single window to monitor data coming from various data sources.

It allows users to better understand the metrics of their data through queries, informative visualizations, and alerts.

Since we already have Grafana defined in our `docker-compose` file, so it's already up and running, and to access that you simply need to do is `http://<host>:3000`.

Once you hit this URL, you would get the following Login screen:

Figure 8.94: Grafana Login

You can use admin/admin as username and password to login to the Grafana. Since it is a fresh installation and we have not configured any data source or dashboard, we would simply get the screen as below, and we are expected to add a data source:

Figure 8.95

Once we click on **Add data source**, it shows us a list of databases that we can use; we would simply select Prometheus and then provide basic configurations such as host and port where Prometheus is running and save the configuration.

Now, if we go to explore options in the left side nav bar and click on **Metrics** dropdown, we would all the operational metrics, but now everything is being presented in the dashboard. We could see that we have selected **chaincode_shim_ requests_received**, and its showing counts as 1:

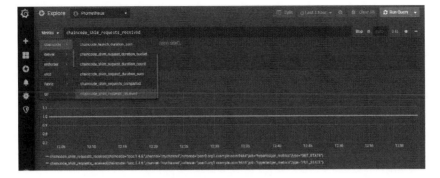

Figure 8.96: Operation Metrics

To see the change in the dashboard, we executed one query of `initCar` and then observed in the dashboard and found that count has changed to 2, and we did observe this in the graph as well in the table:

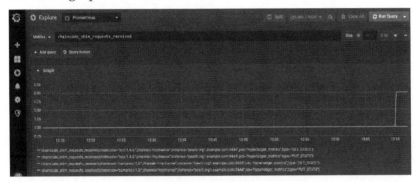

Figure 8.97: Chaincode metrics

Below is the same data in table format:

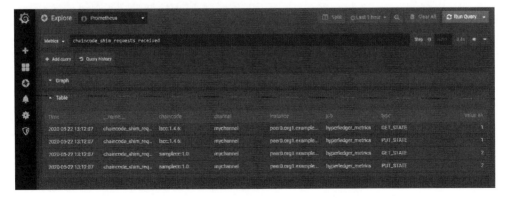

Figure 8.98: Chaincode metrics in table format

I hope, by now, you must have a fair idea of the monitoring aspect of Hyperledger Fabric and how the use of Prometheus and Grafana can increase the experience.

Fabric CA

In all our examples, that we have worked so far, we have generated crypto materials using cryptogen, which is quite fast and easy to use. However, crypto materials generated from cryptogen tools are meant to be used only in the development environment and not recommended for higher environments. Ideally, crypto materials should be coming from a certificate authority. Hyperledger Fabric provides its custom implementation of certificate authority in the form of Hyperledger Fabric CA as an alternative to cryptogen.

This section would give you a high-level walkthrough of the Fabric CA and would recommend going through the official documentation to explore it further. There are two main components of Fabric CA. The first is the Fabric CA Server, and the second is the Fabric CA Client.

Fabric CA server helps in:

- Registration of identities, please recall every participant in the Hyperledger Fabric network is issued an identity to be able to interact with the network. These participants could be peer, orderer, admin, user, or application.

- Issuance of Enrollment Certificates or ECerts that contains every information about the participants.

- Like any other certificate authority, in certificate renewal and revocation.

Fabric CA server exposes a REST API server with all the endpoints that show all the features it provides. You can get the swagger file for Fabric CA server from the GitHub and then explore that in the swagger editor to see what all functionalities it exposes. I have taken the swagger file from **https://github.com/hyperledger/fabric-ca/blob/master/swagger/swagger-fabric-ca.json** and then copied that in the online swagger editor and got the following.

You can see that CA Server exposes a lot of endpoints that can be used for various activities such as register, enroll, re-enroll, and so on. We would also explore some of the APIs, though through the use of Fabric CA clients:

Fabric CA Server API `0.7.0`

Hyperledger Fabric CA Server APIs provides certificate authority services for the blockchain.

Schemes
```
HTTPS    ∨
```

fabric-ca-server Fabric CA server APIs   ∨

GET	/api/v1/cainfo
POST	/api/v1/enroll
POST	/api/v1/idemix/credential
POST	/api/v1/idemix/cri
POST	/api/v1/reenroll
POST	/api/v1/register
POST	/api/v1/revoke
POST	/api/v1/gencrl
GET	/api/v1/affiliations

Figure 8.99: Fabric CA Server API

Hyperledger Fabric CA binaries are separate from main Hyperledger Fabric binaries, and so is their installation. To install Fabric CA binaries, ensure that GO is installed and the **GOPATH** environment variable is set correctly. Just for reference, it is usually as given following; however, you are encouraged to go as per your local settings:

```
export GOPATH=$HOME/go
export PATH=$PATH:$GOPATH/bin
```

Figure 8.100: GOPATH

Once you are sure about GOPATH settings, you can run the following command to get Fabric CA binaries:

```
go get -u github.com/hyperledger/fabric-ca/cmd/...
```

Figure 8.101: Fabric CA installation

Once the above step has been executed successfully, you should be able to see `fabric-ca-server` and `fabric-ca-client` binaries under the `$GOPATH/bin` folder. Since this is set under PATH, so you can run these binaries from anywhere.

Now, since you have server and client available, you can start the server, provide it various configurations, and use fabric ca client to create identities for the network participants.

To start the server, you can run the following command:

```
fabric-ca-server start -b admin:adminpw
```

Figure 8.102: *CA Server start command*

`-b` is bootstrap identity and `admin:adminpw` are the credentials to start the server for the very first time. You can change the credentials if you wish to. Using this command for the first time helps initialize the fabric CA server, and there are a lot of artifacts that get generated when we run this command.

Following is the console that gets print out when we run this command; you can see that it starts listening on port `7054`:

```
ubuntu@ip-172-31-33-127:~/sample_fabric-ca/server$ fabric-ca-server start -b admin:adminpw
2020/05/24 05:31:36 [INFO] Created default configuration file at /home/ubuntu/sample_fabric-ca/server/fabric-ca-server-config.yaml
2020/05/24 05:31:36 [INFO] Starting server in home directory: /home/ubuntu/sample_fabric-ca/server
2020/05/24 05:31:36 [INFO] Server Version: 2.0.0
2020/05/24 05:31:36 [INFO] Server Levels: &{Identity:2 Affiliation:1 Certificate:1 Credential:1 RAInfo:1 Nonce:1}
2020/05/24 05:31:36 [WARNING] &{69 The specified CA certificate file /home/ubuntu/sample_fabric-ca/server/ca-cert.pem does not exist}
2020/05/24 05:31:36 [INFO] generating key: &{A:ecdsa S:256}
2020/05/24 05:31:36 [INFO] encoded CSR
2020/05/24 05:31:36 [INFO] signed certificate with serial number 722866232729500271725234268980039586043476108993
2020/05/24 05:31:36 [INFO] The CA key and certificate were generated for CA
2020/05/24 05:31:36 [INFO] The key was stored by BCCSP provider 'SW'
2020/05/24 05:31:36 [INFO] The certificate is at: /home/ubuntu/sample_fabric-ca/server/ca-cert.pem
2020/05/24 05:31:36 [INFO] Initialized sqlite3 database at /home/ubuntu/sample_fabric-ca/server/fabric-ca-server.db
2020/05/24 05:31:36 [INFO] The issuer key was successfully stored. The public key is at: /home/ubuntu/sample_fabric-ca/server/IssuerPu
buntu/sample_fabric-ca/server/msp/keystore/IssuerSecretKey
2020/05/24 05:31:36 [INFO] Idemix issuer revocation public and secret keys were generated for CA ''
2020/05/24 05:31:36 [INFO] The revocation key was successfully stored. The public key is at: /home/ubuntu/sample_fabric-ca/server/Issu
 is at: /home/ubuntu/sample_fabric-ca/server/msp/keystore/IssuerRevocationPrivateKey
2020/05/24 05:31:36 [INFO] Home directory for default CA: /home/ubuntu/sample_fabric-ca/server
2020/05/24 05:31:36 [INFO] Operation Server Listening on 127.0.0.1:9443
2020/05/24 05:31:36 [INFO] Listening on http://0.0.0.0:7054
```

Figure 8.103: *CA Server start console logs*

Alongside, it generates a couple of artifacts, for brevity we created a separate folder as server and then ran the command. Once the server started up, we checked the listing of the directory, and it showed the following screenshot:

```
ubuntu@ip-172-31-33-127:~/sample_fabric-ca/server$ ll
total 104
drwxrwxr-x 3 ubuntu ubuntu  4096 May 24 05:37 ./
drwxrwxr-x 4 ubuntu ubuntu  4096 May 24 05:36 ../
-rw-r--r-- 1 ubuntu ubuntu   843 May 24 05:31 IssuerPublicKey
-rw-r--r-- 1 ubuntu ubuntu   215 May 24 05:31 IssuerRevocationPublicKey
-rw-r--r-- 1 ubuntu ubuntu   786 May 24 05:31 ca-cert.pem
-rw-r--r-- 1 ubuntu ubuntu 19614 May 24 05:31 fabric-ca-server-config.yaml
-rw-r--r-- 1 ubuntu ubuntu 61440 May 24 05:37 fabric-ca-server.db
drwxr-xr-x 3 ubuntu ubuntu  4096 May 24 05:31 msp/
ubuntu@ip-172-31-33-127:~/sample_fabric-ca/server$
```

Figure 8.104: *Server folder listing*

Fabric CA server maintains all the identities in the SQLite database; this is by default, and however, it gives us the option to use MySQL, PostgreSQL, or LDAP. We can see that `fabric-ca-server.db` file, this is the SQLite database for the Fabric caCA server. One of the important things that it generates is a config file by the name of `fabric-ca-server-config.yml,` and this is the one which provides us with the configurations that we can change and restart the server. These configurations help us customize the ca server behavior as per our needs. We shall just have a look at a couple of important sections.

Following is the registry section, and it shows the details of the bootstrap identity, which is admin. We can use admin to create more identities and specify attributes that shall be a subset of the attributes present here. For example, if admin is creating an identity for a user, then it may make hf.Revoker: false as the user is not required that role. Attributes shown as hf.* are fabric specific attributes, and then while creating an identity, we can specify custom attributes. These custom attributes can be read by chaincode and can help in attribute-based access control, that is, ABAC:

```
registry:
    # Maximum number of times a password/secret can be reused for enrollment
    # (default: -1, which means there is no limit)
    maxenrollments: -1

    # Contains identity information which is used when LDAP is disabled
    identities:
       - name: admin
         pass: adminpw
         type: client
         affiliation: ""
         attrs:
            hf.Registrar.Roles: "*"
            hf.Registrar.DelegateRoles: "*"
            hf.Revoker: true
            hf.IntermediateCA: true
            hf.GenCRL: true
            hf.Registrar.Attributes: "*"
            hf.AffiliationMgr: true
```

Figure 8.105: Registry section

Another section is the database section; you can see that by default SQLite database is configured; however, MySQL or PostgreSQL can also be used. Since SQLite is an embedded database while setting up CA servers is a cluster, other databases are required to be used:

```
db:
    type: sqlite3
    datasource: fabric-ca-server.db
    tls:
        enabled: false
        certfiles:
        client:
            certfile:
            keyfile:
```

Figure 8.106: DB section

Likewise, there are multiple sections in the YAML file that can be configured for `fabric ca server` as per organization needs.

Now, we shall move to Fabric CA client and try to generate an identity that would give us a fair idea as to how this works.

We already have the server initialized, and now we would enroll the admin to the CA server. For that, we shall do:

```
fabric-ca-client enroll -u http://admin:adminpw@localhost:7054
```

It would generate an `msp` folder for admin and yaml file that can be configured for `fabric-ca-client`.

Once the bootstrap admin is enrolled, it can generate different identities. Let's create an admin type identity admin2, and we would generate its msp.

We shall run the following command of registering `admin2` with its name, affiliation, and attributes. Once we register this new identity, it would generate a password or better known as a secret. It needs to be passed on to `admin2` so that `admin2` can generate its msp:

```
ubuntu@ip-172-31-33-127:~/sample_fabric-ca/client$ fabric-ca-client register --id.name admin2 --id.affiliation org1.depart
ment1 --id.attrs 'hf.Revoker=true,admin=true:ecert'
2020/05/24 12:52:59 [INFO] Configuration file location: /home/ubuntu/sample_fabric-ca/client/admin/fabric-ca-client-config
.yaml
Password: QlglLyahgOUx
```

Figure 8.107: Register admin2

Once admin2 gets this password, it needs to enroll with the CA server so that it can get its MSP. Since we are running these commands on the same machine, for brevity, I created a folder admin2, set the FABRIC_CA_CLIENT_HOME as this is the folder where the msp folder would get created. Now, we run enroll command with id as admin2 and password what we got back in the registration process:

```
ubuntu@ip-172-31-33-127:~/sample_fabric-ca/client$ mkdir admin2
ubuntu@ip-172-31-33-127:~/sample_fabric-ca/client$ export FABRIC_CA_CLIENT_HOME=$HOME/sample_fabric-ca/client/admin2
ubuntu@ip-172-31-33-127:~/sample_fabric-ca/client$ fabric-ca-client enroll -u http://admin2:QlglLyahgOUx@localhost:7054
```

Figure 8.108: Enroll admin2

Once we run the enroll command, there is an msp folder that gets created, and it contains the `signcerts` that act as public key and file in Keystore that acts as a private key, along with that we get ca certificate as well:

```
ubuntu@ip-172-31-33-127:~/sample_fabric-ca/client/admin2/msp$ tree
├── IssuerPublicKey
├── IssuerRevocationPublicKey
├── cacerts
│   └── localhost-7054.pem
├── keystore
│   └── 7ff958fd6c6507c49d04b18c0828eb3db59cff2e7149de75a8d78d4461f8b970_sk
├── signcerts
│   └── cert.pem
└── user
```

Figure 8.109: MSP admin2

If you go back and compare it with the `msp` folder of an admin that we created through cryptogen, you would find that we have got the same setup, but this time with the CA server. With this, we have come to the end of this section.

Conclusion

With this now, we come to an end for this chapter, it's been a long one, and at times we saw a lot of complexities. Understanding Hyperledger Fabric from a theoretical perspective is one aspect of learning, but putting that in implementation is a tricky one. From the implementation perspective, there are two parts of Hyperledger Fabric; one is setting up the network and understanding the nuances of various configuration changes, network changes that we might have to do as and when requirements pop up.

In this chapter, we laid down a framework of approaching the setting up of Hyperledger Network. We dedicated separate sections as to how we should be progressing with it. Defining a business network is an important step where we need to put our heads down in understanding and figuring who we are making this network for, what are the kind of identities we need to create, need to design business rules that everyone should agree to and needs to go in chaincode. Once with basics done, we jumped into defining the network and worked out its topology. In doing that, we created a lot of configurations and, at times, made use of fabric provided utilities to generate crypto material and channel artifacts. Then we made use of docker orchestration to come up with the network. Once the network was up and running, we needed to install and invoke a chaincode so that we can do some meaningful business on the network.

We complemented the entire setup with a couple of real-time examples and supporting code and configuration on the GitHub so that readers can play along with the code and try out different things. These examples also allowed us to explore different other utilities by which we could delve into actual configuration files and play around with it.

While setting up the network is an important part of hyperledger fabric, equally important is that we understand the nitty-gritty of smart contracts, in the next chapter we would explore smart contract and the vital APIs that fabric provides us to play with the ledger.

Troubleshooting tips

- **Issue**: Permission denied while trying to connect to the Docker daemon socket at `unix:///var/run/docker.sock`

Solution:
1. Open Terminal.

2. Enter `sudo -H gedit /etc/sysctl.conf` and open the configuration file and add the following lines at the end:

   ```
   net.ipv6.conf.all.disable_ipv6 = 1

   net.ipv6.conf.default.disable_ipv6 = 1

   net.ipv6.conf.lo.disable_ipv6 = 1
   ```

3. Save and exit, then Run:

   ```
   cat /proc/sys/net/ipv6/conf/all/disable_ipv6
   ```

   If it reports, 1 means you have disabled IPV6.

   If it reports 0, then please follow *Step 4* and *Step 5*.

4. Type command `sudo sysctl -p`. You will see this in the Terminal:

   ```
   net.ipv6.conf.all.disable_ipv6 = 1

   net.ipv6.conf.default.disable_ipv6 = 1

   net.ipv6.conf.lo.disable_ipv6 = 1
   ```

5. Repeat above *Step 3* and it will now report 1.

CHAPTER 9

Smart Contracts

This chapter is again going to be deep technical in terms of understanding the smart contract. From the deployment and implementation perspective, the smart contract is the second most crucial aspect of the Hyperledger Fabric blockchain platform other than understanding the core concepts of setting up the network. While setting up the network, we went through orderer, peer, configurations, and so on, and at the same time, smart contracts are the code program that gets deployed on the peer.

Structure

- Introduction to smart contracts
  - o Bird's eye view
  - o Anatomy
- Smart contract (chaincode for developers)
  - o Writing a smart contract
  - o Smart contract unit testing
  - o Dev mode testing
- Advanced concepts
  - o Private data collection

o State database (CouchDB) interaction

o Chaincode queries

- Chaincode (chaincode for operators)
- Logging
- Error Handling

Objective

In this chapter, we shall go through various constructs that we need to keep in mind while writing smart contracts. We would also look into the process of deployment of smart contracts, the use of APIs provided by fabric to interact with ledger, how chaincode interacts with each other, the role of system chaincode, and so on. After reading this chapter, you should be able to write and deploy a chaincode and understand the nuances of that.

Please note that, in Hyperledger Fabric, smart contracts are also called chaincode. There is a subtle difference between the two, as we have seen in earlier chapters, but we may use them interchangeably in this chapter.

Introduction to smart contracts

In the last chapter, we learned about setting up a Hyperledger Fabric blockchain network, where we explored various configurations and mechanisms as to how different organizations can come together and create a network. We also explored a couple of real-world use cases concerning network as to what all we need to do in case there is an organization that wants to join the network in the middle of a running network. Similarly, we also learned about joining a peer node for an organization that is already part of the network.

Whereas setting up the network and knowing it various configurations is an essential part of learning Hyperledger Fabric, the same time, we also need to appreciate the fact that just making a network would not solve any purpose. Recall that organizations do come together if they could derive value out of the network. Also, organizations do come together because they want to achieve a common objective. This common objective turns out to be a business agreement; that is, they see a value in carrying out the business transaction on the blockchain network. Business transactions are bounded by business-driven agreed rules between the organizations. In this chapter, we shall delve into how we can make these business rules available to the different participant organizations.

Hyperledger Fabric or, for that matter, most of the blockchain provides the notion of smart contracts. Smart contracts are nothing but business agreement encapsulated in the code. They are like any other code programs though they are deployed on the peer nodes and get executed as part of transaction execution. We learned in the transaction flow of Hyperledger Fabric how execution plays an essential role in the entire process, and smart contracts are the ones that get executed. Smart contracts get executed as part of the transaction process, and they, in turn, interact with the ledger on the peer to change the state an asset.

The sole objective of a blockchain network is to have a shared ledger, and this ledger maintains the assets, transactions are used to manage the state of the asset. To maintain the state of the asset, business logic is invoked, which governs the rule for managing the state of the asset. The smart contract is something that encapsulates the business rules to manage the state of the asset. In Hyperledger Fabric, the same way chaincode exposes the state management feature for the asset through exposing one or more functions. These functions in the chaincode become the invocation point for the transactions. Applications or client initiates these transactions which in turn invoke these functions of chaincode to manage the state of the asset lying in the ledger. We shall now be looking at the smart contracts from two aspects, first is a high-level view, where how it fits into an overall ecosystem of the Hyperledger Fabric network and the inner composition of the smart contract.

Bird's eye view

In this subsection, we would see what smart contract functions do and how the client interacts with them. Smart contract functions, where on the one hand, gives the flexibility of executing business logic to change the state of an asset and, at the same time, provides the way to read the state of the asset as well.

The following figure describes the interaction between the client and the functions that it invokes on the chaincode side. The chain codes are deployed on **Peer** nodes, and the client invokes chaincode functions through **invoke** and **query**. These invocations can be done either through cli or through the application that makes use of fabric provided SDK:

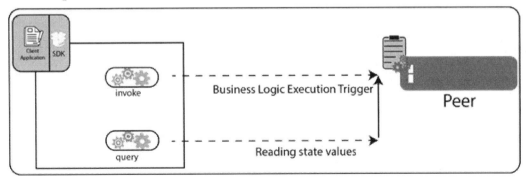

Figure 9.1: Smart Contract invocation

Have a look at the chaincode commands that we ran through `cli` in the last chapter for calling the `invoke` and `query` function:

```
peer chaincode invoke -C mychannel -n samplecc -c '{"function":"initCar","Args":["Ashwani","Blue","BMW"]}'

peer chaincode query -C mychannel -n samplecc -c '{"function":"readCar","Args":["Ashwani"]}'
```

Figure 9.2: Peer chaincode commands

-c denotes the constructor argument. And the input is passed as a JSON parameter; the function is the name of the method that we would want to call, such as `initCar` and `readCar`, and then `Args` is the array of strings.

Let's have a look at the function definition in the chaincode and how it maps to the chaincode call. `readCar` is the function name, and `args` is the string array reference that gets the value being passed as part of chaincode call. So, `args[0]` would give us `Ashwani`. We shall dive deep into all these things, just wanted to give you a glimpse of what we have done in the last chapter while calling the chaincode:

```
func (t *SampleChaincode) readCar(stub shim.ChaincodeStubInterface, args []string) pb.Response
```

Figure 9.3: readCar method definition

We shall be going into the details of these in the following sections.

Anatomy

In real life, when businesses do the transaction with each other, they all need to agree on a standard set of rules, constraints, data, processes, and so on, and that becomes their contract. These contracts then become business guidelines that define and govern the interaction among these parties. Smart contracts help translate these contracts into executable code. A smart contract enforces the agreed governance rules once a transaction happens, and this code gets executed.

A simple example has been shown in the below image; for instance, the `transfer` method shows the change of ownership of a car for one organization to another. It is a pretty straightforward code; however, at the same time, various rules can be enforced during the transfer, such as the given timeframe for a transfer, commitment of funds before the transfer, and so on:

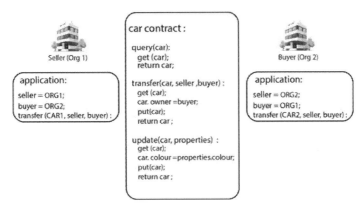

Figure 9.4: *Car smart contract*

Chaincode

We have been using term chaincode interchangeably with a smart contract; however, as discussed in one of the earlier chapters, there is an essential difference between the two:

- Smart contracts are meant to contain the logic that gets executed and interacts with the ledger to manage and maintain the state of the asset
- Chaincode governs the administrative aspects of smart contracts; that is how smart contracts are packaged in a chaincode and then deployed on the network

In the below image, for a vehicle chaincode, there are three smart contracts. So, a smart contract is defined within a chaincode, and there could be multiple chain codes. A chaincode is something that gets deployed on the network, and once a chaincode is deployed, all smart contracts included in the chaincode shall be deployed at once. A chaincode can be thought of as a technical container of a co-related set of smart contracts that are used for smart contracts installation and instantiation.

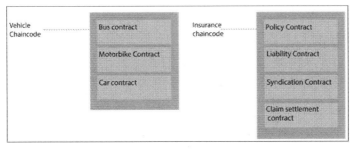

Figure 9.5: *Chaincode comprising smart contracts*

Like we have discussed smart contracts and chaincode, now we shall devote one subsection each to smart contract and chaincode, interestingly they map to *Chaincode for Developers* and *Chaincode for Operators* as per official documentation of Hyperledger Fabric.

Smart contract (chaincode for developers)

In this section, we would delve into the actual writing of smart contracts, and how we could make use of Chaincode SHIM APIs for interacting with the ledger. Once we have written a smart contract, we would then get into the unit testing part of it with an appropriate testing package of Go Lang and SHIM. Once we are through with unit testing, we shall do a dev testing by having a simple network running and then deploying our chaincode there. It shall be of primary interest to developers who would want to write/test smart contracts.

Writing a smart contract

Hyperledger Fabric provides chaincode writing in Go, NodeJS, and Java. Go seems to be popular choice mainly for the reason it is the first one that gets picked up in terms of providing the SDK by Hyperledger Fabric with new features get introduced in Go first. Java was the last to add among three.

In this section, we would go through a smart contract in Go Lang. Though you do not need to be an expert in Go Lang to understand the following code snippets; however, a basic understanding of syntax and how the Go Lang work, in general, would help you easily understand the code. So, before you move further, try spending some time understanding Go Lang. There are enough resources available online to help you grasp the concepts.

Moving on, while writing a smart contract, we need to ensure that the program must implement the *Chaincode'* interface. This interface provides methods that are called when a transaction is received.

The Chaincode SHIM APIs has two interfaces
- Chaincode interface
- ChaincodeStubInterface interface

The following screenshot shows the methods in the `Chaincode interface;` it has two methods `Init` and `Invoke`:

```
// Chaincode interface must be implemented by all chaincodes. The fabric runs
// the transactions by calling these functions as specified.
type Chaincode interface {
    // Init is called during Instantiate transaction after the chaincode container
    // has been established for the first time, allowing the chaincode to
    // initialize its internal data
    Init(stub ChaincodeStubInterface) pb.Response

    // Invoke is called to update or query the ledger in a proposal transaction.
    // Updated state variables are not committed to the ledger until the
    // transaction is committed.
    Invoke(stub ChaincodeStubInterface) pb.Response
}
```

Figure 9.6: Chaincode interface

Hyperledger Fabric requires every chaincode to implement this interface; `Init` gets called when we invoke `peer instantiate` command from cli or client. It helps chaincode to initializes to its internal state.

Now, we would go through a chaincode that we have used in all our sample programs; the import section is like in any other language is required to include the required dependencies for the chaincode. Other than the general use package of Go, we have included shim and peer package.

`SampleChaincode` is a struct that acts as a receiver for Chaincode functions; we have added another **struct** for the `car`, which we shall be treated as an asset for our program. In the `car` structure, we have defined a couple of attributes that are passed by the client to create a record of car on the ledger as an asset:

```go
import (
    "encoding/json"
    "fmt"
    "strings"
    "github.com/hyperledger/fabric/core/chaincode/shim"
    pb "github.com/hyperledger/fabric/protos/peer"
)

type SampleChaincode struct {
}

type car struct {
    ObjectType string `json:"docType"` //docType is used to distinguish the various types of objects in state database
    Owner      string `json:"owner"`
    Color      string `json:"color"`
    Model      string `json:"model"`
}

// Init initializes chaincode
// ===========================
func (t *SampleChaincode) Init(stub shim.ChaincodeStubInterface) pb.Response {
    return shim.Success(nil)
}
```

Figure 9.7: Car struct

Now, if you recall how we did instantiate chaincode, which eventually called the `Init` method of this chaincode and hence ending up by spawning a separate chaincode container for that specific peer, which called up `instantiate` command:

```
peer chaincode instantiate -o orderer.example.com:7050 -C mychannel -n samplecc -v 1.0 -c '{"Args":[""]}'
-P " OR('Org1MSP.member','Org2MSP.member')"
```

Figure 9.8: Instantiate command

Though there are several flags that we are passing with this command and we have discussed them in the last chapter; however, if you –c flag, we are passing no arguments to the `Init` method and so we could see in chaincode that we are doing nothing and just returning success. It has been done here only for simplicity purpose, whereas you should pass arguments here which are required to initialize the asset during this phase.

The second exciting part of the chaincode is the Invoke function, which is also part of the `Chaincode interface.` In this, we could see that we are getting the handle of ChaincodeStubInterface; this was available to us in the `Init` function as well though we didn't use it there:

```
// Invoke - Our entry point for Invocations
// ========================================
func (t *SampleChaincode) Invoke(stub shim.ChaincodeStubInterface) pb.Response {
    function, args := stub.GetFunctionAndParameters()
    fmt.Println("invoke is running " + function)

    // Handle different functions
    if function == "initCar" { //create a new car
        return t.initCar(stub, args)
    } else if function == "transferCar" { //change owner of a specific car
        return t.transferCar(stub, args)
    } else if function == "delete" { //delete a car
        return t.delete(stub, args)
    } else if function == "readCar" { //read a car
        return t.readCar(stub, args)
    }
    fmt.Println("invoke did not find func: " + function) //error
    return shim.Error("Received unknown function invocation")
}
```

Figure 9.9: Invoke function

`ChaincodeStubInterface` helps us to access and modify the ledger; it does have more than 30+ methods that we could leverage. The following snapshot is just part of the interface; Hyperledger Fabric has given enough details with every function as to what it is supposed to do:

```
// ChaincodeStubInterface is used by deployable chaincode apps to access and
// modify their ledgers
type ChaincodeStubInterface interface {
    // GetArgs returns the arguments intended for the chaincode Init and Invoke
    // as an array of byte arrays.
    GetArgs() [][]byte

    // GetStringArgs returns the arguments intended for the chaincode Init and
    // Invoke as a string array. Only use GetStringArgs if the client passes
    // arguments intended to be used as strings.
    GetStringArgs() []string

    // GetFunctionAndParameters returns the first argument as the function
    // name and the rest of the arguments as parameters in a string array.
    // Only use GetFunctionAndParameters if the client passes arguments intended
    // to be used as strings.
    GetFunctionAndParameters() (string, []string)
    .
    .
    .
    .
```

Figure 9.10: *ChaincodeStubInterface*

However, coming back to our Invoke function, we are calling 'GetFunctionAndParameters' on the ChaincodeStubInterface handle, and it returns us with function and string [] in args. This method then checks for function name and parameters as passed in the invoke command. Given out function is initCar, it invokes the chaincode method on initCar and passes the reference of ChaincodeStubInterface and passed arguments:

Recall, while setting up the network, we used the following command; this was an invoke command; that is, we wanted to write something on the ledger. In this case, we were initializing a car asset by passing parameters and calling initCar function:

```
peer chaincode invoke -C mychannel -n samplecc -c '{"function":"initCar","Args":["Ashwani","Blue","BMW"]}'
```

Figure 9.11: *Chaincode Invoke*

In initCar function, we are doing a couple of things, and they are as follows:

- Expected argument number check
- Input verification
- Checking if asset already exists
- Create an asset object, in our case its car
- Saving asset (car) in the ledger
- Once done, returning success

Please note that these are more of vanilla steps that we are doing to make things understand most simply; however, these smart contracts can handle complex of the logic depending on the business requirements like any other programming language, or any other application would do.

Following code snippets are from `initCar` function divided into sections as mentioned above; however, full code is available in GitHub repository in any of the projects you may choose to look into that we have deployed in the last chapter:

```
//     0        1        2
// "Ashwani", "Blue", "BMW"
if len(args) != 3 {
    return shim.Error("Incorrect number of arguments. Expecting 3")
}
```

Figure 9.12: Argument number check

Checking input argument types, you can check for type or range depending on the business need and validity of the arguments:

```
// ==== Inputs verification ====
if len(args[0]) <= 0 {
    return shim.Error("1st argument must be a non-empty string")
}
if len(args[1]) <= 0 {
    return shim.Error("2nd argument must be a non-empty string")
}
if len(args[2]) <= 0 {
    return shim.Error("3rd argument must be a non-empty string")
```

Figure 9.13: Input verification

Populating asset and validating if it already exists in the ledger:

```
// Populating asset (car) struct
owner := args[0]
color := strings.ToLower(args[1])
model := strings.ToLower(args[2])


// ==== Check if car already exists ====
carAsBytes, err := stub.GetState(owner)
if err != nil {
    return shim.Error("Failed to get car: " + err.Error())
} else if carAsBytes != nil {
    fmt.Println("This car already exists for owner: " + owner)
    return shim.Error("This car already exists: " + owner)
}
```

Figure 9.14: Asset check-in the ledger

In the above code snippet, we have used an essential function of `ChaincodeStubInterface` that is `GetState`, which is responsible for getting the asset state based on the key. Likewise, we have `PutState` and `DelState` as an essential function in this interface. I would suggest having a look at the functions of this interface to realize how SHIM API in totality can help us interact with ledgers. Just for quick reference, I am putting the definition of these functions. Hyperledger has provided good enough documentation for these functions:

```
// GetState returns the value of the specified `key` from the
// ledger. Note that GetState doesn't read data from the writeset, which
// has not been committed to the ledger. In other words, GetState doesn't
// consider data modified by PutState that has not been committed.
// If the key does not exist in the state database, (nil, nil) is returned.
GetState(key string) ([]byte, error)

// PutState puts the specified `key` and `value` into the transaction's
// writeset as a data-write proposal. PutState doesn't effect the ledger
// until the transaction is validated and successfully committed.
// Simple keys must not be an empty string and must not start with null
// character (0x00), in order to avoid range query collisions with
// composite keys, which internally get prefixed with 0x00 as composite
// key namespace.
PutState(key string, value []byte) error

// DelState records the specified `key` to be deleted in the writeset of
// the transaction proposal. The `key` and its value will be deleted from
// the ledger when the transaction is validated and successfully committed.
DelState(key string) error
```

Figure 9.15: State-related functions

In the last set, we create a `car` object, marshaling it, and saving it using the `PutState` method:

```
// ==== Create car object and marshal to JSON ====
objectType := "Car"
car := &car{objectType, owner, color, model}
carJSONasBytes, err := json.Marshal(car)
if err != nil {
    return shim.Error(err.Error())
}
// === Save car to state ===
err = stub.PutState(owner, carJSONasBytes)
if err != nil {
    return shim.Error(err.Error())
}
// ==== Car saved. Return success ====
fmt.Println("- end init car")
return shim.Success(nil)
```

Figure 9.16: Saving asset

The entire objective of taking you through one of the methods to help you understand how do we write simplest of chaincode and then invoke it and have also touched upon various essential methods that SHIM API provides. This example by no means is a comprehensive one to understand the smart contracts but for sure, a starting point, and understanding the very basics of the smart contracts.

Similarly, I would encourage you to go through the rest of the functions and understand the basics of a smart contract.

Now, if you were to take a step back and visualize the entire process of how we have used a smart contract that then following are the steps that we did to reach this level:

- We did set up a network through orderer, peer defined in the docker-compose file
- In same docker-compose file, we created a container for `cli` which has the mapping of chaincode from the host VM to docker container
- We provided a script to this cli container that, other than creating a channel and making peers join the channel, install the chaincode on peers.
- Having chaincode installed means, the chaincode build packet was now available to peers. We used the `peer chaincode install…` command with the required parameters.
- We then instantiated chaincode on one of the peers by calling `peer chaincode instantiate…` and required constructor arguments.
- Calling instantiate resulted in `init` method invocation, and chaincode container came up for that peer
- We then called peer `chaincode invoke` … and subsequently, initCar was called, and an asset of type car was created
- We changed the Identity Context of cli for Org2 and then called peer `chaincode query` … and got back the result of asset details on Org2 peer

Smart contract unit testing

While we just talked about the anatomy of the smart contract and did a code walkthrough of our smart contract that we have used in all our examples. Though in real life, we may not have that simple, smart contracts, and we may end up writing complex real-world business solutions. The clear thoughts on fundamentals of any concepts prove to be a stepping stone to move further, so I hope even the understanding of simplest of the smart contract understanding would help you move forward with higher speed.

As a developer, where at one end, you would write smart contracts, the other important aspect being a developer is to write unit tests for your smart contracts. Unit tests, in general, considered as part of code only, and the objective is to isolate parts of the program and test them in a manner that gives us visibility that individual parts are working correctly.

Since we have written our chaincode in Go Lang, we shall be using the Go Lang testing framework for unit testing. Similar testing frameworks are also available for NodeJS and Java. We shall be focussing on Go Lang only. Also, we shall be writing our unit test cases in Go Lang only. It is advisable that while you start working on writing smart contracts, it would be good if you could spend some time understanding Go Language, how we set various environment variables, and then a brief look in the Go Lang testing framework. Learning and understanding Go Lang are out of the purview of this book, yet I strongly recommend you to learn Go that would help you understand develop smart contracts better.

In Go Lang, the unit test framework is available in a package by the name of `testing`. Specific naming rules need to be followed while writing these test cases; also, those who are well versed with unit testing frameworks in other languages such as Java use assertions to verify the test results. In Go Lang, there is no concept of assertions; instead, developers would have to check the result on their own. While we have talked about naming rules:

- Test files follow the naming convention of `*_test.go`; you can follow this in the sample example that we would just talk about.
- Same way, test functions in this test file follow the naming pattern of Test*, for making it more readable, we are using `Test_<FunctionToTest> pattern,` you are free to use any pattern, but `Test` should be the prefix for the function name.

Hyperledger Fabric provides `MockStub`, which is the mock stub version of the `shim.ChaincodeStubInterface`. We make use of this `MockStub` for running the test functions, the instance of the `MockStub` helps us called `Init, Invoke`, and other functions of the chaincode that we want to test.

I would suggest that go and have a look at `MockStub` class in the `shim` package, though just highlighting two of the main functions that we have used in our chaincode unit test code. Have a look at the signature of the function. Both of the functions take the first argument as a string, which is a unique ID and a two-dimensional byte array for arguments:

```
// Initialise this chaincode, also starts and ends a transaction.
func (stub *MockStub) MockInit(uuid string, args [][]byte) pb.Response {
    stub.args = args
    stub.MockTransactionStart(uuid)
    res := stub.cc.Init(stub)
    stub.MockTransactionEnd(uuid)
    return res
}

// Invoke this chaincode, also starts and ends a transaction.
func (stub *MockStub) MockInvoke(uuid string, args [][]byte) pb.Response {
    stub.args = args
    stub.MockTransactionStart(uuid)
    res := stub.cc.Invoke(stub)
    stub.MockTransactionEnd(uuid)
    return res
}
```

Figure 9.17: MockStub functions

We would now have a look at the setup that we need to create to unit test the chaincode, and as well we would go through unit testing code. The setup is quite simple, chaincode and test file (follow the naming pattern) should be in the same package, and then we could do go `test`, and it would automatically pick up the test files and knows about the test functions given the name pattern.

The sample chaincode, the one that we have used in our sample programs, its unit test, along with instructions as to how to run this in `README.md` file at the GitHub location **https://github.com/ashwanihlf/sample_chaincodeUnitTest.git** or **in downloaded code sample.**

If you look at the unit testing file, the name of the file is `samplecc_test.go; recall _test` is required for a file to be made a unit testing file.

Following are the signature of the functions that we have used in the Unit Test; the objective is to use `MockInit` and `MockInvoke` to call actual chaincode methods. Other than that, we have used one another way of calling chain codes as well. Please note that this is not an exhaustive Unit test; however, the objective is to make readers aware of the process of writing Unit Test cases:

```
// Shows the use of shim.MockInit method to invoke init method of chaincode
func Test_MockInit(t *testing.T)

// Shows the use of direct calling of init method of chaincode
func Test_Init(t *testing.T)

// This function shows the iniatialization of the Car through initCar method by way of invoke
// same time we call readCar to check if the asset that we have saved is retrievable
func Test_InvokeInitCar(t *testing.T)


// Calling initCar directly than MockInvoke
func Test_initCar(t *testing.T)
```

Figure 9.18: Chaincode unit test methods

We shall now have a look at one of the `MockInit` and `MockInvoke` methods to get a good hold of the understanding.

Following is the code snippet from the unit test code that shows the `import` statement and `MockInit` method. If you look at the import section, `fmt` package is used for console output, `testing` is an essential package from Go Lang and a pointer to `testing.T'` is that passed to functions. There are a lot of methods that are used from `testing.T`; we have used `FailNow()`, which marks the function as having failed and stops the execution. Similarly, there is a function `Fail()`, which marks the function as having failed but continues execution. There are a lot of new methods; I would strongly suggest to review and use them in your Unit test cases:

```
import (
    "fmt"
    "testing"
    "github.com/hyperledger/fabric/core/chaincode/shim"
)

// Shows the use of shim.MockInit method to invoke init method of chaincode
func Test_MockInit(t *testing.T) {

    fmt.Println("--------Entering Test_MockInit--------")
    sampleCC := new(SampleChaincode)
    mockStub := shim.NewMockStub("mockstub", sampleCC)

    txId := "mockTxID"

    // First argument is uuid as String and second is argument, passing nil
    response := mockStub.MockInit(txId,nil)

    if s := response.GetStatus(); s != 200 {
        fmt.Println("Init test failed")
        t.FailNow()
    }
    fmt.Println("--------Exiting Test_MockInit--------")
}
```

Figure 9.19: *Unit test MockInit function*

The function `Test_MockInit` is used to call the `init` method of our chaincode; we are merely creating a `MockStub` object by calling `shim.newMockStub` method by passing the chaincode instance. `MockInit` method takes two parameters, first is uuid and the second one is the argument list since we are not using any arguments in the `init` method, we are merely passing nil. The return type is `Response`, which has got a couple of methods such as `GetStatus`, `GetMessage`, and `GetPayload`, and so on, to be used for the return type.

The following snapshot is the example of the test case where we are calling `MockInvoke` on shim that calls the `Invoke` method in the chaincode. In the signature, we saw that as arguments, we need to pass uuid and two-dimensional array of the byte that represents the function name and the required arguments. Likewise, in all our samples, we are trying to call `initCar` function with three arguments, and this is what we are doing through the `Invoke` function. Then in the same method execution, we are calling `readCar` method through `invoke`, and this time we are merely passing the name of the argument as `Ashwani` to see if the call before executed successfully and we were able to save the record. We should be able to retrieve it now.

In this method, we have used a `response.Getpayload` method we should get the same response as we were getting when we were running peer query commands. We have kept this simple, but ideally, you should have failure scenarios also to test:

```go
func Test_InvokeInitCar(t *testing.T) {

    fmt.Println("---------Entering Test_InvokeInitCar---------")
    // Instantiate mockStub using SampleChainCode as the target chaincode to unit test
    stub := shim.NewMockStub("mockStub", new(SampleChaincode))
    if stub == nil {
        t.Fatalf("MockStub creation failed")
    }
    // Here we perform a "mock invoke" to invoke the function "initVehiclePart" method with associated parameters
    // parameters are uuid and arguments.
    result := stub.MockInvoke("001",
        [][]byte[[]byte("initCar"),
            []byte("Ashwani"),
            []byte("Blue"),
            []byte("BMW")}})
    // We expect a shim.ok if all goes well
    if result.Status != shim.OK {
        t.Fatalf("Error Invoking method")
    }
    // calling the readCar on 'Ashwani' as we just persisted that
    response := stub.MockInvoke("002",
        [][]byte[[]byte("readCar"),
            []byte("Ashwani")})

    if response.Status != shim.OK {
        t.Fatalf("Error in readCar")
    }
    fmt.Println("Payload: " + string(response.GetPayload()))
    fmt.Println("---------Exiting Test_InvokeInitCar---------")
}
```

Figure 9.20: Unit Test MockInvoke function

Since the unit test is supposed to be run on the developer's machine, I ran the complete set on my windows machine and got the following output:

```
C:\Users\ashkumar9\go\src\sampletest>go test -v --tags nopkcs11
=== RUN   Test_MockInit
--------Entering Test_MockInit--------
--------Exiting Test_MockInit--------
--- PASS: Test_MockInit (0.00s)
=== RUN   Test_Init
--------Entering Test_Init--------
--------Exiting Test_Init--------
--- PASS: Test_Init (0.00s)
=== RUN   Test_InvokeInitCar
--------Entering Test_InvokeInitCar--------
invoke is running initCar
- start init car
- end init car
invoke is running readCar
Payload: {"docType":"Car","owner":"Ashwani","color":"blue","model":"bmw"}
--------Exiting Test_InvokeInitCar--------
--- PASS: Test_InvokeInitCar (0.00s)
=== RUN   Test_initCar
--------Entering Test_initCar--------
- start init car
- end init car
Status: 200
--------Entering Test_initCar--------
--- PASS: Test_initCar (0.00s)
PASS
ok      sampletest      4.125s
```

Figure 9.21: Unit Test cases result

Dev Mode Testing

The above two sections covered writing of the smart contract, so explored the code, and then the second part was around writing unit test cases and testing it. Once this much is done, a developer needs to test the chaincode with the network. Deploying the chaincode on the actual network may be time taking activity given the number of peers and other entities we might be running, so to be able to test the chaincode on a simulated network, Hyperledger Fabric provides dev mode. The usual mode is called net mode. In that case, chain codes are started and maintained by the peer. Though in the case of dev mode, the chaincode is started by the user. This mode helps developers in the development phase as it increases productivity in terms of rapid `code/build/run/debug cycle.`

Hyperledger Fabric has provided chaincode-docker-mode in fabric-samples that contain pre-generated crypto material and orderer block definition etc. which can help us deploy our chaincode on this network quite quickly.

To simplify and to make it easier to understand, for our readers, I have retrofitted the same folder in a separate project with our chaincode. It would help readers to understand the process quite quickly, and using the same chaincode that we have been using all through our sample programs would help them understand the concept faster.

To set up the project, you need to follow the steps as mentioned in README.md file at **https://github.com/ashwanihlf/sample_chaincodedevntest.git** or from downloaded code sample.

We have used the same `samplecc.go` chaincode to deploy it in this network in dev mode, and similarly, we have executed the same queries that we have been doing on our full-fledged network.

The steps are quite simple and mostly what we are doing in this is:

1. Starting the network by giving a simple command of docker-compose and the network with the following four containers would come up. An Orderer with a solo, simple peer a `cli` container and chaincode environment. It would be a running console that shows your network is up, and you can simple *Ctrl* + *C* to kill the environment:

```
ubuntu@ip-172-31-33-127:~/sample_chaincodedevntest$ docker ps
CONTAINER ID    IMAGE                        COMMAND               PORTS                                             NAMES
bb58a8525713    hyperledger/fabric-ccenv     "/bin/sh -c 'sleep 6…"                                                 chaincode
d11f2bf1799f    hyperledger/fabric-tools     "/bin/bash -c ./scri…"                                                 cli
1a3db0260cb3    hyperledger/fabric-peer      "peer node start --p…"  0.0.0.0:7051->7051/tcp, 0.0.0.0:7053->7053/tcp  peer
174570c0e1ed    hyperledger/fabric-orderer   "orderer"               0.0.0.0:7050->7050/tcp                          orderer
```

Figure 9.22: Network in 'dev' mode

2. In the second step, we open up a new terminal and bring up the chaincode environment, build the chaincode, and run the chaincode. At this point, the

chaincode is not associated with any channel, and it should be done in the third step.

3. In this, we open another window and do actual chaincode operations. Even though chaincode container is started though we still need to do chaincode lifecycle commands. Ideally, this should not have been required, but this is the way Hyperledger works for now and maybe get away this step in the future.

Following are the commands that we need to run

```
docker exec -it cli bash
peer chaincode install -p chaincodedev/chaincode/ -n mycc -v 0
peer chaincode instantiate -n mycc -v 0 -c '{"Args":[""]}' -C myc
peer chaincode invoke -C myc -n mycc -c '{"function":"initCar","Args":["Ashwani","Blue","BMW"]}'
peer chaincode query -C myc -n mycc -c '{"function":"readCar","Args":["Ashwani"]}'
```

Figure 9.23: Chaincode commands in 'dev' mode

And once we run the query command, we get the output as we have to get it:

>> "docType":"Car","owner":"Ashwani","color":"blue","model":"bmw"}

See, in this set up of the entire network, we didn't create any crypto material, channel artifacts, and played around with compose or script files. Yet we were able to test our chaincode with a simulated environment. This project can be used as a template for the rapid development of chaincode without worrying too much about testing it and creating networks, and so on, for that purpose.

Advanced concepts

So far, we have seen the basic concepts and understanding of writing smart contracts along with unit testing and running them in dev mode for rapid development. However, when we would be trying to solve real-world problems, then it might not be the case, and we may have to write complex business logic. To help you get an understanding of some more topics, in this section, we would also touch upon a couple of more real-world situations and how we can leverage smart contract techniques to solve them.

Private data collection

We have already discussed the private data collection concepts in Hyperledger Fabric in *Chapter 6*. It's time to see them in action. Before that, a quick recap and a brief look into transaction flow, which is a bit different from normal transaction flow.

Just to recap, there could be a situation where there are multiple parties involved in a blockchain network over on a channel; however, there might be a couple of parties who would want to get involved only among themselves to safeguard their business-sensitive data. In that case, one of the options could be creating more channels among themselves. However, having more number of channels in a network could result in maintenance overhead and maybe performance degradation over some time. Due to this, Hyperledger Fabric came up with the concept of private data collection starting v 1.2.

A private collection consists of two parts, actual private data that gets stored in an individual state and hash of data that are stored in the ledger of every peer. Only authorized peers can access data from the private state. Following is an image that clearly shows how Org1 is maintaining a private data collection and is only authorized to access the data, and Org2 peer can't access that data:

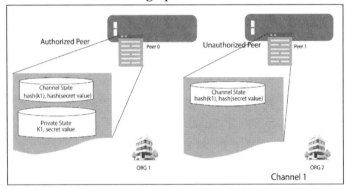

Figure 9.24: Private data collection

Ordering service does not get involved for block dissemination and hence cannot see the private data. Data gets distributed through peer-to-peer gossip protocol in between private authorized organizations. We could see in the above diagram that unauthorized peer still holds the hash of the private data collection on channel state, and this further helps in conflict resolution, should there be a need. Members can choose to share the private data with other parties, which can be used to compute the hash of the private data and to see if it matches the state on the channel ledger, proving that the state existed between the collection members at a certain point in time.

We also had seen the transaction workflow in the usual scenario in *Chapter 7*, the transaction flow in case of private data collection is a bit different, and we would cover that in brief just that you have a good understanding of that.

Transaction flow in private data

- Likewise, as in normal transaction flow, the client application submits a proposal request to invoke a chaincode function only to endorsing peers part of authorized organizations of the collection. The private data is sent in a transient field of the proposal.

- The endorsing peers simulate the transaction and store the private data in a transient data store, which is different from a general ledger or world state. It is a temporary storage local to the peer. Then as defined in the collection policy, it distributes the private data to authorized peers via gossip.

- Now, as in the usual transaction flow, the endorsing peer would send the proposal response back to the client. It shall include the endorsed RW set, including public data, and as well as hash of private data keys and values. Please note that no private data is sent back to the client.

- The next step is to submit the transaction to ordering service, which then includes the transactions with the private data hashes in blocks as usual. Blocks, along with the private data hashes, are then sent to all the peers. All peers on the channel can now validate transactions with the hashes of the private data in a consistent way. That, too, without knowing anything about the actual private data.

- It is a crucial phase of the transaction cycle, during block commit, authorized peers refer to collection policy to figuring out if they are authorized to access the private data. In case of having required privileges, a peer will first look into local transient data store to ascertain if they indeed received the private data during chaincode endorsement. And in case not, next step they would do, try to pull the private data from another authorized peer. Once data is received, they would validate the private data against the hashes in the public block and then move to commit the transaction and the block. Once validation is done, the private data shall be moved to their copy of the private state database and private writeset storage. The private data is then deleted from the transient data store.

Time to go through the sample and running application to make this clearer. The sample code is located at the repository with steps in **https://github.com/ashwanihlf/ sample_pdc.git** or from downloaded code sample.

The code-base for this example is an extension of the three peer networks that we created initially, and it is the same chaincode that we have seen multiple times before. The execution steps are mentioned in the README file, and we would now go through the changes that we have made in the earlier application to apply the concept of PDC.

Private data collection is governed by the collection definition that contains one or more collections. This collection individually forms a structure of policy definition by including a list of organizations and specific other properties. These properties determine certain aspects of private data such as how to control the dissemination of private date at endorsement time when data should be purged and so on. The collection definition is deployed to the channel during chaincode instantiation.

While using the peer CLI to instantiate the chaincode, the collection definition file is passed to the chaincode instantiation using the `--collections-config` flag.

Below is the sample collection config file that we have used in the sample program; we would go through the parameters of the policy. First thing first, this collection definition defines an array, so we could have multiple collection definition that we may want to apply at the channel. We have used only once to keep it simple for understanding:

```
[
    {
        "name": "collectionPrivate",
        "policy": "OR('Org1MSP.member')",
        "requiredPeerCount": 1,
        "maxPeerCount": 3,
        "blockToLive":0,
        "memberOnlyRead": true
    }
]
```

Figure 9.25: Collection Config

Collection definition has a couple of properties; we will go one by one:

- `name`: This is the unique name of the collection, that works like a namespace.
- `policy`: These attributes define which organization's peers are authorized to persist the private data. It is expressed as Signature policy syntax, with the organization name included in an OR signature policy list. In this example, we have included only Org1, so only Org1 peer can save the data and is authorized to access the data. In case we would want to add Org2 peer then we can make this as `"OR('Org1MSP.member','Org2MSP.Member')"`
- `requiredPeerCount`: Minimum number of peers that each endorsing peer must successfully disseminate private data before the peer signs the endorsement before returning the proposal response to the client. In the ideal case, you would require at least some distribution of the private data at endorsement time to ensure redundancy of the private data on multiple peers in the network.
- `maxPeerCount`: To achieve the right level of redundancy, the number of peers that each endorsing peer should try to distribute the private data to. Collection member peers who were not able to receive the private data at endorsement time, can, in that case, would be able to pull the private data from peers the private data was disseminated to.
- `blockToLive`: This property represents how long the data should live on the private database in terms of blocks. Private data will be available for this

specified number on the private database, and after that, it will get purged. To keep private data indefinitely, we can set the blockToLive property to 0.

- memberOnlyRead: A true value for this property indicates that peers belonging to one of the collection member organizations are allowed to read access to private data. In the event of a client from a non-member org attempts to execute a chaincode function that performs a read of a private data, the chaincode invocation is terminated with an error.

Now, with the understanding of property definition, you can go back and have a look at the collection file and relate.

With the collection config defined, we need to make changes in the smart contract to ensure that the same chaincode data operations can be applied to channel state data and private data. There is a different API that we need to use to save and retrieve private data. The APIs that are used are:

```
PutPrivateData(collection,key,value)

GetPrivateData(collection,key)
```

Figure 9.26: Private Data Collection API

In the case of private data collection API, the collection name is also specified, which in our case is collectionPrivate.

In our sample chaincode, where we have been taking the car as an asset, we want to keep the price of the car as private data for Org1, so we have added the following struct to handle this case:

```
type carPrice struct {
    ObjectType string `json:"docType"` //docType is used to distinguish the various types of objects in state database
    Owner      string `json:"owner"`   //the fieldtags are needed to keep case from bouncing around
    Price      float64 `json:"price"`
}
```

Figure 9.27: Struct to handle the price

To test this functionality that while reading `carPrice` it is only accessible to `Org1` as it is the private data we would now add function in the chaincode, which should be called from the invoke like other functions:

```
func (t *SampleChaincode) Invoke(stub shim.ChaincodeStubInterface) pb.Response {
        function, args := stub.GetFunctionAndParameters()
        fmt.Println("invoke is running " + function)

        // Handle different functions
        if function == "initCar" { //create a new car
                return t.initCar(stub, args)
        } else if function == "transferCar" { //change owner of a specific car
                return t.transferCar(stub, args)
        } else if function == "delete" { //delete a car
                return t.delete(stub, args)
        } else if function == "readCar" { //read a car
                return t.readCar(stub, args)

        } else if function == "carPrice" { // get car price
                return t.carPrice(stub, args)

        }

        fmt.Println("invoke did not find func: " + function) //error
        return shim.Error("Received unknown function invocation")
}
```

Figure 9.28: carPrice call from Invoke

However, before we can read the `carPrice` this should also get saved in the private data collection, so we have extended `initCar` function to add this attribute, below are the changed code snippets, there are three snippets that we have changed in `initCar`. The first is to retrieve price, second is to create a construct, and third is to save private data collection:

```
// retrieve the values of price along with other attributes
owner := args[0]
color := strings.ToLower(args[1])
model := strings.ToLower(args[2])
price,err10 := strconv.ParseFloat(args[3],32)

// create a carPrice construct
carPrice := &carPrice{"CarPrice",owner,price}
carPriceJSONasBytes, err2 := json.Marshal(carPrice)

// === Save car price in Private Data Collection
err3 := stub.PutPrivateData("collectionPrivate",owner,carPriceJSONasBytes)
if err3 != nil {
        return shim.Error(err.Error())
}
```

Figure 9.29: Code Snippets for PDC

The exciting part is where we are calling `PutPrivateData` to see we are passing `collectionPrivate`, which is the name of private data collection. The owner is being used as Id, and the complete construction is being saved.

Now, once we have written the code for saving the carPrice as PDC, we need to write the code for retrieving the price as well and should check it both from the authorized and unauthorized peer.

Following is the additional method that we have written to get the carPrice from a private data collection store:

```
// carPrice - get price of a car from private collection
// =====================================================
func (t *SampleChaincode) carPrice(stub shim.ChaincodeStubInterface, args []string) pb.Response {
    var name, jsonResp string
    var err error

    if len(args) != 1 {
        return shim.Error("Incorrect number of arguments. Expecting name of the owner to query")
    }

    name = args[0]
    valAsbytes, err := stub.GetPrivateData("collectionPrivate",name) //get the car basis owner name from PDC
    if err != nil {
        jsonResp = "{\"Error\":\"Failed to get state for " + name + ": " + err.Error() + "\"}"
        return shim.Error(jsonResp)
    } else if valAsbytes == nil {
        jsonResp = "{\"Error\":\"Car does not exist for owner: " + name + "\"}"
        return shim.Error(jsonResp)
    }

    return shim.Success(valAsbytes)
}
```

Figure 9.30: carPrice method

We could see that for retrieving, we are using the GetPrivateData method, and we are passing the collection name and also the owner name, which is working as an Id in this case.

With the collection config ready and smart contract changes done, now we need to put this together to see them in action.

If you see the steps in README file, we are doing precisely the same steps; the only change is when we are instantiating the chaincode, if you look at the script file that we are using to weave the network along with chaincode installation and instantiation, you will notice:

```
peer chaincode instantiate -o orderer.example.com:7050 -C $CHANNEL_NAME -n samplecc -v 1.0 -c '{"Args":[""]}'
 -P " OR('Org1MSP.member','Org2MSP.member')" --collections-config $GOPATH/src/github.com/collections_config.json
```

Figure 9.31: Chaincode instantiation with collection

That we are passing an extra flag of --collections-config and along with, we are passing the absolute location of the JSON file that contains that collection definition. We have kept that in the same folder as we have chaincode.

Once this is done, make sure that chaincode instantiation is successful, you can refer to cli logs as `cli` is the container that runs this command, and you would notice the following logs as given in the below picture:

```
=====================================Instantiating chaincode on =====================
CORE_PEER_LOCALMSPID=Org1MSP
CORE_PEER_TLS_ENABLED=false
CORE_CHAINCODE_KEEPALIVE=10
CORE_PEER_ID=cli
CORE_PEER_MSPCONFIGPATH=/opt/gopath/src/github.com/hyperledger/fabric/peer/crypto/peerOrganizations/org1.example.com/users/Admin@org1
CORE_PEER_ADDRESS=peer0.org1.example.com:7051
CORE_VM_ENDPOINT=unix:///host/var/run/docker.sock
********************************Chaincode instantiation on PEER0******************************************
Org1MSP
2020-04-14 15:56:30.430 UTC [chaincodeCmd] checkChaincodeCmdParams -> INFO 001 Using default escc
2020-04-14 15:56:30.431 UTC [chaincodeCmd] checkChaincodeCmdParams -> INFO 002 Using default vscc
============================Chaincode Instantiation on PEER 0 on channel 'mychannel' is successful. ====================
```

Figure 9.32: cli logs

With this, you would come to know that a smart contract has been built successfully and instantiated with the private data collection definition. Now, we would run the following set of commands:

```
docker exec -it cli /bin/bash
peer chaincode invoke -C mychannel -n samplecc -c '{"function":"initCar","Args":["Ashwani","Blue","BMW","3000"]}'
peer chaincode query -C mychannel -n samplecc -c '{"function":"readCar","Args":["Ashwani"]}'
```

Figure 9.33: Invoke & Query

Looks familiar, by now you must have done in hundred times, we are merely invoking the `initCar` function to save the car asset and then querying it, we would get the result as usual as:

>> {"docType":"Car","owner":"Ashwani","color":"blue","model":"bmw"}

Now, we would invoke our `carPrice` method:

```
peer chaincode query -C mychannel -n samplecc -c '{"function":"carPrice","Args":["Ashwani"]}'
```

Figure 9.34: readCar from Org1

And we get:

>> {"docType":"CarPrice","owner":"Ashwani","price":3000}

Yes, it's working on authorize peers. Remember, `cli` starts with an identity context of Org1, and Org1 peer does have the permission to get the private collection.

Now, we would see how it behaves if we try to access this from an unauthorized peer, you could try it from either of Org2 or Org3.

First, we would change the Identity Context to Org2, and just to ensure that it's set up correctly, we would call `readCar` operation:

```
export CORE_PEER_LOCALMSPID="Org2MSP"
export CORE_PEER_MSPCONFIGPATH=/opt/gopath/src/github.com/hyperledger/fabric/peer/crypto/peerOrganizations/org2.example.com/users
                                                                                          /Admin@org2.example.com/msp
export CORE_PEER_ADDRESS=peer0.org2.example.com:7051
peer chaincode query -C mychannel -n samplecc -c '{"function":"readCar","Args":["Ashwani"]}'
```

Figure 9.35: readCar from Org2

We get the output as:

`>> {"docType":"Car","owner":"Ashwani","color":"blue","model":"bmw"}`

So far, so good, everything is as expected, and you can have a look at the docker processes, and you would see that chaincode for Org2 peer has been successfully instantiated.

Time for private collection method invoke, that is, `carPrice`, that shall be done using the following command:

```
peer chaincode query -C mychannel -n samplecc -c '{"function":"carPrice","Args":["Ashwani"]}'
```

Figure 9.36: carPrice from Org2

And we get the following screenshot:

```
message:"{\"Error\":\"Failed to get state for Ashwani: GET_STATE failed: transaction ID: e6e4c03f480f1199b51813f3b162c3c98691616b5965ba3c79f8e5af5643b606:
  tx creator does not have read access permission on privatedata in chaincodeName:samplecc collectionName: collectionPrivate\"}"
```

Figure 9.37: carPrice output at Org2

Yes, we get the error because Org2 doesn't have permission to access private collection that stores `carPrice`.

I would suggest that you change the identity context of cli to Org3 and try it on your own.

With this, we come to an end to the private data collection feature in Hyperledger Fabric.

State Database (CouchDB) Interaction

We did discuss the Ledger in Hyperledger Fabric in *Chapter 6*, it consists of two parts, one is blockchain, and another one is the world state. We also discussed the options present in Hyperledger Fabric for world state options. Level DB is something that comes by default as in-process State DB. However, following the principle of modularity, the fabric gives us the option of having CouchDB for the world state.

To change the world state options, we need to do two things in docker-compose; first, we need to configure properties in peer were to want to switch to CouchDB, and secondly, we need to have CouchDB configuration defined in compose file as it also comes up as a docker container. It's interesting to see that we have been using CouchDB in all our examples though we have not spoken about that once.

While we are talking about CouchDB, in the same section, we would also talk about additional support that CouchDB provides for rich query support for the chaincode data. Productive queries are an excellent way to understand what's there on the ledger. Modeling assets as JSON and then using CouchDB, it would help us perform complex, productive queries against the chaincode data values through CouchDB JSON query language within chaincode.

We would now look into the changes that need to be done to change the state DB to CouchDB for a peer. CouchDB runs as a separate database process alongside the peer; therefore, there are additional steps that need to be performed to do the setup, management, and operations.

CouchDB configuration

CouchDB can be enabled as the state database for a peer by making the change in the `stateDatabase` configuration option from `goleveldb` (this is provided by default) to CouchDB. Other than that, the `couchDBAddress` is required to be configured to point to the CouchDB to be used by the peer. This CouchDB would be running as a docker container. The credentials (username/password) are required to be given with an admin username and password; this is required if CouchDB is configured with a username and password.

There are also specific other additional options are provided that can be used to provide more flexibility in terms of managing the CouchDB configuration; all of these are in the `stateDatabase` section.

You can refer to **https://github.com/ashwanihlf/sample_couchdb.git** or from downloaded code sample repository that includes the configuration steps; we will discuss them here and also the code changes for queries which we are going to discuss in the next subsection.

This example again is the extension of the sample projects that we have been using so far, the significant change that we have done is enabling of CouchDB as a state database for one of the peer and then the addition of a couple of methods in a smart contract to go through the queries. Following is the snippet of the definition of `peer0` for Org1 (Please note that this is not a complete definition, we have just taken what matters to be on point, for complete definition refers to `docker-compose.yaml` in the same project):

```
peer0.org1.example.com:
    container_name: peer0.org1.example.com
    image: hyperledger/fabric-peer
    environment:
        - CORE_VM_ENDPOINT=unix:///host/var/run/docker.sock
        - CORE_PEER_ID=peer0.org1.example.com
        - FABRIC_LOGGING_SPEC=info
        - CORE_CHAINCODE_LOGGING_LEVEL=info
        - CORE_PEER_LOCALMSPID=Org1MSP
        - CORE_PEER_MSPCONFIGPATH=/etc/hyperledger/msp/peer/
        - CORE_PEER_ADDRESS=peer0.org1.example.com:7051
        - CORE_VM_DOCKER_HOSTCONFIG_NETWORKMODE=${COMPOSE_PROJECT_NAME}_basic
        - CORE_LEDGER_STATE_STATEDATABASE=CouchDB
        - CORE_LEDGER_STATE_COUCHDBCONFIG_COUCHDBADDRESS=couchdb:5984
        - CORE_LEDGER_STATE_TOTALQUERYLIMIT=10
```

Figure 9.38: *CouchDB configuration*

If you see, we have added three properties starting with `CORE_LEDGER_STATE_*`, first one `STATEDATABASE` where we are mentioning that we want CouchDB instead of LevelDB and then `COUCHDBCONFIG_COUCHDBADDRESS` provides the address, couchdb is the name of the server, and it runs on 5984 port. And the third `TOTALQUERYLIMIT` is one of the properties that we would talk about in the queries section. With this additional configuration, now the peer knows that now CouchDB is the state database; however, we also need to bring up the couchdb on port 5984 to which this peer can connect to, and for that, we define couchdb in `docker-compose.yaml` file as well so that all the containers can be brought up during start time.

Following is the simplest definition of `couchdb`:

```
couchdb:
    container_name: couchdb
    image: hyperledger/fabric-couchdb
    # Populate the COUCHDB_USER and COUCHDB_PASSWORD to set an admin user and password
    # for CouchDB.  This will prevent CouchDB from operating in an "Admin Party" mode.
    environment:
        - COUCHDB_USER=
        - COUCHDB_PASSWORD=
    ports:
        - 5984:5984
    networks:
        - basic
```

Figure 9.39: couchdb

Having made these two changes, `couchdb` instance would come up, and `Org1 peer0` would use this as state database.

Now, we would see how we can see data that is going inside CouchDB, in the same project we have made some changes in the smart contract, we have added a method by the name of `initLedger`, this is the extension of the same contract that we have been using so far. The purpose of this method is twofold, one we can load the data at one go to see the entries in CouchDB, and secondly, we can use this data for queries in the next section:

```go
func (s *SampleChaincode) initLedger(stub shim.ChaincodeStubInterface) pb.Response {
        cars := []car{
                car{Owner: "Ashwani", Color: "blue",Model: "bmw" },
                car{Owner: "Raja", Color: "red",Model: "santro" },
                car{Owner: "Naman", Color: "white",Model: "wagonR" },
                car{Owner: "Gurneet", Color: "black",Model: "fortuner" },
                car{Owner: "John", Color: "orange",Model: "pajero" },
                car{Owner: "Bob", Color: "grey",Model: "RangeRover" },
                car{Owner: "Alice", Color: "voilet",Model: "bentley" },
                car{Owner: "Mayank", Color: "ruby",Model: "merc" },
                car{Owner: "Ratan", Color: "green",Model: "audi" },
                car{Owner: "Prem", Color: "seagreen",Model: "kia" },
                car{Owner: "Yoyo", Color: "silver",Model: "thar" },
                car{Owner: "Mini", Color: "gold",Model: "xuv" },
        }
        i := 0
        for i < len(cars) {
                fmt.Println("i is ", i)
                carAsBytes, _ := json.Marshal(cars[i])
                stub.PutState("CAR"+strconv.Itoa(i), carAsBytes)
                fmt.Println("Added", cars[i])
                i = i + 1
        }
        return shim.Success(nil)
```

Figure 9.40

To call this function from `cli`, we called:

```
peer chaincode invoke -C mychannel -n samplecc -c '{"Args":["initLedger"]}'
```

Figure 9.41

Once the successful execution is done, that simply means our data has gone inside the ledger, however since now we have state database running as CouchDB, we shall leverage the UI to see this data. What we need to do simply is, open up a browser and enter:

```
http://<host>:5984/_utils/#/_all_dbs
```

Figure 9.42

And we shall get all the database listed in that CouchDB instance:

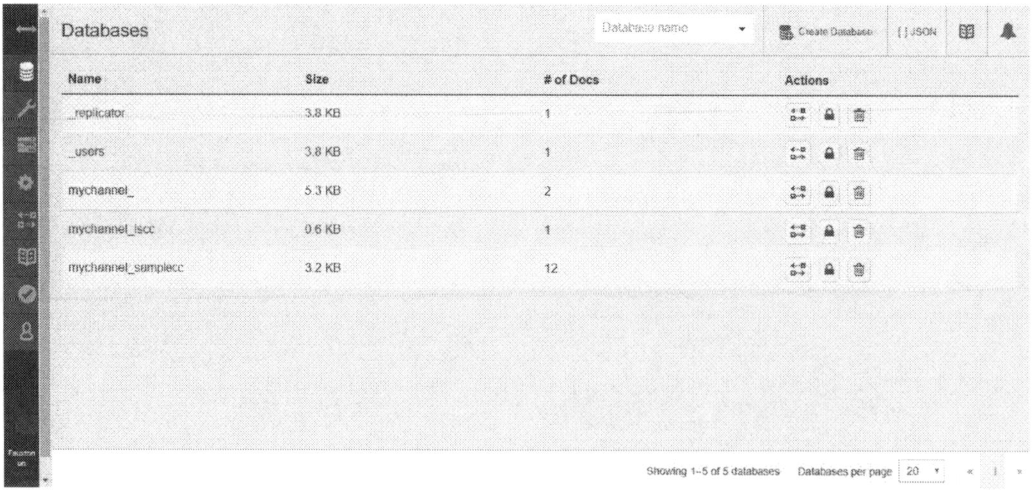

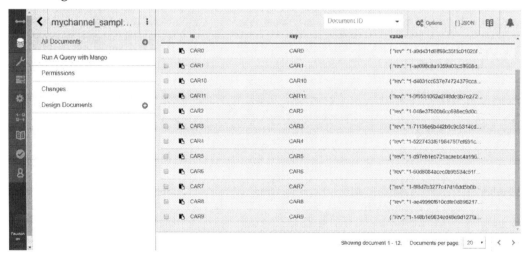

Figure 9.43: CouchDB interface

We can make out our database, which is a combination of our channel name and chaincode, that is, `mychannel_samplecc`, once we click on this, we shall get the following screenshot:

Figure 9.44: mychannel_samplecc database

Yes, we can see the records that we entered through the `initLedger` method. One of the vital keys take away from this screen is that data stored in the database as Key-value pair, and it follows lexical ordering; that is, **CAR10** entry is coming before **CAR2**.

Further, if we click on one of the records as we clicked on **CAR0**, we got the actual information that we sent as shown in the following screenshot:

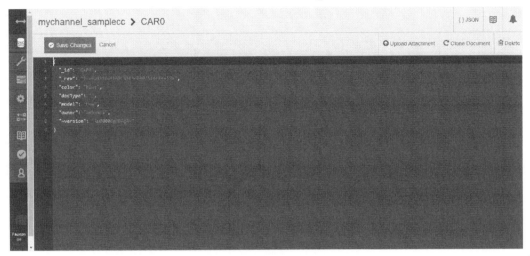

Figure 9.45: CAR0 record

We can see the flexibility that we have just got only by switching the state database from LevelDB to CouchDB. Another advantage that we would get from this is we can execute productive queries against the JSON in the state database by using the API provided by the shim, that is, `GetQueryResult` and passing a CouchDB query string.

Chaincode queries

We would now look at a couple of functions starting from `GetStateByRange` function. This function takes two values, `startKey` and `endKey` and returns `StateQueryIteratorInterface`. `GetStateByRange` function helps us get the values between a specific range. One of the vital keys take away from this method is that whereas `startKey` is included in the result, `endKey` is not available in the result.

We have included one method `getCarsByRange` in our sample smart contract to see the usage of the following functions as they become the standard of getting and iterating through the values.

`HasNext()` method of iterator helps us loop through the result set, and `Next()` gives us the next record, and then by using `GetKey()` and `GetValue()` function, we retrieve the values:

```go
func (s *ChaincodeStub) GetStateByRange(startKey, endKey string) (StateQueryIteratorInterface, error)

type StateQueryIteratorInterface interface {
    // Inherit HasNext() and Close()
    CommonIteratorInterface

    // Next returns the next key and value in the range and execute query iterator.
    Next() (*queryresult.KV, error)
}

type CommonIteratorInterface interface {
    // HasNext returns true if the range query iterator contains additional keys
    // and values.
    HasNext() bool

    // Close closes the iterator. This should be called when done
    // reading from the iterator to free up resources.
    Close() error
}

func (m *KV) GetKey() string

func (m *KV) GetValue() []byte
```

Figure 9.46: Chaincode Query essential functions

Now, we would go through the actual code that we have written as part of the same smart contract to understand how all of this work together. Please note, there is some boilerplate code as well, which I have removed to increase brevity, you can refer to complete code in the sample program:

```go
func (s *SampleChaincode) getCarsByRange(APIstub shim.ChaincodeStubInterface, args[] string) pb.Response {
    startKey := args[0]
    endKey := args[1]
    resultsIterator, err := APIstub.GetStateByRange(startKey, endKey)
    var buffer bytes.Buffer
    buffer.WriteString("[")
    bArrayMemberAlreadyWritten := false
    for resultsIterator.HasNext() {
        queryResponse, err := resultsIterator.Next()
        if err != nil {
            return shim.Error(err.Error())
        }
        // Add a comma before array members, suppress it for the first array member
        if bArrayMemberAlreadyWritten == true {
            buffer.WriteString(",")
        }
        buffer.WriteString("{\"Key\":")
        buffer.WriteString("\"")
        buffer.WriteString(queryResponse.Key)
        buffer.WriteString("\"")

        buffer.WriteString(", \"Record\":")
        // Record is a JSON object, so we write as-is
        buffer.WriteString(string(queryResponse.Value))
        buffer.WriteString("}")
    }
    buffer.WriteString("]")
    fmt.Printf("- getAllCars:\n%s\n", buffer.String())
    return shim.Success(buffer.Bytes())
}
```

Figure 9.47: getCarsByRange

In this function, we are expecting a `startKey` and `endKey` that is getting passed as an argument to this function, and then we are calling `GetStateByRange`. The return type of calling this function is of type `StateQueryIteratorInterface`, which we are capturing in `resultsIterator`. Now, this has two functions `HasNext()` and `Next()`. We are using `HasNext()` to check if we have more records, and then we are looping through; in the loop, we are extracting records by calling `Next()` function, and that gives us an instance of `queryResult.KV` in the `queryResponse` variable. Then we are simply calling `Key` and `Value` on the `queryResponse` to get details of `Key` value of that record, and this goes on in loop till we get all records. Along with we are assembling the complete response in `bytes.Buffer` to send it back to the client.

In the same sample smart contract, we have added another method by the name of `getAllCars`; the only difference between this and `getCarsByRange` is that we are not passing `startKey` and `endKey` in getAllCars instead we are taking them as empty string expecting that we would want all cars from the state.

Now, we would invoke these functions from the cli and see the output, a complete set of instructions are given in the README file.

We are running `getCarsByRange` for `Car0` to `Car5`, and we could see that `Car5` is not included in the result, as we mentioned earlier that `endKey` does not get included. Second thing, which we noticed that `CAR10` and `CAR11` records are also present, and that is because it supports lexical ordering:

```
peer chaincode invoke -C mychannel -n samplecc -c '{"Args":["getCarsByRange","CAR0","CAR5"]}'

result: status:200 payload:"[
{\"Key\":\"CAR0\", \"Record\":{\"color\":\"blue\",\"docType\":\"\",\"model\":\"bmw\",\"owner\":\"Ashwani\"}}
{\"Key\":\"CAR1\", \"Record\":{\"color\":\"red\",\"docType\":\"\",\"model\":\"santro\",\"owner\":\"Raja\"}}
{\"Key\":\"CAR10\", \"Record\":{\"color\":\"silver\",\"docType\":\"\",\"model\":\"thar\",\"owner\":\"Yoyo\"}}
{\"Key\":\"CAR11\", \"Record\":{\"color\":\"gold\",\"docType\":\"\",\"model\":\"xuv\",\"owner\":\"Mini\"}}
{\"Key\":\"CAR2\", \"Record\":{\"color\":\"white\",\"docType\":\"\",\"model\":\"wagonR\",\"owner\":\"Naman\"}}
{\"Key\":\"CAR3\", \"Record\":{\"color\":\"black\",\"docType\":\"\",\"model\":\"fortuner\",\"owner\":\"Gurneet\"}}
{\"Key\":\"CAR4\", \"Record\":{\"color\":\"orange\",\"docType\":\"\",\"model\":\"pajero\",\"owner\":\"John\"}}]"
```

***Figure 9.48**: getCarsByRange function invocation*

Next is we are invoking `getAllCars` where we have not constrained `startKey` and `endKey` instead we have given them as empty string anticipating that we would get all records that we created using `initLedger`, see the command the output below:

```
peer chaincode invoke -C mychannel -n samplecc -c '{"Args":["getAllCars"]}'

result: status:200 payload:"[
{\"Key\":\"CAR0\", \"Record\":{\"color\":\"blue\",\"docType\":\"\",\"model\":\"bmw\",\"owner\":\"Ashwani\"}}
{\"Key\":\"CAR1\", \"Record\":{\"color\":\"red\",\"docType\":\"\",\"model\":\"santro\",\"owner\":\"Raja\"}}
{\"Key\":\"CAR10\", \"Record\":{\"color\":\"silver\",\"docType\":\"\",\"model\":\"thar\",\"owner\":\"Yoyo\"}}
{\"Key\":\"CAR11\", \"Record\":{\"color\":\"gold\",\"docType\":\"\",\"model\":\"xuv\",\"owner\":\"Mini\"}}
{\"Key\":\"CAR2\", \"Record\":{\"color\":\"white\",\"docType\":\"\",\"model\":\"wagonR\",\"owner\":\"Naman\"}}
{\"Key\":\"CAR3\", \"Record\":{\"color\":\"black\",\"docType\":\"\",\"model\":\"fortuner\",\"owner\":\"Gurneet\"}}
{\"Key\":\"CAR4\", \"Record\":{\"color\":\"orange\",\"docType\":\"\",\"model\":\"pajero\",\"owner\":\"John\"}}
{\"Key\":\"CAR5\", \"Record\":{\"color\":\"grey\",\"docType\":\"\",\"model\":\"RangeRover\",\"owner\":\"Bob\"}}
{\"Key\":\"CAR6\", \"Record\":{\"color\":\"voilet\",\"docType\":\"\",\"model\":\"bentley\",\"owner\":\"Alice\"}}
{\"Key\":\"CAR7\", \"Record\":{\"color\":\"ruby\",\"docType\":\"\",\"model\":\"merc\",\"owner\":\"Mayank\"}}]"
```

***Figure 9.49:** getAllCars invocation*

One of the things that we noticed that we had got a total of 10 records, whereas we didn't give any range, so we should have got the complete result set but; however, due to the property `CORE_LEDGER_STATE_TOTALQUERYLIMIT` which we set the value as 10 we got only ten records.

Along with this, there are quite essential methods given in the API that supports pagination, composite keys, and rich query keys. There are ample of examples available for them on various online resources. I would suggest having a good foundation laid out for chaincode queries; readers should go out and try these essential methods of API as that would help them address real-world business problems.

Chaincode (Chaincode for Operators)

The above section was more around the development of chaincode in a particular smart contract, which, as a developer, you need to do. In that course, we learned how to write smart contracts and use of chaincode queries, unit testing of smart contracts, and the use of peer dev mode for the rapid development cycle. However, writing of smart contract is one aspect, and deployment of chaincode on the network is another aspect which is more of an administrator would do; however, as a developer, it's good to know these as well.

In this section, we would learn about the commands and steps that you should know about to be able to perform the admin side of the work related to chaincode. As we understand that chaincode is a program written in the language as supported by fabric, and then it is deployed on the network as a secured docker container, which then makes it usable for carrying out the transaction. However, once a smart contract becomes a chaincode, it follows a life cycle, and that is where operators have a role to play.

We have also seen in the last couple of examples that we use peer binary to manage the chaincode. Additionally, we also know that chaincode follows a life cycle, that is, package, install, instantiate, and upgrade. Just to show you that what all operations are available on chaincode, of course, through peer binary, we simply can run peer on the Terminal, and we could see the following output. Though as of now, we are more interested in chaincode specific commands as we are focussing more on chaincode, then we would utilize this opportunity to see a couple of other commands and other usages:

```
ubuntu@ip-172-31-33-127:~$ peer
Usage:
  peer [command]

Available Commands:
  chaincode   Operate a chaincode: install|instantiate|invoke|package|query|signpackage|upgrade|list.
  channel     Operate a channel: create|fetch|join|list|update|signconfigtx|getinfo.
  help        Help about any command
  logging     Logging configuration: getlevel|setlevel|getlogspec|setlogspec|revertlevels.
  node        Operate a peer node: start|status|reset|rollback.
  version     Print fabric peer version.

Flags:
  -h, --help   help for peer

Use "peer [command] --help" for more information about a command.
```

Figure 9.50: *Peer command*

In this section, now we would go through a chaincode upgrade process along with some other commands. We have a sample code repository with clear steps that would show us how we can upgrade a chaincode even though they are already deployed.

A chaincode may be required to change during the period, maybe because of business requirement change, the addition of some constraints, or maybe a bug fix. A chaincode can be simply upgraded by changing its version. The only thing that we need to keep in mind that name should remain the same; otherwise, that would be treated as a different chaincode.

As like before, a chaincode needs to be installed before it can be upgraded. The upgrade is similar like instantiate transactions, which binds the new version of the chaincode to the channel. One of the other essential things to notice is that Hyperledger Fabric doesn't provide the support for automatic removal of the old version of the chaincode, so this needs to be done manually by the operators.

Now, I will walk you through the steps, as mentioned in the sample application located at **https://github.com/ashwanihlf/sample_chaincodeupgrade.git.**

It is the same project that we have seen and played around with multiple times; however, with the difference that is required us to achieve the upgrade process. Since we would be upgrading the chaincode, so have added a new folder **v2** under the chaincode and copied the same smart contract under that, but with a small change, I have added a console print statement in **readCar** method. I could have changed the business logic or added any other method, but the objective is to learn the process.

Once we have brought the network up after installing and instantiation of chaincode, I ran pure invoke commands on the peers of **Org1** and **Org2**. So far, we have not done anything different than we have been doing so far. And in the process, if we go and see the list of docker containers we could easily see both the chaincode containers for Org1 and Org 2, have a look at the snapshot of my console below:

```
ubuntu@ip-172-31-33-127:~$ docker ps
CONTAINER ID        IMAGE                                                                                                    COMMAND                  CREATED
    STATUS              PORTS                                            NAMES
40b8fa1c1c26        dev-peer0.org2.example.com-samplecc-1.0-[illegible]   "chaincode -peer.add…"   7 seconds ago
    Up 5 seconds                                                         dev-peer0.org2.example.com-samplecc-1.0
c200d1b16005        dev-peer0.org1.example.com-samplecc-1.0-[illegible]   "chaincode -peer.add…"   2 minutes ago
    Up 2 minutes                                                         dev-peer0.org1.example.com-samplecc-1.0
f0c0d4d6edfc        hyperledger/fabric-tools                                                                                 "/bin/bash -c './scr…"   2 minutes ago
    Up 2 minutes                                                         cli
9f3bacb9d043        hyperledger/fabric-peer                                                                                  "peer node start"        2 minutes ago
    Up 2 minutes        0.0.0.0:7051->7051/tcp, 0.0.0.0:7053->7053/tcp   peer0.org1.example.com
305a29850049        hyperledger/fabric-peer                                                                                  "peer node start"        2 minutes ago
    Up 2 minutes        0.0.0.0:8051->7051/tcp, 0.0.0.0:8053->7053/tcp   peer0.org2.example.com
d5f12c1dbe59        hyperledger/fabric-peer                                                                                  "peer node start"        2 minutes ago
    Up 2 minutes        0.0.0.0:9051->7051/tcp, 0.0.0.0:9053->7053/tcp   peer0.org3.example.com
b3ae222a5958        hyperledger/fabric-orderer                                                                               "orderer"                2 minutes ago
    Up 2 minutes        0.0.0.0:7050->7050/tcp                           orderer.example.com
7f0b8d2dc032        hyperledger/fabric-couchdb                                                                               "tini -- /docker-ent…"   2 minutes ago
    Up 2 minutes        4369/tcp, 9100/tcp, 0.0.0.0:5984->5984/tcp       couchdb
```

Figure 9.51: docker ps

The first two entries are of chaincode container, and it follows certain naming conventions, which is a concatenation of a couple of things such as peer name with the full domain, chaincode name, chaincode version, and very long random number.

Peer binary gives us the facility to find out the installed and instantiated chaincode on a particular running peer, so if you have logged into a peer or cli having an Identity Context and you try to run following command. You would get to know about chain codes. It seems okay in our case as we have just installed and instantiated only one chaincode that is samplecc with version 1.0:

```
> peer chaincode list --installed
Get installed chaincodes on peer:
 Name: samplecc, Version: 1.0, Path: github.com/, Id: 85b811c882492bbdb6a41242715902d65d588f7cb62b88de6bc3ea77a5b690107.

> peer chaincode list --instantiated -C mychannel
Get instantiated chaincodes on channel mychannel:
Name: samplecc, Version: 1.0, Path: github.com/, Escc: escc, Vscc: vscc
```

Figure 9.52: peer chaincode commands

Now, we would get into the actual process of upgrading the chaincode. First, we would install upgraded chaincode (in our case it's under `chaincode/v2 folder)`

We shall follow two commands on `Org1` and `Org2` peer; first is the installation of chaincode under `the v2` folder, and in the second step, we are calling `upgrade` instead of instantiating:

```
peer chaincode install -n samplecc -v 2.0 -p github.com/v2/
peer chaincode upgrade -o orderer.example.com:7050 -C mychannel -n samplecc -v 2.0 -c '{"Args":[""]}' -P "
                                                                 OR('Org1MSP.member','Org2MSP.member')"
```

Figure 9.53: Chaincode upgrade

Once we are done with this, we can again go back and run the peer chaincode list --installed and peer chaincode list --instantiated command to see if our version 2 chaincode has been successfully done. Have a look at the below screenshot, and you would see that both the version of chain codes are installed; however, the latest version is instantiated:

```
root@f0c0d4d6edfc:/opt/gopath/src/github.com/hyperledger/fabric/peer# peer chaincode list --installed
Get installed chaincodes on peer:
Name: samplecc, Version: 1.0, Path: github.com/, Id: 85b811c882492bbdb6a41242715902d65d588f7cb62b88de6bc3ea77a5b69010
Name: samplecc, Version: 2.0, Path: github.com/v2/, Id: 169e3f4c1cdc20ba51efcd5819a14d72bbf09f48e744d86055191818b5f9f6b4

root@f0c0d4d6edfc:/opt/gopath/src/github.com/hyperledger/fabric/peer# peer chaincode list --instantiated -C mychannel
Get instantiated chaincodes on channel mychannel:
Name: samplecc, Version: 2.0, Path: github.com/v2/, Escc: escc, Vscc: vscc
```

Figure 9.54: Chaincode status

Now, we can run as usual queries, so we ran `readCar` on the peer of `Org2`. First thing, you could notice by looking at the docker processes that there are two more chaincode containers with version 2.0. Remember, we just talked about that old chaincode container doesn't go on their own:

Figure 9.55: docker ps

Alongside, when I looked into the logs of the chaincode container, I could see the logs getting printed from version 2 chaincode, which ensures that our chaincode has been upgraded:

```
ubuntu@ip-172-31-33-127:~$ docker logs -f 8b7fd8a272e4
invoke is running readCar
readCar called in Sample Chaincode version 2....
```

Figure 9.56: Chaincode logs

Please follow through README on the GitHub repository, and you should be able to run through these steps of the chaincode upgrade.

I would suggest you run through some of the peer commands that would give you more insight into the network.

Logging

Logging is an essential aspect of development where it helps developers, and at the same time, the production support team relies too heavily on the log consoles. Hence, it becomes essential that in any development, we provide adequate and accurate logs. The same goes for Hyperledger Fabric as well. Logging in hyperledger happens at the various level:

- peer and orderer
- shim
- chaincode

If you ever had the chance to look at the logs of docker containers of peer and orderer, you would see they are printing a lot of logs at the console. At the same time, shim also writes log, and as a chaincode developer, you would also want to control how you want to write meaningful logs.

For peer and orderer commands, logging levels are controlled by a logging specification, the environment variable that is used to control the logging is `FABRIC_LOGGING_SPEC`. If you have carefully looked at the definition of peer in the docker-compose file, you will notice that we did set this variable. The severity level that is supported for logging is `FATAL | PANIC | ERROR | INFO | DEBUG.`

Another property that can be useful in the case of peer and orderer logs is logging format that is represented as a `FABRIC_LOGGING_FORMAT` environment variable. It takes a default format, and it can be further customized to print the log as you want.

In the case of SHIM logging, the logging level can be controlled by the property `CORE_CHAINCODE_LOGGING_SHIM`, but this needs to be done in chaincode container definition. Alternatively, this can be controlled by the `SetLoggingLevel(LoggingLevel level)` API in your chaincode. LoggingLevel is a member of enumeration that has values:

- LogDebug
- LogInfo
- LogNotice
- LogWarning
- LogError
- LogCritical

An important point here to note is that, in the context of logging, a logger developer can provide an arbitrary name (string) given to groups of related messages. The name for the shim package logger is a `shim`.

In the case of your custom chaincode, shim package provides APIs that allow you to create and manage logging objects and subsequently for setting the log level, and so on. Below is the signature of the NewLogger and `SetLevel` function:

```
NewLogger(name string) * ChaincodeLogger

(c *ChaincodeLogger) SetLevel(level LoggingLevel)
```

Figure 9.57: NewLogger signature

Below is the snippet of the sample code that `NewLogger` can be used to create an instance of the specific logger with a context, and then various functions can be called:

```
var logger = shim.NewLogger("samplecc")

logger.Debug("Simple Debug Message")
logger.Info("An Info Message")
```

Figure 9.58: Way to create and use logger

Various available functions are listed below that can be used to do logging at various severity levels. Additionally, functions with f give more control over the formatting of logs:

```
(c *ChaincodeLogger) Debug(args ...interface{})
(c *ChaincodeLogger) Info(args ...interface{})
(c *ChaincodeLogger) Notice(args ...interface{})
(c *ChaincodeLogger) Warning(args ...interface{})
(c *ChaincodeLogger) Error(args ...interface{})
(c *ChaincodeLogger) Critical(args ...interface{})

(c *ChaincodeLogger) Debugf(format string, args ...interface{})
(c *ChaincodeLogger) Infof(format string, args ...interface{})
(c *ChaincodeLogger) Noticef(format string, args ...interface{})
(c *ChaincodeLogger) Warningf(format string, args ...interface{})
(c *ChaincodeLogger) Errorf(format string, args ...interface{})
(c *ChaincodeLogger) Criticalf(format string, args ...interface{})
```

Figure 9.59: ChaincodeLogger functions

Error Handling

As in any other application, the chaincode also needs to handle errors gracefully. So far, the simplest of the solution is recommended and being used. May be with new releases we might see some more patterns coming up. Go Lang by itself provides standard error type; however, a vendor package such as `github.com/pkg/errors` can be better used. This package helps generate call stack along with which can be appended with the error message. There are a couple of general directives have been given to how error handling is recommended:

- If the error arises as part of a user request, then it should be simply logged and return

- Since you might end up using some vendor library or external package and if the error comes from vendor package that it is advisable to wrap the error using `errors.Wrap()`

- If there is an error from one of the `Fabric` function, then add context in the error message using `errors.WithMessage()` and leave call stack unaffected.

Below is the snapshot from Hyperledger Fabric documentation:

```
import (
  "fmt"

  "github.com/pkg/errors"
)

func wrapWithStack() error {
  err := createError()
  // do this when error comes from external source (go lib or vendor)
  return errors.Wrap(err, "wrapping an error with stack")
}
func wrapWithoutStack() error {
  err := createError()
  // do this when error comes from internal Fabric since it already has stack trace
  return errors.WithMessage(err, "wrapping an error without stack")
}
func createError() error {
  return errors.New("original error")
}
```

Figure 9.60: Error handling

Conclusion

With this, we have come to an end to our smart contracts chapter. It was purely oriented towards developers who wish to understand and write smart contracts. We started this chapter by making you understand the smart contract for a far and near view. Then we tried to understand the difference between chaincode and smart contracts. While we talked about developing smart contracts, we did look at the ways of unit testing and deploying the smart in dev peer mode to help rapid development for developers. In smart contract development, we went deep into SHIM API and talked about its important methods that, as a developer, we should be doing.

We looked at MockStub that is also a part of the SHIM interface, and how they can help us do the unit testing. Going through the steps of running peer in dev mode was also an exciting aspect as deploying smart contracts on a full-fledged network could be a time consuming and cumbersome activity. Top of all, we tried to present all examples with working samples on GitHub that give you extra confidence in actually running the code. We also talked about Logging and Error Handling, which anyways are an integral part of any development.

We also talked about the role of operators from the chaincode perspective, which is moving from smart contract to chaincode. Chaincode upgrade is the sample that we talked about, and in due course, we learned about other peer chaincode commands as well.

So, I hope this would have been a fulfilling chapter to read through, and it must have helped you clear a lot of concepts for you. The next chapter is an important aspect not from Hyperledger Fabric, but, from the blockchain perspective that is Privacy and security, we shall be talking about that.

CHAPTER 10
Privacy and Security

We have reached the end of the book; I am sure you must have enjoyed reading it and explored Hyperledger Fabric to its core. This chapter covers the aspect of Privacy and Security in general for an open blockchain platform and then specific to Hyperledger Fabric. Hyperledger Fabric employs certain techniques to ensure privacy, given it is an enterprise platform, so privacy is far more critical given the nature of participants and having the possibility of competitors on the same network.

The second important aspect that we shall cover in this chapter is security. Security is at the forefront of any application, and so we would delve into security aspects of Hyperledger Fabric.

Structure

- Privacy
- Privacy in Hyperledger Fabric
- Security
- Security in Hyperledger Fabric
- Conclusion

Objective

We shall be covering Privacy in general for Blockchain as to what it means and how it has evolved over some time. In this chapter, we then again would look into how privacy is achieved in Hyperledger and what components play a role in that. This chapter also covers how security plays a role in general blockchain architecture. We shall refer to security in well-known blockchain platforms. Further to this, we shall also look at security aspects in Hyperledger Fabric

Privacy

In general terms, privacy means the right to enjoy personal space or freedom from uninvited intrusion. Information privacy is the right to have control of one's specific information as to how it is being collected, preserved, and used. In the real world, no one, including organizations or individuals, would be keen on putting all of their information onto a public database that can be arbitrarily read and used without any restrictions.

However, at the same time, there shall be use cases where information needs to be shared with the authorized users in a controlled and timely manner. Think of a use case, where healthcare records are being maintained on a blockchain-based system, while on one side, we would want to keep this sensitive information private. Still, then in the interest of patients and for making better diagnostics and treatment available to them, we would look for ways to share the information with the required parties such as specialized doctors in a controlled and timely manner.

At any point in time, participants would envision leveraging the full benefit of blockchain but with privacy. Following are the key characteristics that would help to achieve privacy in any system:

- **Transaction confidentiality:** While transacting online and more too in case of financial transactions, users would want to limit the disclosure of their transactions and respective account information to a bare minimum, precisely only what is required to fulfill the transaction. This limited disclosure includes users' transaction information that should not be accessible by any unauthorized user (well, they could be a valid and legitimate user on the system but not a valid party to this specific transaction). The user would also want that the system administrator (think of permissioned blockchain where system administrator could be a party), or the participant of the network shall not be in a position to disclose any information to others without explicit permission. Full control of data is expected, such that all data should be stored and accessed consistently and securely even under unexpected failures or malicious cyberattacks.

Such confidentiality is very much expected in financial transactions but desirable too in many non-financial scenarios as well; think of the healthcare system that we just talked about.

- **Anonymity (Privacy of Identity):** Due to its inherent design most of today's (new) blockchain platforms, such as Bitcoin and Ethereum, are designed as open, public and shared ledgers in a way that there are no restrictions on participation and all transaction details are therefore visible to everyone on the blockchain. In this kind of blockchain system, the participant entities are only identified by their blockchain addresses, which are generally derived from the corresponding public keys. Public ledgers are that is why considered to be *pseudo-anonymous,* that establishes the fact that an address is linked to someone; however, that someone is unknown to the public. Whereas, by thoroughly looking at and analyzing the transaction graph and combining with other information, it is quite possible to figure out the true real-world identity behind a blockchain address. It could also indirectly bring the risk of disclosure of the participant's identity. Think of a scenario, having daily coffee morning from a café that accepts bitcoin.

  Again in the real-world, individuals and organizations would prefer to have privacy-enhancing features of anonymity in blockchain transactions.

- **Transactions unlinkability:** Apart from having identity anonymity (not revealing true identity), participants would want that the transactions related to themselves cannot be traced or linked. In case all the transactions of a specific user can be linked, it is quite easy to derive the rest of the information about the user, mainly account balance, transaction type, frequency, and so on. By doing the statistical analysis of data about transactions and related accounts together with some background knowledge about a participant, one could figure out the real identity of the participant behind transactions.

  So, there is a definite requirement of transaction unlinkability as part of privacy enhancement in blockchain platforms o boost up the confidence level of individuals and organizations.

While permissioned blockchain does have a different notion of privacy as participants are known in the system before they have joined the network, there are various techniques that they employ just as channels, private data collection, and so on, in Hyperledger Fabric and Shared fact sharing between intended parties in Corda, a various public blockchain platform and cryptocurrencies are working on adopting techniques that can improve privacy.

The couple of them are listed below.

Mixing

Mixing is one of the earliest techniques adopted by cryptocurrencies to provide privacy; this technique falls under the cryptography of obfuscation. The sole objective of this technique is to obscure the linkage between the inputs and outputs of transactions by way of mixing them with other transaction input and output. As discussed earlier, Bitcoin does not provide anonymity for users. Instead, Bitcoin transactions use pseudonymous addresses, and that can be verified publicly following the behavioral pattern of transaction spend. Thus anyone can relate a user's transaction with other transactions by a simple analysis of addresses. A simple example is of using bitcoin at Cafe when the address of the transaction is linked to the real-world identity of a user, and that could cause the potential leakage of the user's transactions.

Hence, mixing services or also known as tumblers, was designed to prevent users' addresses from being linked. Mixing does a random exchange of user's coins with some other users' coins; as a result, for the observer, their ownership of coins is obfuscated. The technique may not be that simple as it sounds and being used by some prominent cryptocurrency such as Monero, and so on.

Anonymous signatures

We have discussed digital signature technology in our chapter on cryptography. Over some time, there were a couple of variants that were developed for digital signature. As it turned out, some signature schemes by themselves provide anonymity for the signer as an inherent feature. These signature schemes are also referred to as an anonymous signature. Ring signature and Group signature are the two most widely used anonymous signature schemes.

A brief description of the Group and Ring Signature is given below:

- **Group signature:** A group signature scheme facilitates a way that allows a member belonging to the group to sign a message on behalf of the group anonymously. Any member from the group can anonymously sign a message for the entire group by using the personal secret key. The public key of any member within the group can be used for validation purposes. The process maintains anonymity and signature verification, and in due course, it does not reveal anything about the true identity of the signer. Group signature scheme also uses the notion of a group manager who is responsible for adding group members, handling the event of disputes, including revealing the original signer.

- **Ring signature**: Ring signature helps achieve anonymity through the facilitation of signing by any member of a group, which means that no one except the actual signer knows which member has signed the message. Ring signatures are a more sophisticated scheme than typical digital signatures used in other cryptocurrencies such as ECDSA or Schnorr signatures.

  Ring signatures need multiple different public keys for verification, and the word "ring" is used because it consists of a group of partial digital signatures from various users that come together to form a unique signature that is used to sign a transaction. The ring signature is anonymous if it is difficult to determine which member of the group has used the key to sign the message. The ring users (group users) can be selected randomly within the users on the blockchain. A high-level analogy of ring signatures could be having multiple parties signing a check from a joint bank account; however, because of the cryptographic implementation, it is hard to distinguish the actual signer among the group.

Broadly, there are two steps in the ring sign, as shown in the image below:

- o **RingSign(M, PK1, PK2,..., PKr, s, SKs):** It is the step of computing ring signature Q, which would take input of message M, public keys of ring members and signer's private key SKs as arguments

- o **RingVerify(M, Q):** It is verification step of ring signature Q, which takes arguments of message M and ring signature Q, it returns 1, if the signature is correct and 0 otherwise:

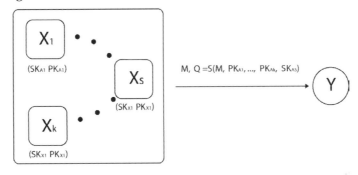

***Figure 10.1**: Ring signature*

Attribute-based encryption

This cryptographic scheme uses one-to-many public key encryption. It is further an expanded way of encryption that makes use of flexible policy-based access controls that are cryptographically enforced. Instead of encrypting data to a single user, data is encrypted in a fashion that it can be decrypted by anyone with credentials satisfying an arbitrary attribute-based access control policy. In this technique, attributes make the defining and regulating factors for the generated ciphertext that has been encrypted using the secret key of the user. Anyone can decrypt the encrypted data using the user's secret key if the attributes are agreed and matched with the ciphertext attributes. Attribute-based encryption also exhibits collusion-resistance security property. It ensures that when a malicious user colludes with other users, he cannot access other data except the data that the user can decrypt with his private key.

Although ABE seems to be quite a powerful concept to provide privacy in some fashion yet very few implementations exist as of date.

As an example, a blockchain can represent permissions by ownership of access tokens. Then participant nodes in the network, who have specific tokens issued to them, will be granted access to the exclusive rights and privileges that are associated with the token. The token provides a way of figuring out specific attributes to perform the operation and access resources.

There are a couple of variants that exist in ABE, such as Content-based Access Control, Role-based Access Control, and so on. In Hyperledger Fabric, we would see that it is known as Attribute Based Access Control or ABAC.

Secure multi-party computation

SMPC has come out as an essential aspect of cryptography and has shown credible potential in enabling real data privacy. In this scheme, a multi-party protocol enables to allow to carry out some computation jointly over their private data inputs without violating their input privacy. It again happens in such a fashion that an adversary learns nothing about the input of an authentic party but the output of the joint computation.

MPC tries to handle the problem of jointly computing a function among a set of (possibly mutually distrusting) parties. In MPC, a group of parties computes an agreed-upon function on their private inputs. For example, suppose three parties, A, B, and C, hold separate inputs a, b, and c, respectively. They agree to compute the value of the function $F(a, b, c) = max(a, b, c)$, while keeping those inputs private. To do so, the parties engage in a protocol to obtain the desired output, that is, the value of the function. In this protocol, all that the parties learn is what they can learn from that output and their input. Thus in the above example, if the output is c, then C comes to know only that c is the maximum value, while A and B learn (if a, b and c are distinct) only that their input is not equal to the maximum, and that the maximum held is equal to c.

The success of employing MPC in distributed voting, private bidding, and private information retrieval has made it a popular solution to many real-world problems.

Non-Interactive Zero-Knowledge (NIZK) Proof

A zero-knowledge proof is another important and quite widely used cryptographic scheme that helps to achieve privacy. The idea is that a formal proof can be formulated which ascertains that a program executed with some input that was known privately to the user can produce some publicly open output without disclosing any other information. In other words, a certifier can establish that to a verifier that provided assertion is valid and correct without giving out any other information to the verifier.

Put merely, and Zero-Knowledge Proofs allow data to be verified without revealing that data.

A transaction would have a *verifier* and a *prover*. In the transaction using ZKP, the prover tries to prove something to the verifier without revealing the verifier anything else about that thing. By providing the final output to the verifier, the prover establishes that he can compute something without revealing the input or the computational process. Meanwhile, the verifier only gets to know about the output:

Prover   **Secret Data & Proofs**   **Verifier**

Figure 10.2: Zero-Knowledge Proof

There are two variants of Zero-Knowledge proof, Interactive and Non-Interactive:

- **Interactive**: In the scheme, the prover needs to perform a series of actions to convince the verifier, of the existence of a particular fact

- **Non-Interactive**: In a non-interactive proof, the prover can deliver proof that anyone can be verified by verifier by themselves. In this case, the verifier picks up a random challenge for the prover to solve. Repeated interaction between the prover and verifier becomes unnecessary since the proof exists in a single message sent from prover to verifier.

One of the prominent variations of ZKP is the zero-knowledge Succinct Non-interactive Argument of Knowledge or better known as zk-SNARK proof, which is being used in one of the cryptocurrency zCash and helps verify transactions while protecting users' privacy.

Zk-SNARK, are Zero-Knowledge because they don't reveal any knowledge to the verifier, succinct as the proof can be verified quickly, non-interactive because there is no need of repeated interaction between prover and verifier and arguments of knowledge because of they present soundproof.

Now, with a brief understanding of what privacy means and different ways by which privacy can be ensured and is being used in different blockchain platforms, we shall move on to the specific topic of our interest in understanding how privacy is attained in Hyperledger Fabric at different levels.

Privacy in Hyperledger Fabric

In actuality, data privacy in a decentralized system where data is supposed to be replicated at every peer, are two different odds of a system. In first permissionless blockchain platforms, mainly Bitcoin and Ethereum, the core objective was to have everything available to everyone, be it transactional data or smart contract for everyone to see and validate. The only notion of privacy available was through pseudo-anonymity in terms of addresses. Then, we saw how different forthcoming blockchain systems, mainly cryptocurrencies, adopted different techniques, especially cryptographic schemes, to ensure some level of privacy.

In permissioned blockchain such as in Hyperledger Fabric, privacy means privacy. In a competitive world where somewhat distrusting parties or for that matter even business competitors who are on a blockchain business network would want to have the privacy of transactional data and contract agreements while leveraging the benefits of blockchain such as no dependency on intermediators, saving time and money on reconciliation effort yet be able to enjoy the benefit of immutable transactional records while agreeing to consensus rules.

In Hyperledger Fabric, privacy is supported at different levels; fabric tries to ensure the following aspects of privacy using different techniques:

- **Transaction Data Privacy**: This aspect of privacy ensures that smart contract data or think of transactional data being sent to the smart contracts to change the state of data of an entity is private and is only visible to concerned parties. It is more of input data to smart contracts.

- **State Data Privacy:** State data is something which is the smart contract is executing, and the resultant change effected by an entity.

- **Smart Contract Privacy**: This privacy aspect covers the actual code of the smart contract, which generally is the translation of the contract between different participants into an executable logic.

- **User Privacy**: Protecting the privacy of the user who is carrying out any action on the platform.

To achieve the level mentioned above of privacies, Hyperledger Fabric provides a couple of constructs; the first one is Channel:

- **Channel**: Hyperledger fabric provides a ledger independent of each other on the per-channel level. Channel is a partitioning mechanism that implements in its broadcast mechanism, and participants who are part of a specific channel can only see the data being shared in the channel or stored in the ledger specific to that channel.

    A channel could be at the whole network level where every participant of the business network and hence the channel can view the transactional data, or it could be between a specified set of participants who still being part of the overall network can establish their network to transact confidential data among themselves. A channel can be thought of as a sub-network of the leading network with limited and chosen participants.

    Channel creation by itself as well is appropriately authenticated and authorized by ordering service, which ensures that the right participant is creating the channel. Privacy is ensured using restricting access to participation in the channel. Participation is governed by policies mainly read policy, write policy, and admin policy for a channel. Channel provides transaction and data privacy to its participants.

The other construct used in Hyperledger Fabric to ensure privacy is:

- Private data collection: While channels have been the right way of protecting privacy by way of separating the ledger and hence the transaction and data, but then it does have its shortcomings; one specifically is around channel management, including maintaining chaincode version, assigning policies, and so on. In a small network with a couple of participants, administrator overhead of creating and managing the channel is workable; however, with a medium to vast participant network and then having a lot of channels in between them may not be easy to manage and control. To overcome this, Hyperledger fabric came up with the concept of private data collection.

  As with channels, private data collection is something that can exist between a set of participants, and in this case, where the transaction is still available on the common ledger of the network, private data is limited between interested parties. In contrast, the hash of the data is still stored on the common ledger of the network. We have seen earlier chapters that a ledger in Hyperledger Fabric consists of two parts, namely transaction log and state. However, in this case, there shall be a third component in the ledger, and that is called private data collection.

  Private data collection, at times, also referred to as a private database or side database, and it contains Key-value stores of the private data that intended parties out of the leading network wish to store. Private data collection is achieved through a policy written in the JSON file and supplied at the time of chaincode instantiation:

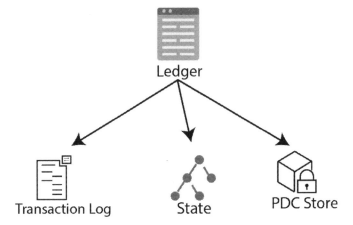

Figure 10.3: Private data collection

A PDC is generally categorized by the combination of two elements. Actual private data and hash of private data:

- **Private data:** This is stored in the private state database of the intended party and is only sent to authorized party peer to peer using the gossip protocol.

- **Hash of private data**: Hash of the private data as part of the transaction cycle in the fabric is endorsed, ordered, and then gets written on to the ledgers of every participant peer on the channel. The hash serves as a basis of proof of the transaction and is further used for state validation and can be used for audit purposes.

The following figure depicts how the content of PDC looks as compare to another peer not having access to a private state. **Peer0** does have private state and hash of the private state in channel state ledger, whereas for **Peer1** does not have private data collection, whereas its ledger still contains the hash of the private state key and value.

Participant members who chose to keep private data collection can decide on sharing the private data with other parties in the network should they choose to or if they have gotten into a dispute. The third party then has the facility to compute the hash of the private data and can see by itself if the resultant matches the state already stored on the channel ledger, hence proving that the state was existing between the collection members at a certain point in time:

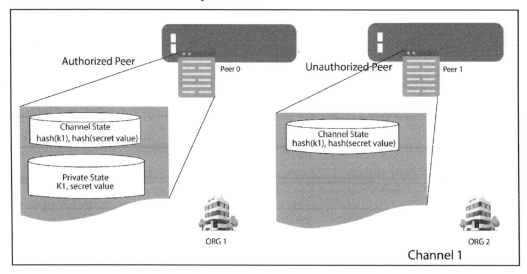

Figure 10.4: *Private state*

Another essential thing to notice here is that any Peer can have multiple private data collection based on the different relationships between different participants of the network and need. An example is shown below, where a Peer on a channel can have multiple PDC with different participants:

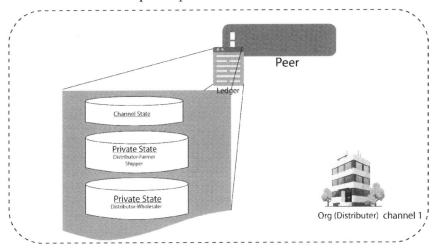

Figure 10.5: Multiple PDC

Other than the channel and private data collection techniques that are used to ensure transaction data and state data privacy, other constructs are used in Hyperledger Fabric to ensure other levels of privacy. Some are given below:

- **Smart Contract Privacy:** To provide contract code confidentiality to ensure that business agreements that have been translated in the code are known only to the right set of participants, Hyperledger Fabric provides smart contract privacy. Chaincode deployment is a two-step process, that is, installation and instantiation.

  The installation of a chaincode on peers (node) is independent of the channel. Instantiation of chaincode is channel-specific and can only be done by authorized entities. Hyperledger fabric follows the concept of endorsement policies, which means that transactions are required to be endorsed by a predefined set of nodes before they can be committed. Only endorser nodes are required to have chaincode instantiated.

  So, even if a in the channel with a limited number of participants only a subset of participants are required to do endorsement, then only these nodes would have the visibility of the smart contract and not everybody on that channel. This way, smart contract confidentiality is preserved in the Hyperledger Fabric network.

- **User Privacy (Anonymous and Unlinkable Transactions):** Identity Mixer is a cryptographic technique that has been provided as a feature to guarantee anonymity and unlinkable transactions in Hyperledger Fabric. Hyperledger

Fabric entities need to have identities to interact with the platform, and these identities are issued by Certificate Authority and used in Fabric by way of **MSP (Membership Service Provider)**, which works as an abstraction for the use of certificates issued by CA.

Usually, the **Enrolment Certificate (ECert)** is something that is used by the user to invoke smart contract operations on the blockchain platform. However, with the identity mixer, the user can use one **time certificates (TCert)** to invoke individual transactions. These TCerts are derived from ECert, so providing the support of non-repudiation. Along with the transactional key, the user can also generate a key for encryption as well. And due to transactions being invoked with different TCert from the same user, it appears that transactions are done by different users and hence achieve unlinkability:

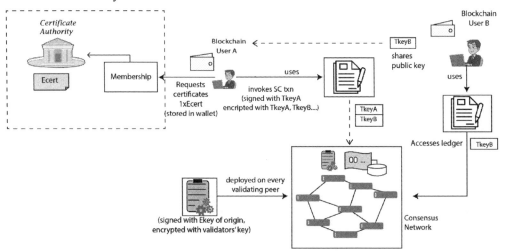

Figure 10.6: Transaction Unlinkability

We did talk about identity mixer in the Cryptography chapter of the book; however, it is essential to note the difference that identity mixer bring into the Hyperledger platform. If a user is not using the identity mixer than it, only the public certificate (X.509) which is used to the signed transaction and this certificate contains a couple of attributes which are visible in all the transaction. Hence, anyone can make out as to the different transaction invocations that are done by the same user.

However, with an identity mixer, the issuance of a certificate from CA remains the same. Still, with the use of identity mixer as provided in Fabric SDK, users can define presentation policy and hence can use which attributes to be used in a specific transaction. So, based on the presentation policy, which defines which attributes to be used, different TCert can be created and used in the transaction. The following figure gives a high-level comparison of transaction flow concerning certificates in the Hyperledger Fabric.

As you can see, in the case of X.509 based certificates, all attributes are the same in different transactions, whereas in the case of identity mixer attributes are hidden and are different in different transaction processing:

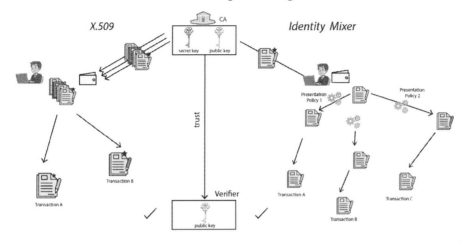

Figure 10.7: Identity Mixer

Security

Whereas data privacy is more inclined towards the use and governance of personal data—mechanisms like putting controls and policies in place to ensure how an individual's personal information is being collected, preserved, and shared. Security features talk about more on protecting data from malicious attacks and the exploitation of stolen data for personal gains.

Public blockchain platforms such as Bitcoin and Ethereum are permissionless and open for the public to join and leave at will. Any computer having a bitcoin node and on the internet can connect with the network. Any wide open system could be vulnerable to attacks, although these systems have grown over time and have numerous techniques implied which help them inherently look secure. The security aspect in permissioned blockchain needs to follow the different ways, which we shall cover in the next section, taking Hyperledger Fabric as an example.

Following are the security considerations which have been kept in mind for public blockchain systems while designing the systems to handle security threats:

- **Tamper resistance:** Tamper resistance is a way to resist any way of change or tampering of the system by any adversary who has access to the entity but with maligned intent. It falls under the integrity property of the CIA triad of security. Correctly, in the context of blockchain, tamper-resistance systems mean that any data or transaction information available in the blockchain cannot be tampered during and after the process of block generation. On a high level, there are a couple of ways that the transaction information may be tampered with, most notably ones are:

- Miners with maligned intention could try to tamper with the information of the received transaction

- Any adversary may attempt to tamper with the information stored on the blockchain

As an instance of tampering, any node working as miner could attempt to, for instance, change the payee address of the transaction to different addresses. Though, in the case of Bitcoin, since each transaction is compressed by a secure Hash function (SHA-256) and then signed by the payer using a secure signature algorithm (ECDSA). After all this, the transaction is sent to the entire network for verification. Now, multiple miners would then receive and pick up the transaction to validate. If a node acting as miner tries to manipulate any information of the transaction, it will be detected by others when they check the signature with the payer's public key. Since the miner cannot generate a valid signature on the modified information without the payer's private key. It is ensured by the robustness of the secure signature algorithm.

Secondly, modifying historical data stored on the blockchain is equally challenging to do. And this is possible only because of cryptographic techniques used in blockchain such as in Bitcoin. These cryptographic techniques employ hash pointer technique, and then there is network-wide support for both storage and verification of the blockchain. Suppose, if any malicious node wants to tamper with the data on some block (say x), this would be mismatch problem, that is, the tampered block x has an inconsistent hash value compared to the hash of the preceding block x maintained in the $x + 1$ block. This reason for this is the hash function used for generating hash pointer, which is inherently collision-resistance. The outputs of the hash function with two different inputs will be utterly inconsistent with each other, and such inconsistency can be quickly figured out by other nodes on the network.

In a nutshell, as every transaction in public blockchain such as Bitcoin is signed and distributed over all nodes of the network through the blockchain, it is nearly impossible to change transaction data without the network knowing about it.

So, this property in the blockchain is usually achieved through the use of hash functions and digital signature, which help it making them tamper-proof.

- **DDoS (Distributed Denial-of-Service) attack resistance:** This is a way of attack where the flood of requests are sent through automated spam system such that host machine or the network resource on the host becomes unavailable to its intended users and it makes the system unusable for valid users or system. In this case, an attacker may somehow get access to an individual's computer to attack another computer by taking advantage of security vulnerabilities. By using a set of such compromised computers, an attacker may be able to spend vast amounts of requests to a hosting system.

The question now really arises is, if a DDoS attacker can make the blockchain unavailable by sending out requests in large numbers and knocking out a partial or the whole network. The answer lies in the fact that due to the fully decentralized nature of the blockchain such as Bitcoin and the requirement of going through consensus protocol for new block generation and addition to the blockchain, which ensures that the processing of blockchain transactions can continue even if several blockchain nodes go offline.

- **Double-spending prevention:** This somehow again falls into the integrity aspect of the security where a node can attempt to double spend the assets allocated to it. The sole reason for this threat is only because duplication of digital information is relatively easy. Specifically, with transactions involving the exchange of digital tokens, such as digital currency, there is a risk that the holder could potentially duplicate the digital token and send multiple identical tokens to multiple recipients. If an inconsistency can be formed due to the transactions of duplicate digital tokens, then the double-spending problem could become a severe security threat.

Blockchain system such as Bitcoin and Ethereum employs cryptographic techniques and by the use of consensus protocol that enables them to prevent double spend. Bitcoin, in particular, evaluates and verifies the authenticity of each transaction using the transaction logs along with consensus protocol. By making sure that all transactions are included in the blockchain, wherein the consensus protocol allows every node to verify the transactions in a block before committing the block into the main blockchain, ensuring that the sender node of each transaction only spends the bitcoins that it possesses. Also, every transaction is signed by its sender using a secure digital signature algorithm. It ensures that if someone manipulates the transaction, the verifier can easily detect it. The combination of transactions signed with digital signatures and public verification of transactions with a majority consensus guarantees that Bitcoin blockchain can be resistant to the double-spending attack.

Security in Hyperledger Fabric

While we have talked about security aspects in open and permissionless blockchain, specifically Bitcoin, security in permissioned blockchain like in Hyperledger Fabric assumes more considerations.

We shall list down some of the considerations below and what aspect of security they address.

Strong identity management

In any typical enterprise application, the first thing to ensure is to know the identity of the participant, which eventually leads to the decision of the authorization and access control of the participant for specified resources on the network. Likewise, in Hyperledger Fabric, strong identity management is enforced so that participant entities are known in the network, and members are known to each other. Having known to each other doesn't mean they trust each other and would want to ensure limits of access control as per agreed terms. With the identity management places, this is beforehand agreed and decided as to which participant can see and access what; this can be achieved by way of configurations done at various levels such as channel, endorsement policies for transaction validation, chaincode deployment by the authorized admin of organizations. It ensures the confidentiality of the transaction data, among other things in the network.

Hyperledger Fabric employs the Public Key Infrastructure model to create or use cryptographic certificates that are linked to organizations, infrastructure network components, and client applications. Result of which, data access control is governed on the broader network and as well on channel levels. It is, in turn, controlled through Membership Service Provider abstraction in the Hyperledger network.

For instance, there are policies as to only admin can install chaincode on peers. Admin has the identity with the rights to deploy chaincode.

Governing Rules (Network)

Hyperledger Fabric network is usually a set of organizations who wish to come together and, in process, create a network to achieve a common business outcome. In-network creation, specific crucial governing rule come into play which inherently provides security features, these rules could be:

- Agreement on the initial set of members from different organizations and what role they shall play such as endorser or committer
- Agreement on the criteria as to how a new member can join the network and with what privileges
- Responsibility around development, verification, and deployment of chain code to ensure no malicious code gets into the system

Again, all of these can be achieved by various configurations at various level of setting up the network, and so these levels of implicit security can be obtained directly. By using these security threats such as spoofing, repudiation, and tampering can be prevented.

We have seen them, for example, in one of our earlier chapters where we took a deep dive into the network configurations, policies attached to those configurations as to who can do what, and then we also looked at the Access Control List.

Scoped chaincode execution

In Hyperledger Fabric, smart contracts or chaincode are installed on the peers that are endorsers and not on every peer node. It ensures that only intended parties could see the smart contract code and able to execute the necessary operations. These, in a way, ensure the *confidentiality* of the code, tampering with could result in wrong data getting into the ledger.

Alongside, since chaincode runs on separate docker containers, care is given to ensure that the inbound and outbound traffic is controlled as per the agreed policy.

Endorsement policies

Another essential aspect in Hyperledger Fabric is a construct of endorsement policies, which enforces that before a transaction could be committed to the ledger, it should be endorsed by a set of agreed participants. Endorsement ensures other than validation of transactions and participants who are authorized to do the specific operation. It somehow contributes to the integrity of the data as endorsers ensure that there is no wrongdoing is happening with the data by any unauthorized participant in the system.

The endorsement process also ensures that they come up with Read Write set as part of transaction execution, and this ensures that keep a tab on the RW version of the data set and hence can eventually avoid a replay attack.

Transport Layer Security (TLS)

To provide security to that data in transit, Hyperledger Fabric also supports TLS. Fabric provides support for secure communication between nodes. TLS can be established one way, that is, for the server only and client-server, which is two-way authentication. In case of one way, a peer can act as a server with CLI, application client, or another peer making the connection to it, and in case of peer to peer connect, client-server relation can be established.

To enable TLS, Hyperledger Fabric provides configuration options that can be used; these configurations are divided into the following categories:

- Peer Node TLS configuration
- Orderer Node TLS configuration
- Peer CLI TLS configuration

We have gone through the configurations required to configure TLS at a different level in one of our earlier chapters.

BCCSP

BCCSP stands for **Blockchain Cryptographic Service Provider** that provides the implementation of cryptographic standards and algorithms. It includes an implementation for encryption, decryption, key pair generation, message digest, and so on. In the Hyperledger Fabric network, the peer and orderer need to carry out a lot of these operations during the transaction life cycle. So, to achieve this in fabric and keeping the design philosophy of modular architecture, fabric provides a way to plug the crypto library. **Crypto Service provider (CSP)** can be plugged in fabric either through a software library or hardware module, also known as **Hardware Security Module (HSM)**. Hardware CSP follows the PKCS#11 standard, which is platform-independent, so HSM vendor can follow these specifications to come up with a hardware module that exposes interfaces for various operations as defined by this standard.

In Hyperledger Fabric, the orderer can use either use any of the crypto service providers, and switch between software and hardware can be controlled through configurations. In configurations, we can provide the name of the hashing algorithm to be used, key size, and so on. These configurations are part of `orderer.yaml` or `docker-compose.yaml` where orderer is defined by way of environment variable such as `ORDERER_GENERAL_BCCSP_*`.

Keep in mind that for using the CSP, the orderer needs to have crypto material such as private key, certificate, and so on, which is provided through MSP and is also provided by way of config parameters as we have seen earlier in the YAML file:

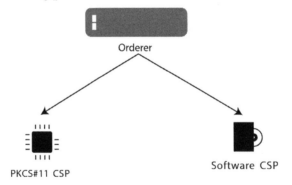

Figure 10.8: Orderer BCCSP options

Likewise, in the same way, as Orderer can use CSP, peer nodes can also use CSP as they also need to carry out signing, and so on, functionalities as part of the transaction life cycle. For peers as well, they can support both software and hardware CSP and need MSP to interact with CSP. All this information is provided through configuration as part of the YAML file.

Other considerations

While there are a lot of security features that come implicitly with the fabric being a blockchain network as cryptography at its helm, secondly, as part of the configurations, there are a lot of security features that can be enhanced at various level.

However, the fabric is not an individual node by itself in the blockchain network; instead, it is a set of components that makes a complete blockchain platform. Whereas fabric components are orderer, peer, CA, and then we need other auxiliary tools such as Kafka, Zookeeper, docker swarm, and so on, to establish a complete network. An eventual Hyperledger fabric network with all components up and running usually occupies more than ten ports in the system; in that case, it becomes essential that we select what all ports need to be exposed and what all are meant for communication among themselves only. Another aspect is the Fabric CA configuration and key management.

Conclusion

Privacy always has been one of the vital keys in applications as it governs who can see what and how information should be used. We did touch upon various privacy characteristics and various techniques that are being used in open blockchain platforms that are being used to ensure privacy by way of mixing, anonymous signatures, Zero Knowledge Proof, and so on. Given business requirements, there could be a case where there might be a difference in the offering of one seller to its buyers, and the seller may want to keep the information private between it and specific buyer while still carrying out business with another buyer. Hyperledger Fabric provides the concept of the channel and private data collection to ensure privacy in transactional data. Then we also looked into user privacy mechanism in fabric by way of identity mixer and as well as smart contract privacy to make sure that business agreements translated in smart contracts are private.

Open blockchain platforms are designed to be secure inherently, more so given in public blockchain any node/user can join the network at any time by just possessing the node software and having access to the internet. We did talk about how confidentiality, integrity, and availability is achieved in open blockchain and how implicitly platforms have been designed to ensure that security is not compromised. We discussed the security features available in the fabric using identity management, endorsement policies, TLS, and so on. A short focus was also given to peripheral components of the fabric network.

Whereas, this chapter was not inclined towards details of achieving security in Hyperledger Fabric using playing around with configurations and other changes that can be done in fabric. Still, the intention was to make the reader aware of the security aspects involved and a starting point for achieving this. The idea is to make the reader conscious of the fact that security is an essential key while developing a fabric blockchain platform, and consideration should be given to achieve that.

CHAPTER 11

Hyperledger Fabric v 2.0

We have covered the Hyperledger Fabric v 1.4 in this book, and that was the latest version when I started writing the book. On January 30, 2020, a new major version of Hyperledger Fabric was released and its v 2.0. Someone rightly said *The only constant in life is change*. In this mini-chapter, I would cover some of the important changes that are worth having a look. There are certain changes that are good to know but may not have a direct impact on us.

Structure

- Decentralized governance
- Chaincode lifecycle
- External chaincode launcher
- Private data enhancement

Objective

I am strongly convinced that if you have gone through the book diligently and have understood the concepts, then you should be able to understand the changes and be able to make required changes for this and upcoming release.

What's new?

In this section, we would go through noticeable changes. At the same time, I would strongly recommend you to go through **https://hyperledger-fabric.readthedocs.io/ en/release-2.0/whatsnew.html** to understand new changes.

Following is the list and brief of the changes.

Decentralized governance

Fabric chaincode has a new lifecycle in Hyperledger v 2.0 which deviates from the install and instantiate pattern as we had seen in v 1.4 and this provides the greater flexibility to decentralize the governance. For instance, in v 1.4 any one organization could have instantiated the chaincode with set endorsement policy and then the option left with other organizations to agree on that or not join the channel. In v 2.0, a new chaincode lifecycle allows organizations to agree on the parameters of chaincode one such example is endorsement policy as we discussed.

The second noticeable change is a more controlled process of chaincode upgrade. Earlier, any org could have upgraded the chaincode whereas now only after a required number of organizations have approved the upgrade, chaincode can be upgraded.

In v 1.4, even change in endorsement policy or private data collection would require reinstallation of chaincode, however now this can be done easily.

Chaincode lifecycle

The new chaincode lifecycle looks like:

- Packaging the chaincode
- Installing chaincode on peers
- Chaincode approval
- Committing the chaincode definition to the channel

This is now supported by the peer lifecycle chaincode command and there is no instantiation command as earlier. However, the peer chaincode of v1.4 still works.

If you look at peer command, you would still see all the commands, you can notice the new `lifecycle` command:

```
ubuntu@ip-172-31-40-141:~/sample/fabric-samples/bin$ ./peer
Usage:
  peer [command]

Available Commands:
  chaincode   Operate a chaincode: install|instantiate|invoke|package|query|signpackage|upgrade|list.
  channel     Operate a channel: create|fetch|join|list|update|signconfigtx|getinfo.
  help        Help about any command
  lifecycle   Perform _lifecycle operations
  node        Operate a peer node: start|reset|rollback|pause|resume|rebuild-dbs|upgrade-dbs.
  version     Print fabric peer version.

Flags:
  -h, --help   help for peer
```

Figure 11.1

And if you see peer `lifecycle` command, then you would see the following:

```
ubuntu@ip-172-31-40-141:~/sample/fabric-samples/bin$ ./peer lifecycle
Perform _lifecycle operations

Usage:
  peer lifecycle [command]

Available Commands:
  chaincode   Perform chaincode operations: package|install|queryinstalled|getinstalledpackage|
                            approveformyorg|checkcommitreadiness|commit|querycommitted

Flags:
  -h, --help   help for lifecycle
```

Figure 11.2

External chaincode launcher

Till Hyperledger Fabric v 1.4, peers needed to have docker daemon access to be able to build and launch chaincode. If you recall, it was a peer who would spin off the chaincode container and then use it. This would have required the peer process to have certain privileges on the docker process, which may not go down well with the system administrators. With the support of external chaincode launcher, we may not need a docker container always and can have a variety of options to launch chaincode.

This setup requires certain changes to achieve that, listing down steps on a high level as to how we can do that:

1. Have Hyperledger Fabric v 2.0 installed with required prerequisites.
2. Buildpack creation – Hyperledger has come up with a concept of Buildpack which is essentially a set of scripts, there are four scripts as part of Buildpack:

- `bin/detect`: This script file determines if this Buildpack should be used to create and launch of the container.
- `bin/build`: This script picks up the chaincode package and converts that into executable chaincode.
- `bin/release`: This provides chaincode metadata to peers.
- `bin/run`: It runs the chaincode.

Sample scripts are available at **https://hyperledger-fabric.readthedocs.io/en/release-2.0/cc_launcher.html.**

3. Once you have all the script files ready in the `bin` folder, the next step is to configure these so that the peer knows that it has the option of external chaincode launcher. For this, service definition in `docker-compose` file or `core.yaml` needs to be changed. Section of the `core.yaml` is shown below:

```
# List of directories to treat as external builders and launchers for
# chaincode. The external builder detection processing will iterate over the
# builders in the order specified below.
externalBuilders:
    - path: ../test-network/external-builder/bin
      name: my-golang-builder
      environmentWhitelist:
        - GOPROXY
        - GONOPROXY
        - GOSUMDB
        - GONOSUMDB
        - GOCACHE
        - GOPATH
        - GOROOT
        - HOME
        - XDG_CACHE_HOME
```

Figure 11.3

4. Map bin path in the service definition of peer in docker-compose file, so that it is available to a peer.
5. Create chaincode package using the peer lifecycle chaincode package.
6. Follow the rest of the peer lifecycle chaincode install commands, etc.

Private data enhancement

In Hyperledger Fabric v2.0, there are new changes introduced related to private data collection. Earlier, we used to define a collection of members whom we may want to share private data and then ended up having a lot of collections depending on the number of combinations we wanted to have. Now, with implicit per-organization collection enhancement we can share data across collections.

Private data now can have a separate endorsement policy that overrides the chaincode level endorsement policy for keys within the collection:

- **CouchDB (State Database) Cache Performance improvement:** A new property of `cacheSize` has been introduced that improves the read performance during the endorsement and validation phase.

- **Removal of 'provisional' genesis method:** When we went through orderer, we read that there are two ways by which we can provide genesis block file to the orderer, either through file or provisional way. The provisional genesis method has been removed from v 2.0 since we have used file everywhere in all our examples, it should not have any bearing on us.

There are also a couple of other changes that as a developer or operator you must know of and the complete list is given at **https://github.com/hyperledger/fabric/releases/tag/v2.0.0.** My suggestion would be to go through that.

Conclusion

This was a small mini-chapter that I introduced to understand the changes that have come in Hyperledger v 2.0. Though it's been since the only couple of months that this version has released and it might take some time to understand and grasp new changes and to see them running. However, going through Hyperledger Fabric v 1.4 would set a strong foundation in understanding fabric concepts and working and would work as a stepping stone to get the understand of the new version.

Printed in Great Britain
by Amazon

65378024R00199